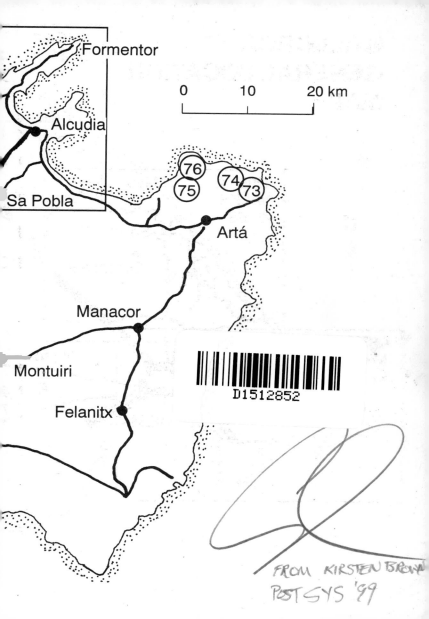

0   10   20 km

Formentor

Alcudia

Sa Pobla

76
75
74
73

Artá

Manacor

Montuiri

Felanitx

D1512852

FROM KIRSTEN BROWN
POSTGYS '99

WALKING IN MALLORCA

WALKING IN MALLORCA

by

JUNE PARKER

CICERONE PRESS
MILNTHORPE, CUMBRIA

© June Parker
ISBN 1 85284 250 4
First published 1986
Reprinted 1988
2nd Edition 1991
Reprinted 1994
3rd Edition 1997

Acknowledgements

June and Alan Parker would like to thank all the friends who have helped in trying out new walk descriptions or in making suggestions on itineraries. We would specially like to thank Mary Clarke and the late George Clarke, Stan and Jan Crawford, Jim and Ann Fielding, Brenda and Joe Lockey, Juan Noguerra, Charles Rhodes and group, David and Lily Rowe, Ernie Shepherd and friends, Stan and Margaret Thompson and Menna and George Vincent. Thanks too to all the walkers, too numerous to mention individually, who have written with comments on the book and the walks.

For this 3rd edition we would like also to thank Ronald Bagshaw, Jim and Sue Bannister, Ken and Chris Bricknell, Derek Fieldhouse, Graham Hearl, David Ormerod, Oliver St. John and Richard Strutt. Special thanks to Geoff Haworth for introducing us to Morey and to Tim Pickles for his walk on the Dragonera Island skyline.

Other Cicerone books by the same author:
Walking in the Algarve

Front cover: Between Cornadors and S'Arrom, the latest path threatened with closure

Frontispiece: Sa Calobra. Walk 27b

PREFACE

THE FUTURE OF WALKING IN MALLORCA

The closure of some traditional routes recently has prompted concern among those walkers who love the island and appreciate the scenic beauty, remote and rugged mountains and rural peace and quiet. In the past many of the private landowners who own large parts of the island have had no objection to small groups of people crossing their land, but it is a different matter when there is an astronomical increase in numbers. One problem is the practice of taking groups of walkers by the coachload into areas which are sensitive because of agriculture, animal husbandry or conservation. This is to be deplored and I would appeal to those who do not wish to walk on their own to join one of the several reputable organisations who arrange walking holidays and restrict numbers to an acceptable level. Naturally it behoves all walkers to keep strictly to the country code and exhort others to do so so that landowners are not further antagonised.

Although many of the mountain areas are farmed for sheep, the island is dependent on tourism economically. Tourist organisations and hoteliers are especially keen to promote 'green' tourism; to encourage walkers, cyclists, photographers, naturalists and all lovers of the countryside to come to the island in the winter and so extend the tourist season. The Consell Insular and one of its dependent branches FODESMA have an active programme designed to encourage walking. First, they are undertaking to restore and signpost many of the traditional named paths on the island and already a considerable number have been completed. These include the Barranc of Biniaraix, the Cami de Castello, the Cami Vell de Lluc and many more. In the course of this work the traditional techniques of drystone walling and the construction of 'margers' or retaining walls for terraces are being kept alive. Second, plans are under way to establish an official long-distance path between Andratx and Pollensa, with a network of mountain huts one day's walking distance apart. The first of these, Tossals Verds, opened in April 1995 and it is hoped that five more will be completed by the year 2000. Third, paths on publicly owned land are being cleared and negotiations are going on for paths on private land to be cleared also.

The 'Agroturismo' programme is also resulting in projects which benefit walkers such as the farm at Balitx d'Avall which offers accommodation under this scheme.

Recently Mallorquin walkers have become increasingly concerned that landowners have closed off routes long regarded as traditional rights-of-way and a new organisation ADIM (Associacion para la Defensa de los Itinerarios de Mallorca) has been formed. British walkers are invited to join and so help to put pressure on appropriate administrations and authorities. ADIM is employing a group of lawyers to work on the restoration of closed routes and needs support from as many walkers as possible. Please write for an application form to: Gabriel Ordinas, President A.D.I.M., c/Jaime Primero 14, Santa Maria 07320, Mallorca, Baleares, Spain.

The author suggests that any walker noticing any new or unexpected obstruction on a walk should report this to the Tourist Office in that area.

Important note: Walks 44, 45 and 46

As this edition goes to press, news has been received that the path between Soller and Cornadors via S'Arrom has been closed by means of large padlocks on all the gates. Local opposition to this closure is strong and as this is a popular and well-known route, it is hoped that it will soon be re-opened. Meanwhile Cornadors (Walk 44) can only be reached as a there-and-back walk from Biniaraix, the Alfabia ridge (Walk 45) can only be done by using Walk 46 to reach Sa Serra and descending via the *barranc* to Biniaraix, and the Circuit of S'Arrom (Walk 46) cannot be done.

Advice to Readers

Readers are advised that whilst every effort is taken by the author to ensure the accuracy of this guidebook, changes can occur which may affect the contents. It is advisable to check locally on transport, bus times, accommodation, shops etc but even rights-of-way can be altered.

The publisher would welcome notes of any such changes

CONTENTS

ROUTES LIST

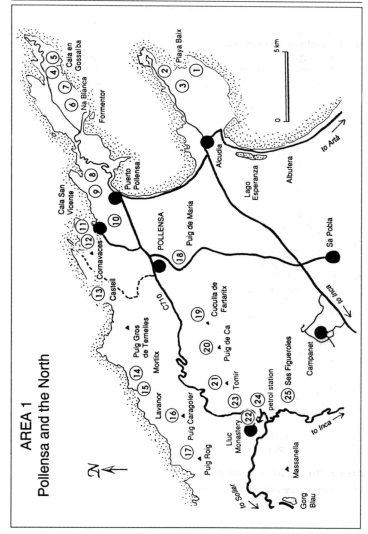

AREA 1
Pollensa and the North

9

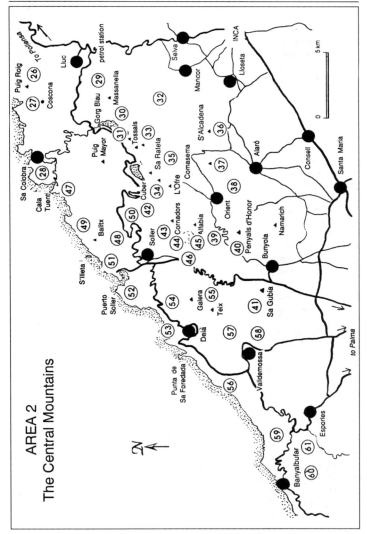

AREA 2
The Central Mountains

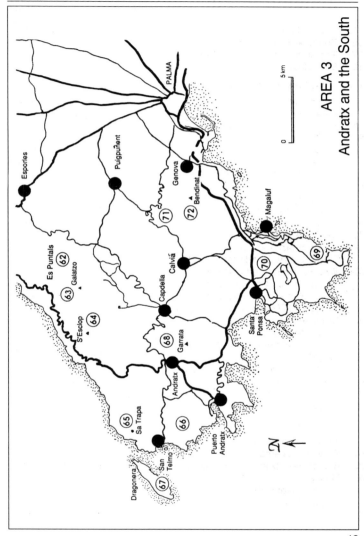

AREA 3
Andratx and the South

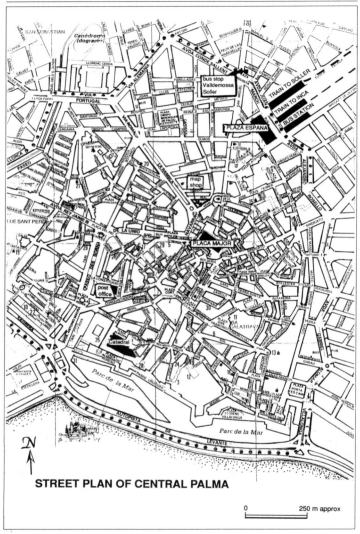

STREET PLAN OF CENTRAL PALMA

0   250 m approx

SKETCH MAPS

KEY TO MAPS

Main roads	
Other roads	
Tracks, private roads	
Footpaths	
Water courses	
Mountain tops	
Springs, fountains	
Approx. contours	
Sandy beaches	
Sea or lake	
Cliffs	

MOUNTAINS AND TOPS OVER 1000m

The heights are taken from the new IGN 1:25,000 maps where these are available. The criteria for separate mountain status are a separation of 1km or over and/or a re-ascent of 100m or more.

Mountains	Tops	Height m	Comments
1. Puig Mayor	Main top Mitx Dia West top Ses Vinyes	1447 1401 1358 1105	In military zone. Outside military zone.
2. Massanella	Main top Twin tops Unnamed Unnamed Ses Bassetes Galileu Sa Mola Es Fronto (w) Es Fronto (e)	1367 1352 1258, 1239 1169, 1058 1216 1188 1182 1009 1061	An enormous massif of two long ridges separated by two valleys leading to the the high Coll des Prat.
3.Tossals group	Tossals Verds South top Sa Font Almallutx Es Tossals	1115 1097 1069 1058 1047	S of Gorg Blau and E of Cuber.
4. Tomir	Main top South top	1103 1086	At head of Pollensa valley.
5. L'Ofre		1091	1.8km from Sa Rateta.
6. Sa Rateta	Main top Na Franquesa	1084 1067	On ridge to L'Ofre.
7.Alfàbia	Main top Palou 'Antennae' top	1067 1049 1029	Centre of long ridge. 1km NE of Alfàbia. 2.1km SW of Alfàbia.

Mountains	Tops	Height m	Comments
7. cont.	Sementer Gran	1014	At N end of ridge.
	Ses Heures	1051	Off-set from ridge.
	(Puig des Jou)		
8. Teix	Main top	1062	Between Deià and
	Teixoch	1062	Valldemossa.
	Puig des Vent	1004	0.75km N of Teix.
9. N'Alis		1035	Separated from Massanella by Coll de Sa Linea.
10. Galatzó		1027	Highest peak in SW of Mallorca.
11.Puig Roig		1002	Most northerly 1000m peak
12.Cornadors		1009	1.6km NE of Alfàbia.

CYCLAMEN BALEARICUM   ASPHODELUS AESTIVUS

INTRODUCTION

General background

The Balearic islands lie in the Mediterranean between Barcelona on the coast of mainland Spain and Algiers on the North African coast. This favoured position is responsible for the sunny, temperate climate attractive to both sun-lovers and walkers alike. Here it is worth pointing out that the temperatures in July and August which are ideal for sunbathing are far too hot for any serious walking by most people. These months are best avoided and the recommended 'season' for walkers is from the beginning of September to the end of May.

Mallorca is the largest of the islands and has long been well known as a paradise for sun-worshippers. That it is also a paradise for walkers has now been discovered by those discerning walkers who enjoy the attractive and varied scenery, the equable climate and the opportunities for walking in quiet places where other people rarely go. Add to this the extensive Mediterranean flora, the spring migration of birds and the opportunities for photography and it is hard to understand why it was neglected as a walking area for so long. This is no longer the case, as witnessed by the increasing number of access restrictions caused by pressure of numbers on popular routes. The inclusion of twenty new walks in this edition will help to reduce this pressure and the author assures readers it is still possible to enjoy walking in quiet areas, especially in the winter months.

The main mountain chain in Mallorca is the Sierra de Tramuntana which lies along the north-west coast and reaches heights of over 1,000m in many places, culminating in the Puig Mayor at 1,447m. The Sierra de Levante in the east, although only topping the 500m contour, also offers walks of surprising length and quality, having the same sort of high mountain characteristics as the Tramuntana. Many of the mountain tops of the island are almost bare of vegetation and the hard, rough limestone gives excellent walking and scrambling with loose rock being extremely rare. There is a varied flora including dense evergreen forests, maquis and garigue in the arid zones, sub-alpine flora on the approach to the peaks, and an enormous number of beautiful flowering shrubs which give an extra dimension to many walks.

The small size of the island means almost every walk is enhanced by views of the coastline and the sea. The sea varies in colour from the palest greens and blues to incredible dark ultramarine and purple, often with small bays of white sand between steep cliffs which plunge dramatically into the water. In fact the coastal walks vie in attraction with the inland mountains and although they may not reach any great height often go through very wild and uninhabited country.

Many of the walks in this guidebook go through pathless and rough areas where some experience of route-finding is needed. Some make use of excellent tracks and paths which are very easy to follow. Most of these are a legacy of the past, being made by those who worked in the now defunct rural industries of snow-collecting and charcoal manufacture. Some of these paths are neglected, overgrown and difficult to find, but some have been repaired and waymarked. The maps are not entirely reliable in the matter of footpaths and these are rarely signposted, except those maintained by ICONA. If using the maps to plan your own walks, care is required. Steep cliffs or very complex ground can be encountered where the map gives no indication of this.

Scope of this guide

This book is written for the experienced mountain walker who is used to walking in mountains like the British ones in all seasons. It is not comprehensive but provides a selection of walks of all degrees of difficulty and should enable those limited to a short holiday to make the best use of their time. Circular walks have been described whenever possible, but sometimes it is necessary to return the same way to the starting point. Most of the walks depend on the use of a hired car, by far the best means of getting about the island. Some walks can be done directly from Cala San Vicente, Pollensa, Puerto Pollensa, Soller and Puerto Soller. Occasionally public transport can be made use of, but in general the buses are more useful for getting to beaches than to the mountains.

Accommodation and travel *(See also Appendix 2)*

Although the development of the tourist industry in recent years has led to the spread of large concrete jungles, these are in the main confined to the coast around the bay of Palma, from Paguerra to El Arenal. However, there is no need to stay in this area, there being plenty of accommodation throughout the island in places that remain comparatively unspoilt. The resorts which are the best centres for walking will be described later. Some people may like to stay in Palma, which has certain advantages. There is an excellent network of roads from the capital in every direction, and also a very good public transport system, provided you are fairly near the centre. Personally I do not like to be tied to catching a bus or train at the end of a walk, but if this doesn't bother you it can be a good system.

One advantage of the tourist development of the island is that a number of tour operators offer package holidays throughout the year, with the effect of keeping prices down to a reasonable level. By far the cheapest way to get there is to take advantage of any special offers that include the use of a car at a reduced rate. These offers only apply to the winter, but then that is the best time to go for a walking holiday.

It is also possible of course to book a flight only and find your own accommodation independently. On the whole it works out more expensive to book into a hotel this way, but less expensive to take an apartment. There are an enormous number of apartment blocks, and some smaller ones often belonging to small bars and restaurants. It is easier to arrange this sort of holiday on a second visit when you know your way around and also if you are able to speak a little Spanish. English is always spoken in larger hotels, but by no means always in smaller places where cheaper accommodation is more likely to be found. Remember that some hotels close in winter, although those that do open are rarely full. The exception to this is Christmas and New Year and also Easter, when booking ahead is advisable.

Those who are able to take advantage of a long stay winter holiday can obtain extremely good rates for stays of up to four months. The best of these offers is usually from November to March, if you can get away for that length of time. There is a regular ferry service from Barcelona to Palma which may be worth considering for a long winter stay, but the costs of two ferries plus overnight stays on route make this quite an expensive option.

There is one official campsite on Mallorca, near Ca'n Picafort, at K8 on the Alcudia-Artà road. It is open all the year round and reservations can be made by telephone on 20-38-61. Those wishing to camp or bivvy in the mountains should ask permission at the nearest farm. Note that in many areas there is a prohibition against lighting fires because of the risk from dry vegetation. All walks can be done easily from a base in a small town or village, but longer two or three day backpacking walks can easily be devised. A popular annual event is organised jointly by walking clubs from Palma and Pollensa, in which a large number of walkers set out on a three day walk from south to north. The route is different each year, but always very tough and only a small number actually complete the whole course.

Choice of base

The best resorts for walkers are Cala San Vicente and Puerto Pollensa in the north, Soller and Puerto Soller on the west coast, and Puerto Andratx in the south-west.

Cala San Vicente is a small quiet resort with sandy beaches and a spectacular view of the steep cliffs of the Cavall Bernat ridge across the sparkling green-blue sea. It is surrounded by pinewoods, good for quiet walks, orchids and bird-watching. Several walks start from here and it is no great distance to drive to the starting points for other walks. There is a bus service, although very limited in winter. Walkers need to catch the 08.45 to Pollensa.

The Oriola is a very quiet family-run hotel by the pinewoods on the edge of the village. There is a home-cooked set meal in the evening and an attractive quiet lounge with a library of English books. Juan Noguera, the owner, is very knowledgable about walking and bird-watching and speaks excellent English. Open February to the end of October (Tel. 53-19-98).

Puerto Pollensa lies on the coast in a very sheltered position. There is a narrow strip of sand and quite a large marina. Much development has taken place here in recent years, so that those who remember it as a small fishing village will doubtless be horrified by all the changes. However, it has not been ruined as some of the resorts on the south and east coasts have been and it still remains an attractive place to stay. Nothing can spoil the splendid backdrop of the Cavall Bernat ridge and the quiet bay with its shallow water and sandy beaches. There are numerous hotels and apartments, a better bus service than Cala San Vicente, and plenty of shops and supermarkets. It is a good choice if there are children or non-walkers in your party. We recommend the Daina and the Ses Pins, and friends speak highly of the Flora Apartments.

Soller lies on the west side of the island between the mountains and the sea. It is an excellent centre for walks and has a good public transport system, with the train to Palma, a tram to the port, a bus service to Deià and Valldemossa, and the bus over the mountains to Pollensa. There is a good old-established hotel near the station, the Guia, which can be personally recommended, but this sometimes closes in the winter.

Puerto Soller has many more hotels and apartments clustered round the attractive circular harbour. It is linked to Soller with a frequent tram service and is a good place for the independent walker.

Unfortunately not many tour operators seem to offer holidays here, especially in the winter. We have found the Hotel Monte Azul quite attractive, and this is open in the winter. The Hostal Es Port makes an excellent base and is usually open all year. This interesting old building preserves an old olive press in the bar and is set in an attractive garden. There are also numerous apartments to let, especially in the winter. See Appendix 2 under Accommodation for the name of an estate agent.

Banyalbufar is a small village about half-way between Soller and Andratx. It is set on a steeply terraced slope between mountains and sea and is a good centre for walking in the southern part of the Tramuntana range. The Hotel Mar i Vent is a family-run hotel with excellent cooking which can be personally recommended. It is open all year except for December and January (Tel. 61-80-00). Two other hotels in the village are open in the summer months, the Baronia and the Sa Coma.

Puerto Andratx at the extreme south of the Tramuntana mountains is another picturesque harbour with a modern yacht marina. There are a number of modest hotels here and it is a good place for walking. The Brismar on the sea-front can be personally recommended. The inland town of Andratx has been saved from development, like Pollensa in the north, by its distance from the sea. It is a charming old town, dating from the thirteenth century, with a weekly market on Wednesdays.

Climate and weather
The climate of Mallorca is a typical Mediterranean one: that is the winters are mild, the summers are hot and dry and there is plenty of sunshine all the year round. The relative humidity is said to be constant throughout the year at about 70%. This, together with the sea breezes, makes even the hottest summer days pleasant and enjoyable, provided you are not trying to walk uphill. There are almost 300 sunny days during the year and even in the winter months there is an average of five hours of sunshine each day. When rain falls it often does so in sharp heavy showers that soon clear up, except for occasional whole days of torrential rain which can occur in the late autumn and early spring. There can, of course, be different weather conditions in different parts of the island. Naturally the rainfall is greatest over the highest mountains, varying from 1,000mm per year near the Puig Mayor to less than 400mm on the south coast. It is thus often possible to find a sunny or sheltered place to walk by avoiding the higher tops on bad days.

Snow is quite common on the mountain tops, or used to be. So common that it was formerly collected during the winter months to make ice for use in the summer. At sea level it is very rare and there was great excitement when several inches fell in January 1985. Local people said it was the first time this had happened for 29 years. That year the snow-fall in the mountains was tremendous and much damage to trees was done, many roads also being blocked for days both by the snow and fallen trees. When the roads were cleared, people from Palma were driving up to the mountains to make snowballs and loading snow on to the tops of their cars.

The central plain, protected by the high Sierras to the north-west, enjoys an almost sub-tropical climate. In winter the average temperature here is 10°C, whereas it is 6°C on the north-west coast.

The following table gives a rough indication of what to expect, but remember that these are averages and apply to Palma. In February 1990 there were 25 days of perfect 'summer' weather and most days the lunch-time temperature was 18-21°C. Then it shot up to 28°C, and plummeted to 5°C two days later.

Temperatures in °C and number of rainy and sunny days each month

	Jan	Feb	Mar	Apr	May	June	July	Aug	Sept	Oct	Nov	Dec
Max. temp.*	14	15	17	19	22	26	29	29	27	23	18	15
Min. temp.*	6	6	8	10	13	17	19	20	18	14	10	8
Average	9	8	11	13	17	21	26	24	22	18	14	12
Sea temp.	13	13	15	16	18	21	24	26	22	19	17	15
Rainy days	8	6	6	7	4	2	2	1	5	8	8	9
Sunny days	23	22	25	23	27	28	29	30	25	23	22	22

*Min. temp. at dawn, *Max temp. at midday

GEOLOGY AND SCENERY

These notes are necessarily very brief and the emphasis is on the scenery. Those interested in the geology are strongly recommended to obtain the new field guides listed in the bibliography.

Brief geological history

The Balearic islands lie on a submarine sill extending north-eastwards from Cap Nao on mainland Spain and are an extension of a chain of mountains in that area known as the Baetic Cordillera. These mountains are part of the Western Mediterranean block, pushed up in a major mountain-building episode at the end of the Carboniferous period, the Hercynian orogeny. It is thought that a ripple fold in a north-east/south-west direction was then thrown up by pressure from the northern land mass and that this fold underlies the main mountain chain of Mallorca, the Sierra de Tramuntana.

Subsequent earth movements raised and lowered this block a number of times, with various land bridges uniting it temporarily with Europe and Africa. It is these land bridges that partly account for the variety of flora and fauna on the islands.

Major events in the Mesozoic period were the laying down of thick deposits of Triassic clays and marls, followed by Jurassic and Cretaceous limestones, when all southern Europe, the Mediterranean and North Africa was a synclinal basin under the sea known to geologists as the 'Tethys'. Even during these times there were periods of uplift when the high land in the north was above water. During the Cretaceous there was probably a land bridge with Catalonia.

In the Eocene period massive earth movements caused folding of vast areas of southern Europe and North Africa. It was at this time that both Alpine and Himalayan folding and uplift occurred. In Mallorca the pressure against the Hercynian block was responsible for further folding on the same axis as the original ripple fold. This and later folding and faulting along the same axis gave rise to steep scarp slopes facing north-west with gentler slopes on the south-east side. A series of lakes was formed at the foot of these slopes when surface water was trapped above impermeable Jurassic rocks. Alluvial deposits dated at 50 million years, or late Eocene, are evidence of this.

A mainland bridge is believed to have existed in the lower Oligocene, then in the Miocene there was a further submergence with deep sea deposits being laid down over a wide area. At the end of the Miocene further elevation brought the mountain chain again up to its present height. The story after this is uncertain, except that the the islands did not achieve their present form until the Quaternary.

Surface features today

Although large areas of the exposed rocks on Mallorca are limestones of various ages and Triassic clays and marls, mention must be made of other rocks that will be observed from time to time when walking in the mountains. There are a number of minor igneous intrusions of a dark doleritic rock, probably of Triassic age, seen for example in the Ternelles valley. In the north-east of the island there are extensive areas of a very coarse conglomerate in which rounded pebbles and boulders with all sorts of angular fragments are well cemented together, giving a 'pudding-stone' appearance. This will be seen on the walk to the Puig de S'Aguila (Walk 11). Here too there is an outcrop of an attractive pink, white and black rock, not a true marble, but the result of pressure and percolating solutions acting on the limestone. Occasional outcrops of cross-bedded sandstones are also seen, for example in the picnic area of the pinewoods at Cala San Vicente.

There are three distinct areas of Mallorca which can be considered as structural-morphological units; these are the main mountain chain known as the Sierra de Tramuntana, the central plains and the mountains of the south-east, the Sierra de Levante.

1. The Sierra de Tramuntana

The Tramuntana is a chain of mountains some 80km long which lies in a north-east/south-west direction along the line of the original ripple fold. There are 12 peaks and 37 tops more than 1,000m in height. There are many ridges showing the same directional trend as the whole chain. The Cavall Bernat ridge (Walk 9) is one of these. The steep north-west scarp slopes are a striking feature, particularly the coastal scarp which makes much of the shoreline inaccessible. This feature is well seen on the circuit of the Puig Roig (Walk 17). As pointed out elsewhere, these scarps are not always marked on the maps and this should be borne in mind when planning independent walks.

Many of the rocks at the surface high up in the mountains are deep sea calcareous rocks dating from the Miocene. They are hard medium-grey rocks often sculpted into fantastic pinnacles and with conspicuous 'flutings' due to rainwater erosion. This phenomenon can easily be seen when driving along the C710 from Pollensa to Lluc, here developed on massive conglomerates. There are many areas of typical karst or limestone pavement, where percolating water has enlarged the joints of the rock into deep fissures called grikes. The ridges between, known as clints, can be knife sharp, and negotiating this sort of terrain calls for great care from walkers. By far the most badly dissected limestone we have ever seen is up on the Puig Gros de Ternelles between the summit and the Coll de Tirapau. It is so bad that this walk is no longer recommended. Walks 16 and 17 both traverse areas of impressive rock scenery and are highly recommended.

There is only one major watercourse on the island. This is the Torrente de Pareis (Walk 27), and it has worn through great thicknesses of rock to expose earlier Jurassic strata of a very dense, hard limestone, sometimes dolomitic.

2. The central plains

The central plain or *es pla* consists of Miocene and late Plio-Pleistocene deposits which are poorly exposed. Large areas are completely flat and covered with a layer of terra rossa, a red and very fertile soil consisting of the insoluble residue left behind after the solution of limestone by ground water. The red colour is due to the accumulation of iron oxides. When recently ploughed this earth is bright red and makes a striking contrast to the pale blossom of the almond trees or the dark green of the carobs.

Elsewhere there is an undulating relief, and at the south-eastern border of the Tramuntana is a belt of low hills derived by erosion from the Sierras themselves. Occasional inliers of folded Triassic and Jurassic rocks rise up prominently from the central plain, such as Randa (Walk 77).

3. The eastern hills

The Sierras de Levante are a lower range of hills running from the Artà peninsula towards Manacor and Felanitx. They only just exceed 500m in height. The folding here is considered to be more recent than that of the Tramuntana. Triassic and Jurassic strata are overlain by Cretaceous limestones and by the mid-grey Miocene limestone. There are extensive areas of karst and some large Jurassic cave systems near the coast. These are the caves of Drach, Hams and Artà: all open as showcaves.

Mallorca: simplified geolgical history

PERIOD	EPOCH	EVENTS	MYA
Quaternary	Recent Pleistocene	Mallorca sep. from Menorca Ibiza sep. from Formentera.	2
	Pliocene	Bridge betw. Ibiza and Mallorca broken.	7
	Miocene	Elevation & uplift to present height. More deep sea deposits.	19
Tertiary	Oligocene	Partial re-submergence, but with land bridges.	38
	Eocene Paleocene	Major folding & earth movements.	63
Cretaceous	Upper Lower	Land bridge to Catalonia. Deep sea limestones dep.	136
Jurassic		Deep sea limestones dep.	190
Triassic		Thick deposits of clays and marls laid down.	225
Permian		Ripple fold in NE/SW direction.	280
Carbonif.		Hercynian mountains formed.	345
Devonian		Fossil plants show earliest evidence of life.	410

MYA = Million years ago

Rafal de Ariant (Walk 17) (Author)
On Puig de Maria (Walk 21) (W.Unsworth)

In the Pareis Gorge (Walk 28b) W.Unsworth)
On the approach to Massanella by the Coll des Prat
(Walk 30) (Author)

NATURAL HISTORY

The pleasure of walking on Mallorca is greatly enhanced by the rich variety of plant and animal life. Wherever you go you cannot fail to notice the immense variety of flowers and shrubs and how different the vegetation is from that seen in Britain. Ornithologists have been visiting the island for many years, mainly in the spring and the autumn to catch the migrants, but there is plenty to interest the walker with a casual interest in bird-watching all the year round. The notes which follow are necessarily very brief and the reader is referred to the bibliography in the appendices for further reading.

Flora

Only five varieties of native tree are found in the woodlands of Mallorca: pine, oak, olive, carob and dwarf fan palm. Others, such as black poplar, London plane, ash, elm, hawthorn and blackthorn, will be observed on the banks of streams. A striking feature of the forests is how green they are in winter, not only because of the preponderance of evergreens but because the autumn rains wash off all the summer dust which gives a drab grey appearance to the trees. Both the pines and the oaks are perfectly adapted to the long, hot and dry summers, the pines having leaves reduced to narrow grooved cylinders and the oaks having thick leathery leaves with a waxy coating, so that both types of tree cut down on loss of moisture by transpiration.

The Aleppo Pine, *Pinus halepensis,* grows from sea level up to 1,000m and is abundant everywhere. It can be 20m high with a straight trunk but is frequently bent and twisted in windy situations. It often grows in fairly open stands but is sometimes in mixed woodlands with evergreen oaks. Two other pines are seen but are not common: the Stone Pine or Umbrella Pine, *Pinus pinea,* recognisable by its umbrella shape, and *Pinus halepensis var.ceciliae* recognised by its upwardly growing branches.

Of the five different evergreen oaks the most common is the Holm Oak, *Quercus ilex.* It has been much used in the past for the making of charcoal but is still abundant. Other varieties are the Kermes Oak, Cork Oak, Lusitanian Oak and *Quercus rotundifolia.* Bonner gives full details of how to recognise them and where to see them all.

It is not known whether the olive, *Olea europea,* existed wild on the island before it was domesticated. The sub-species *Oleaster* does exist and it is believed that the cultivated olive was developed from this in Syria. Another sub-species, *var.sylvestris,* also grows on the island.

The cultivated olive grows up to 10m in height and has a distinctive silver-grey foliage. Olive trees are seen everywhere, on the central plain and on terraces levelled out of the mountain slopes, where they will be noticed on many of the walks. Some of the trees are very old, 1,000 years or possibly older, and their gnarled and twisted trunks are very striking.

The carob tree is also very common. It is a beautiful tree with thick shiny leaves. The new growth is a lighter green than the old, so that the tree often has a two-toned appearance. The fruits are conspicuous, being large pods which are green at first but become brown on ripening and eventually almost black. They have a high sugar content and are used to feed cattle.

The dwarf fan palm, *Chamaerops humilis,* is most distinctive with its sharp lance-like leaves arranged in fans. It occurs only in three localities in Mallorca, but is abundant in these areas which are the north-east around Pollensa and Alcudia, Artà, and the south-west near Andratx.

Although trees are few in variety, there is such a wealth of flowering shrubs that it is impossible to list them all here. Of the more outstanding ones which are to be seen on the walks in this book, the most common is the Lentisk or Mastic Tree, *Pistacia lentiscus*, a dark spreading evergreen shrub which grows from 1-3m high and has a resinous smell. This grows in all situations from sea level to high in the mountains. It is said that keeping a sprig between the lips wards off thirst on hot days. The leaves have 3-6 pairs of dark green leaflets with blunt tips. The flowers occur in the leaf axils and are either reddish or brown, followed by fruits which are first red and then black.

Very noticeable too are the beautiful deep blue flowers of the common rosemary, *Rosmarinus officinalis,* a dense aromatic shrub which seems to bloom somewhere all the year round. The deepest blue flowers have been noticed on Formentor and on the Serra de San Vicens, with swarms of bees humming around each plant.

In March and April the yellow brooms burst into flower, making golden splashes of colour across the hillsides. First seen is *Genista lucida* in March, localized in the Artà area and the south-west, then the thorny broom, *Calicotome spinosa,* in April, easily recognised by its trifoliate leaves and by its long sharp spines.

Hypericum balearicum, an endemic St. John's wort, is another common shrub found on mountain slopes, in woodlands and by the roadside. The yellow flowers may be seen sporadically all the year round but it is at its best in spring. The leaves are deep green, narrow and crinkled. There is another endemic St. John's wort, *Hypericum cambessedessii,* which grows in the beds of mountain streams. It has the same flowers as *Balearicum* but the leaves are long and flat and of a beautiful pale, almost luminescent green.

Asphodels are everywhere, growing along roadsides and on barren wasteland from the seaside to the mountain tops. The tall spikes of white flowers with a reddish-brown vein on each petal are very conspicuous. In spite of its name, *Asphodelus microcarpus,* it may grow as much as 2m high. The plant is not eaten by animals and its presence is a sign of neglected and overgrazed ground. There is a smaller variety, *Asphodelus fistulosis,* which is less common. The flowers may be pink, but it is most easily identified by the leaves which are round in cross-section, those of microcarpus being V-shaped.

One of the most attractive groups of shrubs are the rockroses which are commonly found in the oak woods as well as in more open spaces. Most common is *Cistus albidus,* or grey-leaved cistus, which has velvety leaves and large pink flowers with a crumpled appearance. It flowers in April-June and is very aromatic. *Cistus monspeliensis* or narrow-leaved cistus with smaller white flowers is also common and starts to flower in March. Slightly less common is the sage-leaved cistus, *Cistus salvifolius,* with large white flowers.

The strawberry tree, *Arbutus unedo,* is not a tree but a striking tree-like shrub with big shiny leaves and fruits which turn first orange and then deep red in October and November. The fruits, which are edible but tasteless, ripen at the same time as the white flowers of the following year's crop are in bloom.

Tree heather, *Erica arborea,* grows up to 3m high and is dense but feathery looking with hundreds of tiny white or pale pink flowers in terminal heads. Some of the euphorbias are very striking, especially the tree spurge, *Euphorbia dendroides,* which forms hemispherical bushes with bright yellow glands surrounding the flowers. *Euphorbia characias* is smaller, but very attractive with reddish-brown glands. Bonner says there about twenty different species in the Baleares but only these two are easy to identify.

Two 'hedgehog' or 'pincushion' plants will be noticed by all walkers. Their sharp spines are an adaptation to wind as well as a protection against being eaten by grazing animals. These are *Teucrium*

31

subspinosum and *Astralagus balearicus* and they are very difficult to tell apart when not in flower. In fact in Mallorquin they are both called *coixinets de monja* or nuns' sewing cushions.

Smilax aspera or European sarsaparilla is a climbing plant with hooked spines on the stems, growing up through shrubs and hedges to 1-2m high. The leaves vary enormously in size according to the conditions, being very large in cool shady places and small and narrow in sunny ones. *Smilax balearica* is an endemic variety growing in the mountains. It has minimal leaves and is extremely prickly, becoming a great nuisance to walkers as it often fills the crevices in otherwise bare limestone. The backward curving thorns are notorious for lacerations to flesh and clothes and are one good reason for not wearing shorts on some of the rougher walks. The Mallorquin name is *Aritge*, and there are thousands of them in the aptly named 'Pla des Aritges' crossed on the walk along the archduke's path (Walk 57).

One of the commonest mountain plants is *Ampelodesmus mauritanica,* a pampas-like grass. It's easier to use the short Mallorquin name, *carritx*, for these grasses which form enormous clumps covering large areas. From a distance a green hillside sometimes gives the illusion of being close-cropped turf, but it never is. The tall narrow leaves curve over to reach the ground and it is very easy to step on them with one foot and trip over them with the other. You soon learn to lift your feet high when walking on a narrow path between clumps of *carritx*.

So far we have concentrated on the trees and shrubs and some other plants which make their presence obvious to the walker, but there are a number of smaller, less conspicuous plants which are well worth seeking out. A tiny plant, *Crocus minimus,* shows its lilac-pink flowers before the leaves as early as December, for example on the approach to the west top of the Cavall Bernat ridge. The very common but delightful and delicate little *Cyclamen balearicum* can be found in flower in March, if you look under the sheltering leaves of other shrubs, on the mountains and in the woods. The leaves, not unlike house plant cyclamens, are a mottled greyish green and will be seen everywhere. They are a little like the leaves of another common plant, *Arisarum vulgare,* or Friar's Cowl, which flowers in winter and is very common. Similar in leaf shape are *Arum italicum*, *Arum pictum* and *Dranunculus muscivorum*. The latter is particularly striking with a spotted reddish-purple 'spadix' and 'spathe' and strangely incised leaves. (A spadix is a fleshy spike bearing flowers and a spathe is a large bract enclosing the flower head.)

There is no space here to describe plants of other habitats such as the sea-coasts, the sand dunes, the cliff faces and the marshlands. For these the reader is referred to the books listed in the bibliography in Appendix 4. Before beginning the next section, though, there are two striking plants which deserve a mention although they are not native. One is the prickly pear, which is sometimes used as a dense protective hedge and whose fruits are edible, and the other is *Agave americana*. This plant has huge leathery leaves which may be as long as 2m. After about ten years it sends up an enormous tree-like flower spike up to 10m high, after which it dies. Finally, Mallorca is a wonderful place for orchids, flourishing in the pinewoods near the sea, inland in the mountains and even thrusting up through tarmac at the side of the road.

Birds

These notes are written for walkers and not for experts, who are referred to the books listed in the bibliography. Even those with a minimal interest in birds are likely to find this interest stimulated by the number and variety of birds to be seen on nearly every walk. Binoculars and an identification book are a must. Some of the walks described coincide with good birding areas e.g. Na Blanca (No.6), Boquer valley (No.8), and Castell del Rei (No.13). There is a good chance of spotting birds on many of the other walks too. In fact the only birds missed would be ducks and waders etc., some of which can be seen at the S'Albufera in north-east Mallorca. A visit to this area is highly recommended; see Note 1 at the end of this chapter.

The best time for birdwatchers to visit the island is the peak migration season in April and May with the last half of September and the first two weeks in October as a second choice. Bird meetings are held at the Hotel Pollentia on the sea-front at Puerto Pollensa, every Monday and Friday during these periods, starting at 9.0 pm., when others birdwatchers can be met and information exchanged. Graham Hearl, who runs these meetings, is also the GOB/RSPB representative and can be contacted at APTDO 83, Sa Pobla, Tel. 86-24-18. Graham also leads small groups on birdwatching excursions.

There is a local birdwatching organisation on the island, the Grupo Ornithologia Balear, or GOB, based in Palma, which is very active. Amongst other things they are responsible for the management of the Albufera, have acquired land at Sa Trapa for conservation, cooperated on the black vulture re-establishment programme (see Note 2), and produce an annual review and other publications. Incidentally, the filming of nesting birds is subject to Spanish law. Anyone planning to do this should ask advice from GOB or SECONA.

Although GOB is well supported locally, many other local people are more interested in shooting birds for the pot, both in and out of the official season, which is from the end of August to the end of January. Thrushes are regarded as a serious pest in the olive groves and the traditional practice of *caza a coll* or thrush-netting is still allowed. Thrushes may be seen hanging up in bunches on market stalls. A plateful of robins has been sighted in a domestic refrigerator. However, many birds are protected by law and if any illegal shooting is observed it should be reported to GOB with evidence such as photographs or car-numbers. All eagles, vultures, harriers, owls and flamingoes are protected. Eddie Watkinson described how, with the help of GOB, two men were heavily fined for shooting a flamingo.

Of all the birds of Mallorca, the hoopoe always arouses great interest, even after many sightings. It is extremely striking with its barred black and white wings and tail and erectile crest. It is quite common in many localities, and is often flushed out of hedges as you drive along. Most exciting of all the birds on the island, though, are the large birds of prey, especially the black vultures which may be seen soaring over the Tramuntana, for example on Tomir (see Note 2).

Besides the resident black vultures, other raptors to be seen in winter are red kites, peregrines, kestrels and booted eagles; more rarely the golden eagle and short-toed eagle. Marsh harriers are resident and breed on the larger marshes. Hen harriers and Montagu's harriers are occasional visitors. Ospreys are frequently seen on the marshes and sometimes inland at the Gorg Blau and Cuber reservoirs. One of the most interesting birds is the Eleanora's falcon which breeds in large colonies on the coastal cliffs all the way from Formentor in the north-east to Dragonera in the south-west. These birds arrive in late April but do not breed until later in the summer. The young birds then feed on tired migrants, an activity which may be observed during September and October in the nesting areas. Other birds of the mountains include the fairly common crag martin which might be seen on many walks and other places including the marshes, where flocks of about 1,000 may be seen catching insects on mild winter days.

Alpine accentors may be seen in small flocks in the northern mountains, but personally we have only seen them singly. One accepted some of our lunch high up on Massanella on a cold New Year's Day. The blue rock thrush is resident in fair numbers, but not easily seen. In spite of its bright metallic blue plumage it tends to disappear behind rocks or bushes as soon as sighted. Pallid swifts breed on the cliffs and small colonies of alpine swifts may be seen in a few places, such as the Artà peninsula, near the Puig Mayor, and on the Castell del Rei walk.

In the woodlands the most common winter residents are blackcaps, black redstarts, crossbills and goldfinches. Also white wagtail, meadow pipit, hoopoes, serins and greenfinches, linnets and great tits are common, and robins and chaffinches are abundant. Firecrests and blackcaps are found as high as 800m. Rock doves are fairly common and nest on cliff faces e.g. at Formentor, as well as in the woods.

The many areas of maquis and scrubland are the preferred habitat of a large number of birds including many warblers. The sardinian warbler is a very common resident, as is the fantailed warbler. The marmora's warbler is resident but somewhat elusive. It may be seen in the Boquer valley, and Walk 6 to Na Blanca passes the nesting sites near the Cases Veyas valley.

During the winter there is a big influx of birds from further north in Europe, including starlings, thrushes, finches, waders and wildfowl. Goldcrests are numerous and may even outnumber the resident firecrests.

Other wildlife

July and August are the poorest months for wildlife, apart from grasshoppers and cicadas, but walkers will want to avoid these two months anyway. Even in midwinter there are numerous butterflies and moths and they are abundant the rest of the year. Parrack (1973) mentions that 32 species of butterflies and 250 of the larger moths have been observed. Red Admirals may be seen in the winter, Clouded Yellow and Painted Ladies more commonly in the spring. Some exotic species such as the Two-tailed Pasha arrive in May from North Africa, and the Mediterranean Skipper is found from May onwards (see Note 3 on the processionary caterpillar).

Other invertebrates include the shell-bearing molluscs, with the gastropods or snails being of particular interest. In the mountains snails form the basic diet of the Blue Rock Thrush and it has been noticed that the colours of the shells vary in different areas and from season to season. This colour variation is probably of survival value, depending on the colour of the background vegetation.

A large number of frogs live in the marshes and up to a height of 800m in the mountains. Many breed by the outlet from the Cuber reservoir. Most of the frogs are an endemic form of the marsh frog, *Rana ridibunda,* but there is also a green tree frog and three species of toad: the Green Toad, the Natterjack and the Midwife Toad. They mostly hibernate in winter, but can be heard croaking on mild days at the Gorg Blau or below the dam at Cuber.

There are four species of snake: Grass Snake, Viperine Snake, Ladder Snake and Cowl Snake, none of them capable of causing fatalities. The only snake I've ever seen was high up on the south ridge of the Puig Roig. It was no more than two feet long and slithered away into a rock crevice so fast I could not recall its appearance afterwards. It should have been hibernating, but must have come out to enjoy the hot sun.

Two species of broad-toed lizards or geckos are found. The Wall Gecko lives mainly in lowland areas but it is the Disc-Fingered Gecko which is more common in the mountains. The latter is the more bold of the two, but they both disappear quickly when approached. Both are eaten by hoopoes. Both hibernate, but also come out of hibernation on sunny winter days.

There are few large mammals on Mallorca due to two natural calamities since the severance of the island from the mainland some 800,000 years ago. The first of these was a rising of the water level with widespread flooding and the second was climatic changes associated with the mainland glaciations during the Quaternary. After this the final doom to a number of species was brought by man, not only as a hunter but as a destroyer of the forests through charcoal burning and cultivation. The wild boar and the red fox probably survived until this century. The pine marten and the genet survive along with true wild cats, feral cats and weasels. Pine martens are still being trapped or shot. (Once we saw one hanging by its neck from the branch of a tree.) Of the smaller mammals shrews, hedgehogs, bats, rabbits, the brown hare and various rodents are quite common. Rabbits provide food for man as well as the birds of prey who also do well off the smaller rodents (although extra food is being provided to aid the survival of the black vultures).

The feral goats are the animals most frequently met with on mountain walks, and the tracks they make through the prickly scrub and the *carritx* are often a help to the walker. They are frequently hunted.

From some of the cliff walks it is worth looking out to sea for whales and dolphins. There are occasional sightings of Sperm Whales and Killer Whales but mostly it is the common dolphin and sometimes the Bottle-nosed and Risso's Dolphin that are seen. Pilot Whales are rare and Rorquals more likely. On rare occasions they have been beached after heavy storms.

Note 1. The Albufera (see map p38)

The Albufera is the largest wetland area in the Baleares and one of the most important in Spain. It is on the north-east coast of Mallorca between Alcudia and Ca'n Picafort and covers an area of about 4,000 acres. In the 1960s the northern part came into the hands of property developers and at one time it was thought this might be the fate of the whole area. However, in 1985 the autonomous Balearic Government purchased a large area (almost 2,000 acres) and it is now a well-managed nature reserve with an information centre, seven hides and an observation tower. There is a hide overlooking the deep fresh water at the *Depuradora* (water treatment works) on the southern edge of the Albufera, with access to this by car from K8.9 on the Ca'n Picafort Muro road. More than 200 species of birds have been observed, most of them marsh birds, but also woodland species and others among the dunes and the trees bordering the canals. It is well worth spending some time here and there are many paths and tracks providing quite long walks. A circular walk can be made by returning along the coast which is bordered by pinewoods. The reserve can be reached by bus from Puerto Pollensa. Ask for 'El puente Inglesos' (the English Bridge), or look out for the Hotel Esperanza on the left just before the bridge. If driving, start signalling a right turn before the bridge, as it is a very sudden and narrow turn. There is a car park (with toilets) near the information office (see map of the Albufera). From the English Bridge cars are only admitted from 09.00 to 17.00 in winter (19.00 in summer), although there is always access for walkers and cyclists through a gap in the wall by the main gate. Occasionally, on weekends in peak periods, cars are not admitted at all.

Note 2. The Black Vulture recuperation programme

Since the beginning of the century the resident population of Black Vultures on Mallorca has seriously declined. In recent years attempts have been made to reverse this tendency and already some success

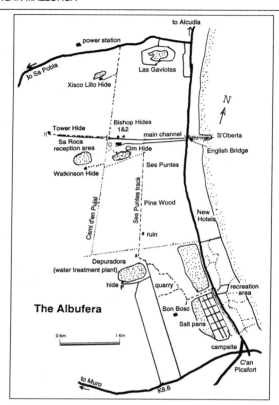

to Alcudia

power station

to Sa Pobla

Las Gaviotas

Xisco Lillo Hide

N

Tower Hide

Bishop Hides 1&2

main channel

S'Oberta

Sa Roca reception area

Cim Hide

English Bridge

Ses Puntes

Watkinson Hide

Ses Puntes track

Pine Wood

Camí d'en Pujal

New Hotels

ruin

Depuradora (water treatment plant)

hide

quarry

recreation area

The Albufera

Son Bosc

0 Km   1 Km

Salt pans

campsite

C'an Picafort

to Muro

K8.6

has been achieved. The first and simplest method has been to put out food for them high up in the mountains. Since tractors have replaced horses and mules there is less carrion which would have been a natural source of food in the past.

The second method has been the introduction of immature and injured birds recovered on the mainland. Twelve of these were introduced between 1984 and 1987.

The third method has been to release chicks hatched in captivity into the wild through the technique known as 'hacking'. Fledgling chicks are put into an artificial nest with a tame vulture who cannot fly. They

38

are fed under cover of darkness so that they do not become accustomed to human beings. The chicks teach themselves to fly and already a number of them have successfully integrated with the local population.

These birds live, breed and feed in the high mountains. They are wonderful and exciting to watch but it is essential that they are not disturbed. For this reason, walkers in the area between the Puig Roig and Ternelles should take special care to keep to footpaths, to avoid undue noise, and preferably to limit numbers in walking parties to less than six. The area of Lavanor is particularly sensitive and discouraged during the long breeding season from January through to May. Hopefully at some time in the future observation hides may be provided so that the vultures can be seen without disturbance.

Note 3. Processionary caterpillars

A number of curious features will be noted when walking through pinewoods. These include strange grey nest-like objects hanging from branches, wooden boxes also suspended from branches, and in some areas large numbers of dead pine trees lying on the ground and riddled with holes.

The fact is that the pinewoods of Mallorca are under serious threat by attacks from 'processionary' caterpillars. The caterpillars get their name from their habit of walking in single file when searching for food, and can form chains many metres long. They have voracious appetites and devour the leaves of pine trees (and other trees) and eventually the trees die. They secrete fine silk threads which are used for returning to the nests, which are the grey bags seen in the trees.

Various attempts have been made to eradicate the caterpillars at enormous cost. At one time cartridges were issued free by the Ministry of Ag. and Fish to encourage people to shoot the nests out of the trees. This was stopped when it was found the free cartridges were being used in normal hunting pursuits. Cutting off and burning branches with nests on has been tried but is only effective if the burning is done on concrete, as the caterpillars can burrow into the ground and chrysalids can survive there for a year, to emerge as moths. Large areas have been treated with insecticides, but the best results are being obtained with biological control, using traps containing pheromenes. These are the boxes seen on the trees in many woodlands. The pheromenes attract the female moths, who can lay up to 200 eggs. They get trapped in the lure and die. No damage is done to other flora and fauna.

MAN AND HIS IMPACT ON THE LANDSCAPE

There is evidence that Mallorca was inhabited more than 6,000 years ago, making use of natural caves. In the 1960s bones of extinct antelopes mingled with human remains were found in the Cueva de Muleta near Soller. The human remains were dated at 3985 BC+ 109 years. This cave is in a Jurassic limestone outcrop and consists of two levels connected by a vertical chimney, forming a natural animal trap. Another major site, even older, is that of Son Matge, near Valldemossa. This is dated at about 4730 BC and has been used as a corral for animals, then as a habitation, a burial site and a workshop.

These caves are not easily accessible, but in the village of Cala San Vicente there are some caves partly natural and partly man-made, the former probably dwelling caves and the latter long rectangular rooms, probably burial chambers. These caves are to be found in a small park full of flowering shrubs, at the western edge of the village. The date of these is probably about 2,000 years later than the Muleta cave.

In 1979 a very important find was made on the ridge of La Punta which separates the San Vicente valley from the road between Pollensa and the Port. Local climbers found the entrance to a large cave which had been used as a burial chamber. It was very carefully excavated and the objects found sent to various museums on the mainland for evaluation. Some have now found their way back to the museum in Pollensa. The most interesting finds at La Punta were the remains of two wooden bull-like creatures with hollow bodies. These have been carbon-dated at 320 BC and are assumed to have contained human ashes. Reconstructions of these can be seen at the museum.

Some time during the 2,000 years before the Romans arrived, the Balearic people progressed from living in caves to building stone dwellings, megalithic structures containing towers or *talayots*. Not a great deal seems to be known about these times, but there are a number of sites where they can be seen. Near Artà there is the Talayot de Ses Paisses, but the largest and best documented is that of Capacorp Vey or Vell, near Lluchmayor. This is maintained as a national monument by the Institute of Catalan Studies and is well worth a visit. It contains 28 dwellings and five *talayots*, two square and three circular. One of the square *talayots* has an opening at ground level from which a low tunnel descends in a spiral to a small room partly roofed by olive wood branches. (To go in here means hands and knees and a torch held between the teeth.) The function of this room was probably religious. This village has been dated at about 1000 BC and was thought to be occupied well into Roman times.

Mallorca has no mineral resources, so the finding of ingots and bronze implements, such as the bronze button at La Punta, shows that trading must have occurred with merchants from the civilisations of the eastern Mediterranean. There would have been settlements on or near the sites of most of the present ports. The Carthaginians provided garrisons to protect their trading posts, recruiting from among the local warriors armed with slings. The name of the islands, the Balearics, comes from the Greek verb, *ballein*, meaning 'to throw'. The leather slings fired stones the size of tennis balls, carried in a leather pouch. Legend has it that boys were trained in this art by having to shoot down their daily food from where it had been placed high up in the trees.

The Romans invaded the island in 123 BC. They built the cities of Palma and Alcudia (then known as Pollentia). The remains of the Roman town of Alcudia include the theatre on the road to Puerto Alcudia and other buildings near the Tucan crossroads. In the Pollensa area there is a Roman bridge on the north side of the town, near the starting point of several walks in the area. The remains of a Roman aqueduct, which was thought to take water all the way to Alcudia, are seen in the Ternelles valley.

The fact that there are so few Roman remains is partly due to the depredations of the Vandals after the island was abandoned by the Romans. During this time too the main settlements began to develop a few kilometres inland from the ports, which is why today there are still the towns of Pollensa, Alcudia, Soller and Andratx each with its own port. Watch towers too were built on headlands and hills so that warning of approaching invaders and pirates could be given. These watchtowers or *atalayas* are seen on many walks. They are usually circular and can often be climbed by iron ladders to a viewing platform at the top. One of the best preserved, and recently restored, is that of Albercutx, on the Formentor peninsula.

After the rout of the Vandals in North Africa by the Byzantine general Belisarius, the Balearics were incorporated into what is now Tunisia. Mallorca again became a trading post protected by military stongholds, this time of the Byzantine Empire. This period was followed by very unsettled times and constant strife between the Moors and the Christians, beginning with Arabic raids in AD 707. This is still re-enacted today in various folk festivals, such as is held in Pollensa every 2nd

August. Arabic influence on the development of agriculture during times of peace is still to be seen in the countryside. They introduced the *norias* or water-wheels used to pump water from underground reservoirs and wells, and the *seguias* or open water channels used to irrigate the fields. They also began the terracing of the steep hillsides with massive drystone walls that enable cultivation of otherwise impossible places.

Placenames on the map are another legacy of the Arabs. *Bini* in a name means 'the house of', as in Binisalem and Biniraitx. In Palma the arches of the Almudaina palace and the Arab baths are still to be seen and there is a Moorish influence on many country houses.

The modern history of Mallorca dates from 1229 when Jaime I of Aragon (known as 'the conqueror') led an expedition of 150 ships and 16,000 men to re-claim the island. The landing was made at Santa Ponsa, after storms diverted them from the original plan of landing at Puerto Pollensa. After several months the reconquest was complete and a new state proclaimed in March 1230. Although a modern style government was introduced this was not the end of Mallorca's troubles but the beginning of new ones. When Jaime I died in 1276 he left his estates of Aragon, Catalonia and Valencia to his eldest son Pedro III and the Balearics, Rousillon and Montpellier to his younger son Jaime II. Pedro III's son and successor, Alfonso III, then invaded Mallorca and proclaimed himself king. The castle of Alaró (Walk 37) was one of the last strongholds to hold out against him. Alfonso committed such terrible atrocities in this siege that he was excommunicated and eventually Jaime II returned to the throne and proved an excellent ruler.

During his reign Palma cathedral was built and so was Bellver Castle. He patronised the great scholar Ramon Llull who founded the hermitage on Randa and wrote his major works there. He encouraged the development of trade and agriculture by granting charters to 11 market towns. His son Sancho continued his father's enlightened policies, but owing to bad health had to spend much time away from state affairs. The Aragonese under Pedro IV again invaded the island in 1343 at Paguerra. Sancho's nephew and heir Jaime III tried to regain possession but was killed in battle in 1349. That brought to an end the reign of the independent kings of Mallorca, which became part of Aragon. (In 1716 Mallorca lost the title of kingdom and became a province of Spain.)

From 1349 until the present Mallorca has had a chequered history, with invasions, rebellions, and natural disasters such as earthquakes, floods, and outbreaks of cholera and bubonic plague. This chapter is not a history of Mallorca, but aims to point out the significance of some of the features seen on the island, so for further details of the history, see some of the books listed in the bibilography. The castles and the watchtowers are some of the most striking features, but other buildings also found on mountain tops are the *ermitas* or sanctuaries. One such is on the Puig de Maria, near Pollensa (Walk 18). Many others are in use and some of them offer refreshments and accommodation.

Cultivation

One of the most impressive sights in Mallorca is the blossoming of the almond trees in early spring when large areas of the island become pink and white. If you arrive by plane during daylight in February you may even observe this from the air. There are said to be over six million trees and most of the crop is exported. Planting of the almonds began in 1765, but the olive tree has been cultivated for much longer. Some of the trees are believed to be 1,000 years old or more, and their gnarled and twisted trunks will be seen on many of the walks. Sometimes you may see almonds or olives being harvested, the almonds being shaken from the trees onto sheets spread on the ground and the olives being knocked down by long poles.

Orange trees and other citrus fruits too are another sight to delight and interest the walker. The main crop is in January but fruit seems to be on some trees all the year round. The scent of the blossom is wonderful. Sometimes in the winter you can see blossom, green unripe fruit and bright orange (or yellow) ripe fruit all at the same time. Soller is famous for its orange groves, but they can be seen in many other parts of the island too, for example in the *huertas* or market gardens near Pollensa on the way to the Ternelles valley (Walk 13).

Potatoes are another crop grown for export, many of them on the central plain near Inca and Sa Pobla, including earlies for export to England. Strawberries are already ripening here under cloches in February and March. Other fruits grown are mandarins, peaches, apricots, melons and figs. Vines grow at Binisalem and near Felanitx where some very good wine is made. Fresh vegetables grow all the year round, thanks to the sunshine and the irrigation system. Often vegetables such as broad beans and peas are grown on terraces between the fruit trees. Several crops can be grown in succession and the first peas and beans will be harvested in February. The village markets all have a fine display of fruit and vegetables, most of them grown locally. It is a splendid treat to buy delicious fresh oranges, still with leaves attached, two or three kilos at a time.

The methods of cultivation too are a pleasure to watch. Horses and mules can still be seen pulling a primitive plough along narrow terraces where it would be impossible to use a tractor. Seed too is often hand sown from a sack hanging round the neck in a manner which may be archaic but is obviously still efficient. Corn and cereal crops are grown too, and grass for grazing is often sown on the olive terraces.

There are few cattle on Mallorca and much milk and dairy products are imported from Menorca. However there are large flocks of sheep and many goats in the mountains. These are usually belled and sometimes hobbled. Pigs are sometimes seen foraging about in oakwoods in a semi-wild state. Besides acorns they dig up roots and can make a real mess of some of the woodland paths in their search for food. One of the main animal markets is at Sineu, near the centre of the island, and is held on Wednesdays. Here can be seen magnificent rams, tiny lambs and goats, cages of birds and all manner of livestock.

Rural Industries

There were two major 'rural industries', the remains of which will be seen time and again on many walks in this book. In fact they are intimately connected with these walks because many of the footpaths were made by workers in these occupations. These two activities were snow-collecting and charcoal-burning and knowing something about these adds greatly to the interest of the walks.

Snow collecting

The highest man-made paths on Mallorca were all built by the *nevaters* or snow-collectors. Snow was collected on all the highest mountains to make ice for use in the summer, and conserved in pits or buildings known as *casas de nieve*. There were 7 on the Puig Mayor, 7 on Massanella, 2 on Tomir and on Teix and several on the Alfabia ridge. Most of them were at a height of over 900m. These structures are sometimes circular and sometimes rectangular, usually partly or wholly below ground level. The most unusual is the one on Tomir, below the Coll dels Puig des Ca, which is roofed over.

In winter when the mountains were covered with snow, groups of men from the nearest villages went up to gather the snow in carriers and baskets made from cane or grass. To make collecting easier flat platforms were often made and cleared of vegetation. These can still be seen. Here the snow was arranged in layers and trampled down hard to pack it into ice, in time to the following rhyme:

pitgen sa neu, pitgen sa neu
i tots estan dins ses cases
peguen potades, peguen potades
en Toni, en Xisco, en Juan i N'Andreu

Tramp the snow, tramp the snow
and throw it in the pit
Beat it down, beat it down,
on Tony, Harry, John and Andrew.

The packed snow was put in the pit and each layer covered with thin layers of grass (probably *carritx*), to make it easier to extract the blocks when required. When the pit was full, it was protected with a layer of ashes and finally a thick covering of branches. One man remained on duty all the year to maintain the covering in perfect condition. In the summer nights, huge blocks of the snow-ice were taken down on muleback to the villages and towns. It was not only used for ice-creams and cooling drinks, but also medicinally. An emulsion with olive-oil was used for dressing wounds and was believed to stop bleeding.

The local authority controlled the price and limited the production of ice, supposedly to prevent speculation. There was a specific tax on it. Sometimes ice had to be imported from Cataluña by boat, but other years there was overproduction and ice was exported to Menorca. It appears that the last occasion in which a snow-pit was used was in 1925 on the Puig de Massanella. The *casa de nieve* on the Son Moragues estate was built in the seventeenth century, but abandoned in the eighteenth century as it was not really at a high enough altitude. This one is seen on Walk 57. Nearby, the hut where the *nevaters* lived has been made into a shelter for walkers.

Charcoal production

Many other paths used by walkers today were made by the charcoal workers. Almost every wood of evergreen oaks was formerly used in the production of charcoal and there are still plentiful signs of this activity. The former charcoal hearths or pitsteads appear as flat circular areas often ringed by stones and covered with bright green moss. Many have been pointed out as landmarks in route descriptions. They are known as *sitjes* (singular *sitja*). The production of charcoal in Mallorca continued until butane gas became popular, roughly in the 1920s, although in some areas it continued for longer and there are still people alive today who worked in this industry in their youth. Occasionally pieces of charcoal can still be found on the sites. Its only use in Mallorca was for cooking, preferred rather than wood because it gives a cleaner and steadier heat.

The charcoal burners began work in April and lived and worked all summer in the woods with their families. They could not leave the site because charcoal burning is a delicate operation and everything could be ruined in a moment of neglect. For this reason they built huts to live in, the remains of which are often seen in the woods, together with a stone oven used to bake bread. These ovens are a beehive shape, instantly recognisable. They can be seen on Walks 30, 31, 57, 58 and others.

The process of making charcoal began with the felling of large oaks, of a diameter stipulated by the landowner. Each *carbonero* had his own area known as a *ranxo*. Axes and enormous two-handed saws were used to fell the trees. Meanwhile a perfectly flat and circular site had to be prepared. Stones were carefully arranged so that sufficient circulation of air would carbonise the wood without igniting it. On this platform the cut logs and branches were arranged in a 'cupola', leaving a narrow central chimney. Over all this was arranged a covering of gravel and clay. A ladder was needed to reach the top of the chimney through which the *carbonero* dropped live coals to start the process, and to feed the fire from time to time with small pieces of dry wood. Constant vigilance and expertise were needed on the part of the worker.

During the process the weight of the wood was reduced by 75-80%. Each firing lasted for 10-12 days, and would produce around 2,800 kilograms. When the operation was complete the covering was removed and very hot pieces extracted with a shovel and rake. Sieved earth was used for quenching as using water caused a loss of quality. Finally the charcoal was sorted into a number of different grades and taken by muleteers for sale at special shops in the villages. As a by-product, bark from the oak trees was collected and used for tanning.

A fine reconstruction of a charcoal-burning structure can be seen on the Son Moragues estate (Walk 57).

Lime-burning

Brief mention must be made of the limekilns which will be seen from time to time. There are three of them in the Cairats valley (Walk 57), but they will be seen in almost every woodland. They are rather different from those seen in the British Isles in that they are normally cylindrical. Lime is used for whitening houses, something which used to be done every year, and also for making mortar in the construction industry.

Great heat is needed to initiate the reaction $CaCO_3 \rightarrow CaO + CO_2$, so these *hornos de calc* were always built near a plentiful supply of wood. Great destruction of woodland was often the result. Although there is a vast amount of limestone on Mallorca, stones used to produce lime were always chosen very carefully and were known as *piedra viva* or living stones.

From the base of the circular pit used as a kiln, a cupola was built up of large stones with spaces left between them so that the flames could pass through. Above the cupola the rest of the oven was built up of stones and the space between the cupola and the outer walls of the kiln filled with pieces of limestone for calcining. The whole structure was then covered with slaked lime and soil. The interior was filled with wood and the fire lit. It was kept burning for a period of time varying from 9 to 15 days, wood being thrown in continually. The quantity required is impressive: up to 10 tons of branches during one firing. A firing would produce around 100-150 tons of lime. It was very hard work, the fire needing to be fed day and night. Nor was it financially rewarding, according to the old proverb *Qui fa calc, va descalc* (he who makes lime goes barefoot).

QUERCUS ILEX (HOLM OAK)

QUERCUS COCCITERA
(KERMES OAK)

WALKING IN MALLORCA

Equipment and clothing

Although the winters in Mallorca are mild and the weather is normally ideal for walking, bad weather is not unknown as in any area of high mountains. There are days when a warm sweater, anorak, hat, gloves and waterproofs will be appreciated, especially on the higher tops. There will always be days when these extra clothes will stay in the rucksack, even in January, the coldest month, but it's as well to be prepared. Boots are advised for most walks, although for those graded 'C' some may prefer trainers or strong shoes. Shorts are not advised because of the extremely prickly vegetation unless long trousers are taken along too. Sunglasses and a sunhat might be needed even in winter for those sensitive to hot sun. It is advisable to carry water or other drinks as dehydration can be very unpleasant and debilitating. The local oranges are both thirst-quenching and cheap.

Snow falls on the high tops most years, but it is very rare for it to fall at sea level as it did in December and January 1984-5. When this happens, the roads to the mountains are cut off for days on end, not only by snow but by fallen trees. The snow is usually wet and soft, so ice axes and crampons can be left at home. Of standard walking equipment take a whistle, compass and torch. Darkness falls early in midwinter, 17.30 on the shortest days, and some of the walks are long.

This book deals only with walks and occasional scrambles, none of which requires a rope, although some parties prefer to take a short length for the Cavall Bernat ridge (Walk 9) and the Torrente de Pareis (Walk 27). The whole island abounds in steep rock and there is much good rock climbing, with many crags hardly developed (see *Rock Climbs in Majorca, Ibiza and Tenerife* by Chris Craggs, Cicerone Press).

Maps

One of the best maps for getting about the island is the Firestone map, *Baleares: Map Turistico*, scale 1:125,000. This is available at petrol stations, newsagents and some general stores throughout the island. Another good general map is *Majorca Leisure Map: What to see - where to go,* scale 1:120,000. This has the bonus of 66 coloured photographs on the back of places of interest, with brief descriptions. This is also commonly available.

There are no ordnance survey maps of the high standard of the

British O.S. maps or the French IGN maps. However, since the first edition of this guidebook, new Spanish IGN maps have been published on the 1:25,000 scale. These are based on an aerial survey of 1979, and the contouring seems more accurate than on the military maps which were the only ones available previously. However, it is disconcerting that many roads and paths are missed out, especially where they are hidden by trees - and not only when they are in woodlands, as even the well-known path up the barranc from Biniaraix to the Cases de L'Ofre is missing. This means that the serious walker will want to have both sets of maps. The military maps are available on the scale of 1:50,000 as well as 1:25,000. To avoid confusion when ordering it is best to quote the quadrant by compass point rather than number. A list of the relevant military maps with the IGN equivalents is given at the end of this chapter.

The most important maps for walkers are Pollensa, Soller and Inca on the 1:50,000 scale. Of the 1:25,000 maps Son Marc, Pollenca, Soller, Esporles, Alaró and Selva are the most relevant. All maps, folded and in a plastic wallet, can be ordered from The Map Shop, 15 High Street, Upton-upon-Severn, Worcs WR8 0HJ (Tel: 01684 593146). When in stock they will be supplied by return of post (£3.00 each, plus postage, in December 1996). Stanfords' International Map Centre at 14 Long Acre, London, also stocks them, or they can be bought in Palma at the Libreria Fondevila at 14 Calle Arabi.

When using any of the maps for exploration, remember that the terrain is frequently more complex than is indicated by the map. Steep cliffs and crags are not always shown, new roads appear and old ones fall into disuse. Always leave time to get back to your starting point in case of unforeseen difficulties.

Grading definitions

All the walks in this book have been done by the writer. An attempt has been made to assess the difficulties in such a way that anyone using the book can form a reasonable idea of what to expect. Such assessment is obviously very subjective and can be influenced by weather conditions at the time and many other factors. When heavy rain occurs dry stream-beds can become raging torrents, landslips may occur, rocks can fall and the ground can become very slippery. At such times it is better to wait for things to improve, and once the sun is out again all the surface water quickly disappears.

Assuming normal conditions, the walks have been graded into three

49

categories which can be called difficult, average and easy or A, B and C. These categories refer to the terrain and the route-finding difficulties. The approximate times, distances, and heights involved are given separately in addition to the grading. Under the heading 'type of walk' a description gives details of what is involved. It cannot be over-emphasised that much of the walking in Mallorca is over very rough ground and this often takes much longer to negotiate than expected. Even the paths are usually rough and stony and require care. The walking times allow photography, some birdwatching and flower identification but do not include long stops for refreshments. On the whole they are for slower-than-average walkers, more interested in enjoying the scenery than setting up speed records.

The grades

A   A strenuous walk, often pathless in places and on rough ground with considerable route-finding and/or some scrambling. Normally only for experienced walkers.

B   An average mountain walk which may call for some skill in route-finding, but mainly on paths.

C   Easy walking along well-defined paths or tracks and with no route-finding difficulties.

Access

Many of the walks in this book go across private land. The maps do not show rights of way. However, by Spanish law, there is a right of way on any track leading to the sea, to a mountain top, or to monasteries, hermitages, towers, castles, or other famous landmarks, which just about covers every walk. That is the theory, but in practice it seems to be slightly different. For example, access restrictions have been imposed on the Ternelles valley and visitors are only allowed through the entrance gate on Saturday. In certain areas walkers have even been threatened in a very unpleasant manner. However, we personally have met with nothing but friendliness from the landowners we have encountered. On occasion they have gone out of their way to point out routes, and obviously appreciated our attempts to speak a few words of their language.

One fact worth knowing is that the ubiquitous sign *coto privado de caza* only means 'private hunting' and can be ignored by walkers. However, if there appears to be a lot of shooting going on, it might be more prudent to choose another walk. The black and white rectangular sign divided diagonally often seen on fence posts and gates also means private hunting.

Many tracks have a standard 'no entry' sign which means that cars are prohibited and this must be respected, but should not stop walkers. Often access gates or stiles are provided when the gate is a locked one, but more of these are needed. On the other hand there are some private estates where walkers are distinctly unwelcome. Exploration stops short when faced with 3m high fences and heavily padlocked gates topped with barbed wire and iron spikes.

There is no access to the summit of the highest mountain of Mallorca, the Puig Mayor, because it is occupied by a military radar station. The western spur, the Penyal de Mitx Dia, is outside the boundary and the ascent was described in the previous edition of this book, but the descent route was not satisfactory and so it has been omitted this time round. At one time there was a popular annual excursion to the top of the Puig Mayor itself to see the sunrise at the time of the summer solstice. A long walk was made of it, starting at Biniaraix and following the old road up to Monnaber, going up at night to avoid the scorching heat of the sun.

Walkers' 'country code'

It goes without saying that all walkers should have the utmost respect for the countryside through which they walk and for the people who live and work there. Although the vast majority of walkers have this ingrained in them, the fact remains that there are always a few people about who are careless or antisocial and by irresponsible actions can do serious damage to natural resources and private property. For this reason I am spelling out this code here, in the hope that the responsible readers of this book will not only continue to abide by the code themselves but take an active part in seeing that others do so. Even if this is only in minor ways, such as taking back an extra bit of litter or closing a gate left open by others, it can all help. Watching out for carelessness in use of matches in dry areas could even prevent the devastation of a fire.

The Country Code

1. Guard against all risk of fire.
    Forests, woodlands and scrub are all highly inflammable. Take every care with matches and cigarette ends and do not light fires except in recognised fire places.

2. Fasten all gates.
    Even if the gate is found open, unless obviously fastened open by the farmer.

3. Keep dogs under control.
    Keep dogs on leads whenever there is livestock about. Some farms have clear pictorial signs not allowing dogs at all.

4. Keep to the paths across farm land.
    Crops can be ruined by people's feet.

5. Avoid damaging fences, hedges and walls.
    Repairs are costly. Keep to recognised routes, using gates and stiles.

6. Leave no litter.
    All litter is unsightly and some is dangerous to livestock, such as glass, tins and plastic. Take all litter back to the town.

7. Safeguard water supplies.
    Avoid polluting water supplies in any way. Never interfere with wells, springs or cattle troughs.

8. Protect wildlife, wild plants and trees.
    Wildlife is best observed, not collected. To pick or uproot flowers, carve trees and rocks, or disturb wild animals and birds not only destroys other people's pleasure but can irrevocably damage the ecology.

9. Go carefully on country roads.
    Country roads have special dangers: blind corners, high walls, deep drops at the edge, slow-moving tractors, sheep and goats. Drivers should reduce their speed and take extra care; walkers should keep to the left, facing oncoming traffic.

10. Respect the life of the countryside.
    Set a good example and try to fit in with the life and work of the countryside. In this way good relations between walkers and landowners are preserved and those who follow are not regarded as enemies.

The importance of the Country Code cannot be too strongly emphasised. There is already some evidence that increasing numbers of walkers have resulted in landowners being antagonised and discouraging access across their land. Large parties should take special care over closing of gates, as it is only too easy to assume that the next one through will see to it. Leaders should try to ensure there is a responsible person at the rear. Large parties in themselves, with their tendency to chatter and spread out over a long line, can be resented as an intrusion into the landscape. Every effort should be made to keep numbers in guided parties to a minimum.

ICONA

This is the national institute for nature conservation (El Instituto Nacional para la Conservacion de la Natureleza). They are doing a lot of good work on the island and have acquired several tracts of land which are being conserved for public use, constructed some excellent paths and provided well-equipped picnic sites with shelters, cooking facilities and toilets. One of their largest undertakings is the purchase of the Son Moragues estate near Valldemossa which has become an open-air museum with reconstructions of charcoal-burning sites etc. (Walk 57).

SECONA

This is the nature conservation office of the Balearic government.

Mountain Rescue

There is no mountain rescue organisation on the island. In the event of an accident the Guardia Civil should be contacted (Tel. 46-51-12). Walking alone in the mountains is not recommended. There are many places where you could break a leg or worse and not be found for days or even weeks.

Guides

1. Pere Llobera, Calle Costa i Llobera, 40, Pollensa. Tel. 53-03-65. Walking, rock-climbing and caving.
2. Biel Ordinas, Calle Jaime I, 24, Santa Maria. Tel. 62-01-62. Walking and rock-climbing.

Relevant military maps and their IGN equivalents

Military maps		IGN maps
1:50,000 645 CABO FORMENTOR	1:25,000 645 IV (NW) Cabo Formentor 645 III (SW) Aucanada	1:25,000 645 I (NW) Cap de Formentor 645 III (SW) Alcanada
644 POLLENSA	644 I (NE) Cala de San Vicens 644 III/IV (SW) Son March 644 II (SE) Pollensa	644 II (NE) Cala de Sant Vicenc 644 III (SW) Son Marc 644 IV (SE) Pollenca
670 SOLLER	670 I (NE) Soller 670 III (SW) Esporlas 670 II (SE) Alaró	670 II (NE) Soller 670 III (SW) Esporles 670 IV (SE) Alaró
671 INCA	671 IV (NW) Selva 671 III (SW) Inca	671 I (NW) Selva 671 III (SW) Inca
698 PALMA	698 IV (NW) 698 III (SW) Calviá	698 I (NW) Sa Vileta 698 III (SW) Calviá
697 ANDRAITX	697 I & IV (NW & NE) Dragonera 697 II (SE)	697 II (NE) n.y.p. 697 IV (SE)n.y.p

1. PLAYA BAIX, ALCUDIA

The Playa Baix is a small, sheltered and unspoilt beach on the Alcudia peninsula where the sea is an incredible turquoise colour. It is not safe for bathing as there is a very strong undertow, but it is an excellent place for a picnic on a sunny day in winter or early spring. The approach through a sheltered valley with both woodland and open scrub is good for birdwatching.

To reach the starting point, take the Mal Pas road from the second traffic lights in Alcudia, if approaching from the direction of Puerto Pollensa. This means going straight on at the first lights, then at the second lights turn right and immediately left as the junction is slightly offset. Drive along this road for almost 2km then turn sharp right at a minor crossroads where there are two bars, the Bodega del Sol and Ca'n Tomeu. Keep straight on along this narrow country road to the Parque de Victoria, going through the double iron gates (usually open) and parking just inside.

Type of walk: A short easy walk along a level forest track with a gentle rise to the Coll Baix. The narrow path down to the sea is a good one, but there is some rough bouldery ground where it reaches the beach. (This path passes below steep cliffs with some loose rock; beware falling stones.)

Starting point:	Parque de Victoria entrance
Time:	3hr
Distance:	9km
Highest point reached:	148m
Total height climbed:	211m
Grade:	C
Map:	Aucanada 1:25,000

Follow the main forest road into the park, ignoring all side turnings. At first there are pinewoods on the left, then open scrub, and fields with almond trees and carobs on the right, sheltered by a low ridge. Further on the track runs through more pinewoods which are fairly open and

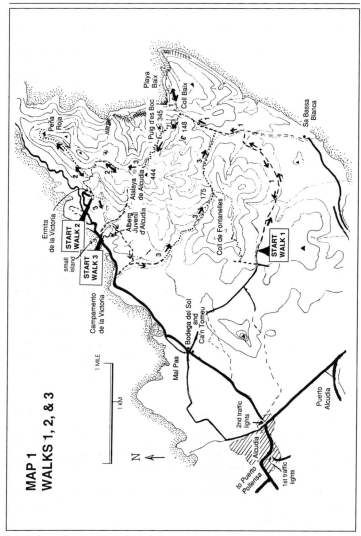

MAP 1
WALKS 1, 2, & 3

N

1 MILE

1 KM

Ermita de la Victoria

Peña Roja

Playa Baix

Coll Baix

Sa Bassa Blanca

Puig d'es Boc

345

148

444

175

Atalaya de Alcudia

Alberg Juvenil d'Alcudia

START WALK 2

small island

START WALK 3

Campamento de la Victoria

Coll de Fontanelles

START WALK 1

Bodega del Sol and Ca'n Tomeu

Mal Pas

2nd traffic lights

Alcudia

Puerto Alcudia

to Puerto Pollensa

1st traffic lights

have an undergrowth mainly of lentiscs and narrow-leaved cistus. There are dwarf fan palms, carritx, euphorbias and asphodels and a few giant orchids too.

About 30 minutes after the start there is a private road on the right signposted to Sa Bassa Blanca. Ignore this and keep on the main track which soon rises up to the Coll Baix, where there is a shelter provided by ICONA. Follow the path down to the beach. This goes quite a long way to the right before descending in zigzags, to avoid the steep and loose cliffs which are in the way of a straight descent from the col to the beach.

Park entrance - Coll Baix	1hr	5min
Coll Baix - Playa Baix		20min
Playa Baix - Coll Baix		30min
Coll Baix - park entrance	1hr	5min

(The Atalaya de Alcudia can easily be ascended from the Coll Baix by a good path if a longer walk is wanted. See Walk 3.)

2. PEÑA ROJA AND ATALAYA DE ALCUDIA

The Alcudia peninsula lies between the bays of Pollensa and Artà. It is hilly and wooded and although the Cap del Pinar at the end is a military area and out-of-bounds, part of it forms a national park and provides some easy and very attractive walks. Although only a low stump some 2m high is all that remains of the original watch-tower, it is still a wonderful viewpoint. There is a shelter below the top with a well on the flat terrace outside. The first part of the walk to the Peña Roja makes a worthwhile short excursion on its own, along an attractive path undulating below red cliffs and overlooking the sea. The barrel of an old cannon still lies on the flat circular top. At one time this had a low stone parapet and a cobbled floor.

Leave Alcudia by the Mal Pas road by going straight on at the second traffic lights if coming from the Puerto Pollensa direction. The junction is slightly off-set so that it is necessary to turn right then immediately left. Follow the coast road, turning right after approximately 4km to the *Ermita* where there is a large parking area, picnic places and a restaurant with a terrace overlooking the sea.

Type of walk: Easy, along wide tracks and well-made footpaths kept in good repair by ICONA. There are even handrails along the exposed places. The last ten minutes to the top of the Peña Roja is by a rocky path which is a little steep and a bit of a scramble.

Starting point:	Ermita de la Victoria
Time:	3hr 10min
Distance:	6km
Highest point reached:	444m
Total height climbed:	409m
Grade:	C+
Map:	Aucanada 1:25,000 or
	Cabo Formentor 1:50,000

Go up past the *Ermita* buildings by a wide track from the corner of the car park. After 20 minutes this makes a sharp bend to the right. Almost immediately turn left along the Peña Roja path which is signposted. This path contours along the base of the reddish cliffs and eventually rounds the end of the ridge by going through a short tunnel. Round the corner the path leads to an old stone shelter with an empty water storage tank behind it. Near this is found the start of the rough steep path which leads up in about ten minutes to the top of the Peña Roja.

Return by the same way to the wide track, turn left along it and continue up to a broad col at 315m. From here a stony ascent leads to a well-built path with protective handrail. This winds up to easy ground below the summit. Near the top, by the *Ermita* signpost, will be seen a very good path coming up from the Coll Baix, used in Walk 3. From the top, drop down a short way on the south side to reach the shelter.

Ermita - Peña Roja	1hr 5min
Peña Roja - Atalaya de Alcudia	1hr 15min
Atalaya de Alcudia - Ermita	50min

3. ATALAYA DE ALCUDIA BY FONTANELLES

This is a circular walk making use of a disused footpath in the Fontanelles valley which goes over the Coll de Fontanelles to join a forest road on the south side of the Atalaya. The road, formerly a forest track but surfaced in 1991, leads through the forest and up to the Coll Baix where there is an ICONA shelter. A footpath goes down to a small beach from here, described in Walk 1, and this could be followed if a longer walk is wanted. From the Coll Baix there is a good path built by ICONA up to the Atalaya. This is an excellent viewpoint, described in Walk 2.

Leave Alcudia by the road to Mal Pas, by doing a right and immediate left at the second traffic lights if arriving from the direction of Puerto Pollensa. The starting point is 4km further on from here. It is found 700m after crossing a stream-bed next to a disused bridge and almost immediately opposite a small island close to the shore. Park here opposite to the Bar S'Illetas.

Type of walk: Fairly easy on tracks and paths, but route-finding quite difficult in places, especially if trying to do the walk in reverse.

Starting point:	Alberg Juvenil d'Alcudia
Time:	4hr
Distance:	9km
Highest point reached:	444m
Total height climbed:	559m
Grade:	B
Map:	Aucanada 1:25,000 or
	Cabo Formentor 1:50,000

Turn right towards the hostel and then left into the woods by a track closed to cars by a chain. Turn right again and go up the low pine-covered ridge parallel to the road to the hostel. The path is not obvious at first, being obscured by pine-needles, but soon becomes evident at the point where it levels out. Follow it through open ground with newly-planted trees and ignore a cross-track. About 5 minutes after this cross-track turn right at a T-junction and roughly one minute later turn left along a track coming from the Campamento de la Victoria. The tennis courts at this children's holiday place are seen from here.

Follow the track across fairly level ground towards some new houses on the far side of the Fontanelles valley where the old and little-used track is picked up. Although slightly overgrown it is easy to follow and continues right up to the col.

The descent from the col is not all that easy to find. At first the path slopes down to the right and then back left. A side-stream on the left is crossed and at a second stream the path crosses the stream-bed at the junction. After this the path becomes a little easier, sometimes following the bed of the stream and finally meeting a forest road at a T-junction. Turn left and in about 15 minutes the Coll Baix will be reached. The path to the beach begins on the far side of the shelter, although it is probably best left for a separate excursion. The path to the Atalaya rises up through the trees on the north-west side of the col. This well-made path passes close to the top of the Puig d'es Boc which is an excellent viewpoint, before going on to the top of the Atalaya with its shelter and well.

From the summit return to the signpost and go straight down the steep path to a wide col, from where a forest road leads down to the *ermita*, below which is a large parking area. The last part of the descent begins at the corner of this car park at the exact point where the forest track joins it. No path is seen at first, but after a very short but quite steep descent a good path will be found. This leads down steadily to a stream-bed which is crossed and re-crossed and eventually joined and followed to reach a wide cross-track. Turn right along this to return to the starting point in a further 5 minutes.

Youth hostel - Coll de Fontanelles	1hr 10min
Coll de Fontanelles - Coll Baix	40min
Coll Baix - Atalaya de Alcudia	1hr 10min
Atalaya de Alcudia - Youth hostel	1hr

4. EL FUMAT AND ROCA BLANCA

The Fumat is a spectacular peak which overhangs the Formentor road near the tunnel. This short excursion is mainly pathless but not very difficult and on a good day the views are outstanding. It can easily be combined with Walk 5 to the Cala en Gossalba and this is strongly recommended. Alternatively there are easy walks down to the sea at Cala Murta and Cala Figuera which are quite short. The route makes use of an old track which was used to reach the lighthouse before the new road and tunnel were constructed in 1968. (Note that the old zigzag track continues down from the col between the Fumat and the Roca Blanca into the Cala Murta valley, but this is not a recommended route. The gradient is tedious, being made for a heavily laden mule, and the lower part has almost disappeared.) To reach the starting point drive through the tunnel towards the lighthouse and park at the viewpoint on the cliff-edge at K14.9.

Type of walk: Although only short the pathless nature of this route gives it a 'B' grade.

Starting point:	Viewpoint, Formentor road
Time:	2hr 35min
Distance:	4km
Highest point reached:	334m

In the Boquer Valley (Walk 8). Photo: W. Unsworth

Cala San Vicente and the Cavall Bernat Ridge (W.Unsworth)

On the ridge of La Coma (Walk 10a) (W.Unsworth)

Total height climbed:	300m
Grade:	B
Map:	Cap de Formentor 1:25,000

Walk back along the road from the viewpoint towards the tunnel and at a point marked by a cairn scramble up the hillside to reach the old lighthouse track which is just above the road. Follow this narrow track which leads up to the col between El Fumat and Roca Blanca at a gentle gradient. The top of the Fumat is reached quite easily from this col, up rock slabs and stony ground at an easy angle. After enjoying the view descend to the col and go straight up the ridge ahead to the Roca Blanca. There is no path but there are no particular difficulties. From the last top on the ridge continue downwards in the same direction, avoiding steep rocks when necessary on the south side. The ridge ends in a short cliff, but an easy way down can be found leading back to the right.

Once on easy ground walk along to the foot of the cliff, then make for a large pine tree in the valley below. Follow the red earth path back left to the viewpoint, or turn right to reach the Cala en Gossalba as in Walk 5.

Viewpoint - El Fumat	45min
El Fumat - col	15min
Col - first top Roca Blanca	25min
First top - last top	25min
Last top - viewpoint	45min

5. CALA EN GOSSALBA

This tiny bay of bright water on the south side of the Formentor peninsula is an unspoilt gem, inaccessible by car. The excellent path down to Cala en Gossalba was used to supply the lighthouse in the days before the new road was built, and also for the extraction of wood from the forest of pine trees. Some of these pines still stand to provide welcome shade in hot weather. This walk is ideal for a lazy day, or it can be done after the walk over the Fumat and Roca Blanca to give a longer excursion.

Type of walk: Easy, on a well-made path.

Starting point:	Viewpoint at K14.9, Formentor road
Time:	1hr 15min
Distance:	3km

The Fumat on the Formentor peninsula

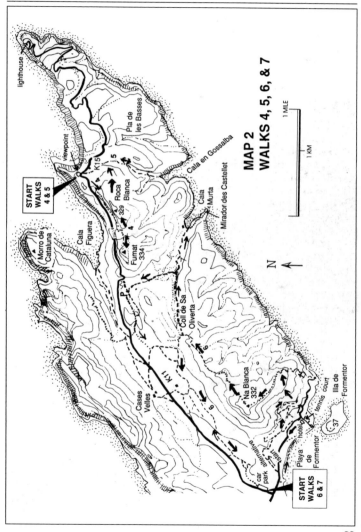

MAP 2
WALKS 4, 5, 6, & 7

1 MILE

1 KM

N ←

lighthouse

viewpoint

Pla de les Basses

START WALKS 4 & 5

K15

5

Roca Blanca

329

4

Fumat 334

Cala en Gossalba

Cala Murta

Mirador des Castellet

Cala Figuera

Morro de Cataluna

P

Coll de Sa Oliverta

6

Na Blanca 332

K11

Cases Velles

9

start
alternative

Playa de Formentor

hotel

tennis court

Illa de Formentor

37

car park

START WALKS 6 & 7

Total height climbed:	Descent and re-ascent of 176m
Grade:	C
Map:	Cap de Formentor 1:25,000

Go down the path from the viewpoint: it is slightly indistinct at first, but soon develops into an excellent and well-made mule track. It follows the river bed, which it occasionally crosses. There are no turnings and no cross-tracks, and the path ends on some rocks on the right-hand side of the little bay. To reach the shore, which is of boulders large and small, go down the last part of the stream-bed.

6. NA BLANCA

This pleasant hill on the Formentor peninsula provides a delightful and varied walk. The broad and rocky top overlooks the colourful waters of the Formentor beach and on clear days there are views across to the Alcudia hills and beyond them to Artà. The return route passes the nesting-sites of the Marmora's Warblers and goes through the sheltered wooded valley near the Cases Veyas where migrants rest during the spring and autumn migrations. During the winter this is a good place for residents such as hoopoes, black redstarts, firecrests, crossbills, linnets and great tits.

Note: In December 1996 new fencing had been completed along the Formentor road and locked gates (one a narrow pedestrian gate) placed across the track at the back of the car park. Hopes that this was a temporary measure have now faded and for the time being Na Blanca can only be done as a there-and-back walk from the Formentor car park.

Type of walk: Mainly easy walking on paths and tracks, but there is a pathless section on the ascent and it is rough and rocky for a short distance on the top.

Starting point:	Formentor car park
Time:	3hr 30min
Distance:	8km
Highest point reached:	332m
Total height climbed	342m
Grade:	B
Map:	Cala de Sant Vicenc 1:25,000 and Cap de Formentor 1:25,000

From the large car park at Formentor walk along the footpath to the jetty and turn left along the sea-front. At one point you have to go on to the sand, then up some steps to the walkway in front of the Formentor hotel. Although the grounds are private it is permissible to walk past them along the coast. At the end of the grounds go round the end of the fence and follow the road inland. Take the second turn to the right, where the main road bends left by a house called Casa Desiderata, after passing the hotel tennis courts. This branch road goes through a gateway with a chain for cars and ends by the gates of a house on the Punta Caseta. Immediately before the gate and on the right of a stream-bed, go through the bushes and up some rough ground. An old path is very soon found, leading back right to the wooded ridge near an old gate. Follow the path up the ridge. It is well marked with cairns. Higher up avoid following a branch path off to the right and keep going up the ridge, where a stony path leads along the edge of steep rocks to the top.

Alternative start:

Walk towards the Formentor hotel along the road and take the first turn left about 100m past the landing stage. About 20 minutes after the start join another track coming from the left. About one minute later turn left where the main track descends to the right, just after passing a house called Quinta Bareta. The track now keeps at a fairly constant height and makes a sharp bend left at a point where a private chained road goes straight on. The track then rises before crossing a torrent bed, branches right and re-crosses the torrent bed to contour again. A workman's hut is passed and in 5 minutes the track rounds a corner and comes to an end. Exactly at this point look out for red paint marks on rocks and pine trees. There is no path but it is easy to pick out a route using the paint marks to give the general direction. Make for a metal pylon supporting electric cables, the first metal one above some wooden ones. From the pylon look uphill and further red marks will be seen ahead. When a group of cairns on a large rock slab are reached it is best to traverse right to join the ridge which rises from the Punta Caseta.

From the top, follow the ridge down in a north-easterly direction to join a path at an unnamed col at 188m. A few cairns mark the way, which in any case is well defined by the proximity of steep crags on the left. Follow the track along from this col to the Coll de Sa Oliverta and continue down into the wooded valley below. Ignore a right and then a left turn, but take the left fork at a junction reached about 10 minutes after leaving this col and at the corner of the cultivated fields. Take another left fork after a further 10 minutes. Ignore a right turn which leads to the road and continue to a flat sports field, the 'Campo de Desportes, Formentor.' Cross the field at its left-hand edge to find a track leading to the right. After 100m fork left at a minor cross-track and follow this down to the car park.

Car park - Na Blanca	1hr 50min
Na Blanca - Coll de Sa Oliverta	50min
Coll de Sa Oliverta - Car park	50min

7. CALA MURTA AND MIRADOR DES CASTELLET

Cala Murta is a small cove on the south side of the Formentor peninsula which can only be reached on foot. Picnic tables and barbecue sites have been provided at the back of the stony beach and a newly restored footpath leads to a mirador looking out to the detached rock El Castellet. The approach through the woods in the sheltered Cases Veles valley is delightful and also an opportunity for some bird-watching. In fact it is one of the best areas on the island for observing migrants in both spring and autumn. Look out for crossbills, linnets, black redstarts, warblers, flycatchers and many others.

Type of walk: Very easy on good tracks and paths.

Starting point:	Formentor car park
Time:	3hr
Distance:	11.5km
Total height climbed:	240m
Grade:	C
Map:	Cala de Sant Vicenc 1:25,000 and Cap de Formentor 1:25,000

Walk up through the woods from the back of the car park where there is a pedestrian access gate. (These woods have recently been fenced off to prevent vehicles driving using the tracks. During forestry operations the access gate for walkers has also been locked. If this is the case then you can either walk or drive up the road and park near K11 by the Cases Velles. The gate here should not be locked and allows you to join the track near the substation.)

Assuming the gate at the top end of the car park is open, follw the wide track heading north-east into the woods. Turn right at a cross-track by a limekiln and pass below a landfill site. After passing a shelter built under an overhanging rock veer left across a flat area towards a ruined building. Bear right and after about 200m ignore a branch track left and keep on the main tack to an electricity substation. Just past this fork right (at the point you would join the route if walking in from the gate at K11) and then fork right again after about 600m. Fork right yet again after 200m, after which the track zigzags uphill to the Coll de Sa Oliverta.

Turn left on a wide track by a sign painted on a boulder. This leads down into the valley and joins a narrow surfaced lane which is followed downhill right to reach the small bay of Cala Murta. The path to the mirador is on the right and is signposted. To return, go back up the lane for about 1.5km, passing the turn to the Coll de Sa Oliverta, until there is a sharp right turn by a children's camp. Turn left at this point and follow the track which rises over a low hill and then bends right to go through a metal gate. Half a minute later turn left on a minor track which runs parallel to a stone wall. After about 500m turn left again, then take the first branch right in about 200m. After a further 350m turn right at a T-junction where the outward route is joined and followed back to the start.

If a shorter walk is required, then there is some parking at about K 12.8, near the Cases de Cala Murta. Walk down the road from here which leads to a locked gate with an opening at the side for walkers and simply follow the narrow traffic-free lane down to Cala Murta and back.

8(a). BOQUER VALLEY FROM PUERTO POLLENSA

This attractive and sheltered valley is much favoured by migrant birds, and in winter is always a good place for seeing some of the residents such as the beautiful Blue Rock Thrush. It is also interesting botanically and the flowers of *Cyclamen balearicum* can be found within a few feet of the valley wall under the shelter of other shrubs. The valley is bounded on the north-west by the splendid Cavall Bernat ridge in which there are several spectacular holes or windows. One of these is easily seen from the path. There is a good path right down to the small shingly beach of Cala Boquer. The end of the Cavall Bernat ridge dips steeply into the sea and there are views across the bay to the detached rock of Es Colomer. (The beach itself is disappointing, with debris washed in by the sea.)

Type of walk: Very easy, along good paths.

Starting point:	Puerto Pollensa
Time:	2hr
Distance:	6km
Highest point reached:	84m
Total height climbed:	168m
Grade:	C
Map:	Cala de Sant Vicenc 1:25,000 and Pollensa 1:25,000

If arriving by car, turn right where the Pollensa road meets the sea-front and park in one of the sea-front car parks. Walk along the sea-front to the left and go straight on along a footpath in front of a terrace of small hotels. Turn left along the Avenida Bocharis at the end of this terrace and cross the main road opposite the stone gateposts at the entrance to the Boquer farm track. The avenue of old trees that once led through the fields is now surrounded by building sites, but the trees have been preserved. Follow the track to the farm and pass in front of the farmhouse to go through the iron gate at the end of the courtyard.

Turn right immediately, go through another gate and follow the track between some immense boulders into the Boquer valley. The track then continues through gaps in the stone walls and over the low Coll de Moro, from where it continues as a narrow and less defined path down a wide shallow gully to the sea. It is possible to walk on past a fisherman's shelter to a small platform overlooking the bay.

8(b). BOQUER VALLEY FROM CALA SAN VICENTE

Walkers staying at Cala San Vicente can get to Puerto Pollensa by public buses, or sometimes by a courtesy bus provided by local hoteliers, or else over the Coll de Siller, an easy walk taking one hour.

From the Molins beach go up the steps near the telephone booths to reach an unsurfaced track. Turn right at the top, then left past the small hotel Los Pinos and turn right again. Go through an old gate at the beginning of a level section, then turn left by an electricity sub-station, then first right by a red arrow. This leads to a cairned footpath across level ground. After going down into and up out of a little stream-bed this re-joins the main track. (This track is a continuation of the road running south along the coast from the Molins beach, which can be followed for easier walking or for variety.) This wide track continues past the white Water Board building on the Siller Pass for about 200m

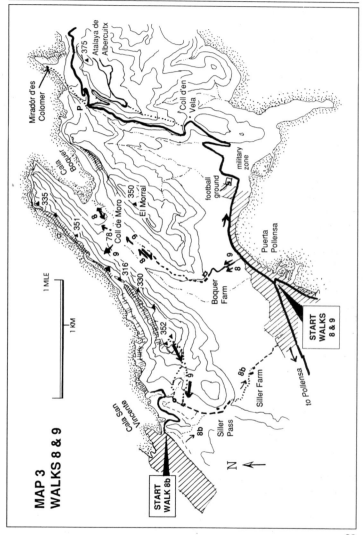

MAP 3
WALKS 8 & 9

1 MILE

1 KM

N

Mirador d'es Colomer

375
▲ Atalaya de Albercuitx

P

Coll d'en Vela

military zone

football ground

Cala Boquer

335
351
352
330
316
78
350

Coll de Moro

El Morral

8
9

Puerta Pollensa

9
8

Boquer Farm

START WALKS 8 & 9

to Pollensa

8b

Siller Farm

Siller Pass

8b

START WALK 8b

Cala San Vincente

then ends abruptly.

From the end of the track there are several alternative ways all marked by a superfluity of cairns. Go roughly straight on, all paths leading to the left of a large private house. Go through the iron gates at the side of the house and follow the lane to a T-junction at the Siller gateway. Turn left and keep following the road, unpaved at first, until the main road is met. Turn left towards the sea-front.

In returning to Cala from the port, the easiest way to find the Siller track is to walk along the Pollensa road to a small bar almost opposite the petrol station and turn right there.

9. SERRA DE CAVALL BERNAT

The Cavall Bernat ridge lies between the bay of Cala San Vicente and the Boquer valley. Although its maximum height is a modest 350m it has very steep cliffs and those on the Cala side plunge the full height vertically into the sea over a length of 2km. In the evening light the slanting rays illuminate their intricate structural detail and they glow with changing shades of amber, orange and pink. A most spectacular and beautiful sight. From the other side it is also a splendid back-drop to Puerto Pollensa, seen to particular advantage when driving along the coast road from Alcudia. The double tower about half-way along the ridge looks quite astonishing from many viewpoints. The traverse of the full ridge from end to end is a major undertaking, requiring rock climbing experience.

Type of walk: The route described here is not long, but includes exceedingly rough walking and some quite difficult scrambling. The ascent of the tower is not technically difficult, but it is sensationally exposed and requires a good head for heights. It could be classed as an easy rock climb rather than a walk. Nevertheless it is highly recommended to experienced scramblers who will find it interesting, strenuous and enjoyable. Those wanting an easier approach are recommended to approach the ridge from the Cala San Vicente side, leaving the Siller Pass road just before the large turning area at a cairn by the stream-bed. It is then comparatively easy to reach the west top and to follow the ridge as far as you wish before returning the same way.

Starting point:	Puerto de Pollensa
Time:	4hr 20min

Distance:	8.5km
Highest point reached:	352m
Total height climbed:	466m
Grade:	A+
Map:	Cala de Sant Vicenc 1:25,000 and Pollensa 1:25,000

Leave Puerto Pollensa by walking along the sea-front and into the Boquer valley as in Walk 8. Continue along the Boquer valley track as far as the second wall crossing the valley; this is opposite the obvious col on the ridge to the right of the impressive double tower in which lies one of the 'windows'. A narrow path on the inland side of the wall leads to some ruined buildings. From the corner of the fields here find a way up a shallow gully towards the col using goat tracks and scree between the vegetation.

From the col turn left and climb up the steep rock tower near the edge overlooking the sea. This is a very spectacular and exposed situation, but easier than it looks. The topmost section of the tower is avoided by taking to a sloping ramp leading up to the left. This arrives at a cairn quite near the top. From this point onwards the exhilarating route continues westwards along the ridge. To reach the 'window ledge' look for a small cairn which shows the easiest way down on the eastern side, then regain the ridge the same way to continue the route.

An alternative way to reach the window without climbing the tower is by the 'Ledge Route'. From just below the col turn left and follow an obvious rocky ledge at the foot of the tower. This becomes narrow in places, but is not difficult and leads across a subsidiary ridge to a broad sloping shelf below the window. Walk along this, passing below the window until it is possible to scramble up to the top of the ridge. Walk back along the ridge to find the way down to it at the eastern side.

Continuing westwards along the ridge, the most difficult part is an awkward move on the descent of the double tower. Perhaps this is technically the most difficult part of the route. It has to be said that even after making several traverses of the ridge finding the best way is not easy. In places there are cairns and flattened vegetation to indicate the way, but trial and error as well as route-finding skills will be called upon.

A second window is found just before reaching the last col. On the rise up to the final top, either continue along the edge of the cliffs, or choose easier walking in the shallow valley lying between the main ridge and another on the left. A short way up this valley and on the right

On the Cavall Bernat ridge, looking towards Formentor

a large hole in gently sloping ground penetrates the sea-cliff to form another impressive window. The final top is double and a line of cairns can be followed down from the dip between the two peaks, crossing a wall. Turn right along the second wall to pick up another descending line of cairns at the end of it. When the angle eases the best way down is to go right, below some steep rocks, and pick up traces of a path which follow a kind of subsidiary ridge down towards the sea, then curve left to reach the Cala-Siller road at a stream-bed below the large circular turning area. Another way is to follow the line of the main ridge and then drop into the shallow depression on the right. When the cairns end, make a slightly rising traverse towards a white building on the Siller Pass road and turn left here to return to Puerto Pollensa, or right to Cala San Vicente.

Puerto Pollensa - col on ridge	1hr 30min
Col - 375m top	1hr 30min
375m top - Coll de Siller	50min
Coll de Siller - Puerto Pollensa	30min

10(a). LA SERRA DE LA PUNTA: RIDGE ROUTE

This low ridge with several tops (named La Coma on the military maps) lies between the Cala San Vicente valley and the main road between Pollensa and its port. Some years ago local cavers found a hitherto unknown cave in this area which proved to be a most important archaeological find. Reconstructions of the wooden burial urns in the form of bulls found in the cave can be seen in the museum in Pollensa.

As a walk, people seem either to love it or to hate it. Those who like wandering along easy paths should give this one a miss, but it appeals to others who like the challenge of making their way over rough country. The terrain is almost wilderness, yet it is within sight and sound of the road and village of Cala San Vicente.

Type of walk: Easy walking along tracks and road to the beginning of the ridge, then pathless on difficult ground, but no route-finding problems. Sometimes easy walking on bare rock, but some boulder hopping and negotiation of scrub cannot be avoided.

Starting point:	Cala San Vicente
Time:	4hr 30min
Distance:	8.5km
Highest point reached:	315m
Total height climbed:	393m
Grade:	B+
Map:	Pollensa 1:25,000

From the Molins beach go up the steps behind the telephones and turn right along the track through the woods. Follow this track through a gate and cross the stream to join the main road just outside the village. Turn left and follow the road to the junction with the road to the port. Go up behind the notice boards and follow the well-defined ridge over several tops. Most people are surprised by how long and rough this ridge is.

The last top has a distinctive cairn standing on a circular wall. Follow the ridge down towards the Coll de Siller. The easiest way is to keep to the ridge at first, then look out for a way off to the left, following the white cairns which avoid the steep lower end of the ridge. The well-marked path leading down to Cala San Vicente is then followed.

Cala San Vicente - road junction		50min
Road junction - main top	2hr	25min
Main top - Cala San Vicente	1hr	15min

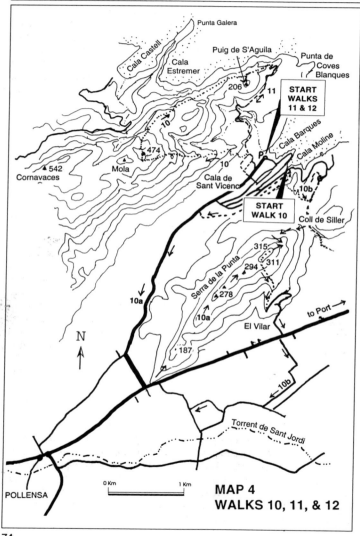

MAP 4
WALKS 10, 11, & 12

10(b). LA SERRA DE LA PUNTA: FROM SILLER PASS

This alternative route is much shorter and less strenuous than the ridge route. It follows the ridge leading up to the highest top from the pass, but avoids the lower part of it which is very steep and rocky. All the same it is still no hands-in-the-pocket stroll and provides a good introduction to the type of terrain often encountered in Mallorca. If the suggested return route is followed then typical market garden countryside is also seen.

Starting point:	Cala San Vicente
Time:	3hr 40min
Distance:	8km
Highest point reached:	315m
Total height climbed:	315m
Grade:	B
Map:	Pollensa 1:25,000

Start either from Cala San Vicente or Puerto Pollensa and go up the Siller Pass by the ordinary way. Some 200m on the Cala side of the pass a white arrow points to the start of the route, and some conspicuous white cairns can be seen higher up. There is no path, but it is easy to choose a way using the cairns as a general directional guide. A large white mark indicates the place where the ridge is most easily gained and followed to the top.

From the top walk along the ridge for about 5 minutes to the second little top. Make a sharp left turn here and the houses of El Vilar soon come into view. Go down the broad ridge, heading between a prominent house on the left and what appears to be a narrow path on the right. Easy walking is found near the remains of an old electric fence with its ceramic insulators still attached. After reaching some cairns on a rocky outcrop bear right to pick up the path, which is in fact the edge of a wide but overgrown track. Follow it down to the road, through the houses of El Vilar.

To return to Cala San Vicente without walking on the busy main road, turn right then immediately left towards the Club Tropicana. At the end of the straight road by a black gate, turn right, then left, then right again. After 500m turn right where another road comes in from the left. There are good views of the ridge route on this stretch. The road now makes several bends before swinging right at a fork and then turning left. Turn right at a T-junction by a square-arched gateway and follow the road along until it re-joins the main road about 100m from the Cala road junction. Either walk back into Cala San Vicente or wait for a bus.

Cala San Vicente - summit	1hr 30min
Summit - road at El Vilar	1hr 10min
El Vilar - road junction	1hr

11. PUIG DE S'AGUILA

This small hill (Eagle Peak) overlooking the sea makes a worthwhile short excursion from Cala San Vicente. There are excellent views, especially in the afternoon when the sun is shining on the magnificent rocks of the Cavall Bernat ridge across the bay. This view is irresistible to painters and photographers. Take a torch if you are interested in exploring the rock tunnels leading to some old ammunition stores.

Since 1996 access is permitted only on Mondays, Wednesdays and Fridays from mid-day onwards. The land is leased to a consortium of hunters and no hunting is allowed on these days.

Type of walk: Easy, along a good but stony track as far as the tunnels; then a narrow path to the top, only a short distance but rather steep.

Starting point:	Cala San Vicente
Time:	2hr 15min
Distance:	6km
Highest point reached:	206m
Total height climbed:	200m
Grade:	C
Map:	Cala de Sant Vicenc 1:25,000

From the circular car park at Cala Barques walk up the main road inland for about 100m and then turn right up a flight of steps between two houses. At the top of the steps turn right and go right again at a T-junction. The track leads to a locked gate at the entrance to the quarry road. Access used to be by a gap in the wall but this has been closed by a locked gate with a notice in three languages explaining the new access restrictions, but since the hunting season closed at the end of February the gate has not been locked and it is expected that the restrictions will not be enforced again until the new season starts in the autumn. If the gate has not been unlocked there is a way round the fence on the left. Follow the wide but stony track which makes several bends to cross stream-beds, then passes an old quarry where a beautiful white, pink and black rock has been extracted. After a sharp bend left the first tunnel leading into the old ammunition store is reached. This runs straight in for some 40m, then makes a right turn and divides, one part going straight on and the other turning left, then right and right again to meet up with the first part. Do not attempt to explore without a torch.

When the road comes to a sudden end, a well-made path marked by cairns and red paint continues horizontally at first and then zigzags up to the lower top of the Puig de S'Aguila. Care is needed near the top as there is a deep shaft, easily recognised by the gravelly spoil heap at the side. The prominent cairn on this little summit is the point of return for many walkers and is a worthwhile objective, but continuing to the main top is highly recommended. Follow the narrow path on across a small depression and then fairly steeply up to another small top with a large cairn and a fine view of the Punta Galera, a long and bare rocky point jutting into the sea. Away to the west Cornavaces can be seen and so can the Castell del Rei, with the cairned route to Mola ahead. From this viewpoint leave the main path and turn left to cross a low saddle and rise easily to the Puig de S'Aguila, to be rewarded by outstanding views.

To return, either retrace your steps or vary it slightly by going down the shallow valley on the north side where another line of cairns marks the way back towards the lower top. Just before reaching this you can if you wish take a short cut down the gully towards the quarry road.

12. MOLA

The area between Ternelles and Cala San Vicente is mountainous and uninhabited except for wild goats. The mountains are not high, but give some very rough walking. They are in the form of parallel ridges with very steep cliffs on the north-western side. Mola, at the eastern end of the Serra de Sant Vicenc ridge, is the most accessible of the tops and this circular route is a good introduction to the sort of terrain often encountered in Mallorca. **Since 1996 this walk has been restricted to Mondays, Wednesdays and Fridays from midday** (see note at beginning of Walk 11).

12(a). NORMAL WAY BY THE EAST RIDGE

Type of walk: Rough and rocky ground with occasional traces of paths. Easy return along the quarry road from the Puig de S'Aguila.

Cala San Vicente from Mola

Starting point:	Cala San Vicente
Time:	4hr 15min
Distance:	6.0km
Highest point reached:	474m
Total height climbed:	493m
Grade:	B+
Map:	Cala de Sant Vicenc 1:25,000

Begin the walk as for Walk 11. From the car park overlooking Cala Barques walk inland and turn up the steps on the right after 100m. Turn right at the top and then right again and go through the new gate (or round the fence at the left). Immediately after this turn left on a rough path going inland. After about 100m leave it and make for the ridge to the left of the end tower. Walk up the first section of the ridge on easy bare rock to reach a cairn, then cross a stretch of level ground to the right to reach the offset continuation of the ridge. At the top of this section there is another cairn. Continue up in the same direction, passing the top of a gully which goes down steeply on the right. Go up the broken ground ahead towards a shoulder slightly to the right of the little peak ahead. Occasional goat tracks and some outcrops of solid rock are a help. From this shoulder it is worth making the short diversion to the little top on the left from where there is a clear view back down the ridge to Cala San Vicente and the Cavall Bernat ridge.

Ahead is a rock tower, steep at the bottom. Cross the little col and go up to the left of the tower on easy rock and scree below the steepest rocks. A path is beginning to develop and there are some cairns. Higher up look for a break in the steep rocks which allows a rising traverse right to be made to the top of Mola. This top is the highest of the three, all marked as 457m on the old maps, now promoted to 474m on the new IGN map.

Leave the summit by descending to the north and cross the hollow straight ahead to a small rocky top on the far ridge. Turn right (NE) along this ridge and descend on good rock, keeping to the edge of the steep ground on the left. After about 500m make for a low rocky outcrop in the middle of a slight hollow, following bare rock ribs when possible for easier walking. Continue in the same general direction, getting closer to the edge of the cliffs again. A short rise is followed by a descent towards a wall. Ignore the red arrow pointing towards the right. A cairn marks the beginning of quite a good but narrow path going up along the edge of continuous and impressive cliffs overlooking the sea. This leads towards an indefinite top from which can be seen two further tops. Make for the left of these and continue on to the lower top of the Puig de S'Aguila. On this top is a hollow and a deep shaft and further on a group of three shafts with an easy path on either side.

Reach the quarry track either by keeping straight on towards the sea and bearing slightly right, or go down the path on the west side of the top used in the ascent of Aguila. At the end of the quarry track, go through the new gate and turn left to reach the steps back down to the road.

Cala San Vicente - Mola	2hr
Mola - Puig de S'Aguila	1hr 30min
Puig de S'Aguila - Cala San Vicente	45min

12(b). MOLA BY A ROCK SCRAMBLE

This route gains the Serra de San Vicenc ridge by a pleasant scramble up an unnamed rock tower, reaches the top of Mola from the northeast, then descends the east ridge of Mola back to Cala.

Starting point:	Cala San Vicente
Time:	4hr

Distance:	5.5km
Highest point reached:	474m
Total height climbed:	480m
Grade:	A+
Map:	Cala de Sant Vicenc 1:25,000

Leave Cala San Vicente by the quarry road as for Walk 11. In about 20 minutes two bridges are reached, close together. Follow the dry streambed from the first bridge and make for the foot of the right-hand rocky peak at the valley head.

The route goes up by the ridge which forms the right-hand skyline and this can easily be gained if the rock is dry by climbing the head of the gully direct. If wet, go up diagonally left, then back right to the notch above the steep section. The ridge is mainly good clean rock with ample holds, although there are one or two patches of dense and trying vegetation.

The scramble ends at a pleasant little rock tower. From the top cross two small rocky knolls and keep going in the same direction to a wall. After crossing the wall continue up the vague ridge ahead, choosing bare rock for the easiest walking and making for the cliff edge on the right as soon as desired. From this cliff there are spectacular views down to the sea and up the Ternelles valley to the Castell del Rei, with the steep face of Cornavaces forming the continuation of the cliffs.

Follow the ridge up until the ground levels out a little with a rocky top on the left. Go up this by a small but obvious groove to reach one of the three tops of Mola, which have between them a grassy depression. Cross over to the east and highest top which has a prominent cairn. To descend, go down at first towards the south-east to avoid some steep ground and find the obvious break in a little escarpment, then down to the right to reach some bare rock ledges. From here go back left and continue in this direction at the foot of some steep rocks to arrive at a small col. Cross this col to the left of a small top ahead and continue down by easy rocks and boulders to another small col. Continue over the next little top and on down towards the end of the ridge. Descend to easy ground on the right before reaching the final tower and make for the gate to the quarry road.

Cala San Vicente - Unnamed top	1hr 10min
Unnamed top - Mola	1hr 20min
Mola - Cala San Vicente	1hr 30min

13(a). CASTELL DEL REI

The situation of the ruined Castell del Rei, overlooking the sea from the edge of very steep cliffs, is extremely impressive. It was an important stronghold of the Arabs, but was taken by Jaime I in about 1230 by offering good terms to the defenders. Later it was besieged by Aragonese invaders in 1285 and again in 1343, but eventually had to surrender. The ruins cover an extensive area and it is well worth spending some time here. Black vultures are sometimes seen on this walk, especially up near the castle.

The walk goes through the wooded and beautiful Ternelles valley which is privately owned. Although according to Spanish law there is a right of way to visit historic monuments such as this, **access is now restricted to Saturdays 08.30 to 15.00hrs**, and then for a few weeks only in the autumn and again for a few weeks in the spring. Sometimes conditions have been imposed, such as showing of passports at the gate or obtaining a permit in advance. At the time of writing the practice is for the guard to make a note of the name of your hotel and the number of people in the party. It is recommended that before setting out on this walk enquiries are made locally as to the current position. These restrictions only apply to visitors. Residents are allowed access at any time but may have to show identity card or passport. A few years ago an extensive programme of restoration on the castle itself began and it is only possible to go as far as the col just below the entrance, although there is a fine view from the rocks nearby.

Type of walk: Although quite long, the walk is easy along country roads and a forest track. The uphill gradients are mainly gentle and nowhere very steep. Only the last five minutes require a little effort up a stony path.

Starting point:	Crossroads on C710 near Roman bridge, Pollensa
Time:	4hr 15min
Distance:	13km
Highest point reached:	491m
Total height climbed:	430m
Grade:	C
Map:	Pollensa 1:50,000

The narrow road to Ternelles begins just outside Pollensa at a signposted crossroads on the Lluc road C710, near the Roman bridge.

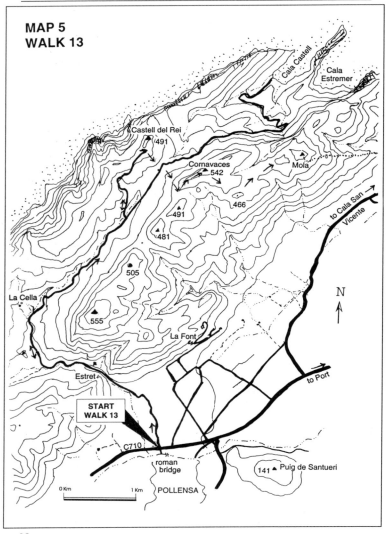

MAP 5
WALK 13

Cala Castell

Cala Estremer

Castell del Rei
▲491

Cornavaces
▲542

Mola

466

▲491

▲481

to Cala San Vicente

505

La Cella

▲555

La Font

N
↑

to Port

Estret

START WALK 13

C710

roman bridge

141 ▲ Puig de Santueri

POLLENSA

0 Km   1 Km

It is possible to park in the town near here, by going into Pollensa from the crossroads and turning first left. (N.B. To walk here from the bus station, turn left and go up through the main square, the Plaza Mayor, up to the right of the church, then right into a small square with a distinctive cockerel fountain, left here, then right into the Calle de la Huerta. Follow this long street to the edge of town where it crosses a bridge to reach the crossroads.)

On the way to Ternelles the road goes through a very attractive area of market gardens with almond orchards and orange trees. As it enters the 'Narrows', the remains of a Roman aqueduct may be seen. At the entrance gates to the Ternelles property, there is a guard on duty who may ask to see your permit or your passport or want to write down the name of your hotel.

After going through this gate, the road becomes unsurfaced. About 100m after passing the large house drinking water may be obtained from a brass tap on the right. This is spring water which local people collect in large plastic containers.

Another access gate is provided at the second locked gate, after which the track begins to rise. Shortly after crossing a cattle grid the track divides into two; take the right fork which is signposted 'Castell del Rei' and continue uphill until the trees thin out and the castle can be seen in the distance. The left turn that leads to the castle will be found 100m beyond the start of a fenced area on the right. (The main track continues over the Coll de Miquelet and down to the sea at Cala Castell.) The track to the castle ends at a flat area from where a narrow path leads to the gateway arch which is the entrance to the ruins.

Most walkers are content to return the same way, but a more adventurous alternative is to return by the Pas dels Pescadors to Cala San Vicente. This is an A+ walk and not recommended except to strong walkers used to some hard scrambling. To do this, go down the track towards Cala Castell to a sharp hairpin bend and follow the paint marks up towards the cliffs. The scramble makes use of a natural ledge and then goes steeply up a kind of chimney which is quite exposed. At the top of the cliffs follow the edge left and return along the Puig de S'Aguila route.

| Pollensa - Castell del Rei | 2hr 15min |
| Castell del Rei - Pollensa | 2hr |

13(b). CASTELL DEL REI AND CORNAVACES
The steep northern face of Cornavaces is part of an almost continuous

line of cliffs extending eastwards right to the Puig d'Aguila. It is a fine viewpoint, guarding the Ternelles valley on the east as the castle does on the west. This walk starts in Pollensa and ends in Cala San Vicente. There is a morning bus from Cala to Pollensa at 08.45 and an evening bus at 18.45.

Starting point:	Pollensa crossroads near Roman bridge
Time:	6hr 30min
Highest point reached:	542m
Total height climbed:	727m
Grade:	A
Map:	Pollensa 1:25,000 and Cala de Sant Vicenc 1:25,000

Go to the castle as in Route 13(a). From the broad track just below the castle go down the hillside to the Coll de Miquelet. There is no path but it is not difficult ground. Go up the hillside opposite on the outside of the wall bounding the cultivated area. Turn right along the wall from the corner and then strike up to the col between Cornavaces and Barrancada. Turn left at the col and follow the edge of the cliffs up to the top. Keep near the edge for striking views of the north-east face of Cornavaces.

From the top it is an easy walk across a dip and up to the 478m top of the Serra de San Vicens ridge. Follow this ridge along to Mola, a triple top with a high point of 474m being the most easterly. Go down the east ridge to Cala San Vicente as in Walk 12(b).

Pollensa - Castell del Rei	2hr 15min
Castell del Rei - Cornavaces	1hr 45min
Cornavaces - Mola	1hr
Mola - Cala San Vicente	1hr 30min

14. RAFAL DE ARIANT AND MORTITX GORGE

The area of the Mortitx gorge is one of the roughest and wildest places in the Sierra de Tramuntana. The area is important ecologically and is now under the protection of ICONA. The property occupies some dozens of square kilometres, sloping down from the foot of Tomir towards the sea. There are incredible rock formations in the karst landscape, and old olive trees with gnarled and twisted trunks. The sea cliffs are pocked with caves and holes. The gorge itself is interesting botanically with plants that prefer moister conditions than those that prevail elsewhere.

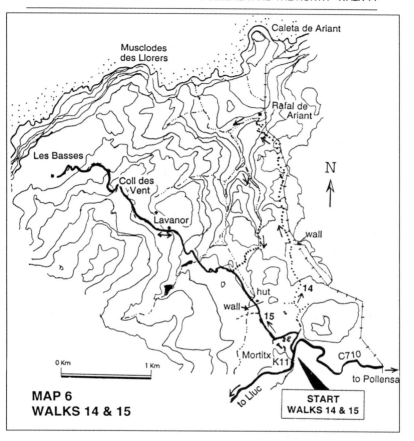

MAP 6
WALKS 14 & 15

The abandoned house Rafal de Ariant is situated on a flat shelf overlooking the sea, where sheep graze on the once cultivated fields among a few almond and fig trees. Remote, quiet and utterly peaceful, this place is about as far removed from the crowded and noisy resorts of the south of Mallorca as it is possible to be. As such it has an irresistible appeal to all lovers of wild country and solitude.

Type of walk: Very rough and rocky, with difficult route-finding.

Starting point:	Mortitx gates, K10.9 on C710
Time:	4hr
Distance:	8km
Total height climbed:	275m descent and re-ascent
Grade:	B+ (A to return by the gorge)
Map:	Son Marc 1:25,000

There is room for several small cars by the Mortitx gates at K10.9. Go through two gates, pass the tennis court, then turn right through another gate on the left of a stone building and continue between orchards to another gate with an access stile over the fence. There is a new notice here (end 1966) warning about hunting, but do not be deterred. The track rises slightly and then bends right. At this point turn left as indicated by a cairn. After about 50m, in an area where new trees have been planted, a cairn marks a branch path on the right. Follow the path down through olive trees, thorny broom and other shrubs. There are a few red paint marks and cairns, but they are not very easy to see.

Go through a gate at a junction of two stone walls and continue to follow the path through this wild and rocky area. Cairns and red paint marks will be found in places, but it is still difficult to find the way. The path twists and turns in a tortuous way through the incredible landscape, but makes steady progress downhill towards the coast. Look out for two places where the path makes a sharp right turn. The path rises slightly to cross two spurs on the right-hand side before later reaching a stone wall.

The path now turns left and descends a cliff in tight zigzags to the plain behind Rafal de Ariant. From the house it is a further 10 minutes or so to the edge of the cliffs with a view of an impressive cave high up on the right. Another narrow path leads from the house over the low Coll de la Caleta and then descends towards the coast. This becomes steep and loose, but is worth the effort for the view of the coast at the Caleta de Ariant (*caleta* = small bay.) The Cova de Ses Bruixes, or witches' cave, is high up in the cliff on the left and cannot be seen except by crossing very rough ground on the right of the path, leaving this at a very large boulder encountered some 20 minutes after leaving the house. Allow an extra hour if you want to do this.

Most walkers will be content to return to Mortitx by the same path used on the descent. Finding the way back is not all that easy owing to the confusing nature of the ground; it is as well to pay attention to the twists and turns on the way down. However, a return by the Mortitx gorge makes a rewarding and slightly more adventurous alternative. This involves some easy scrambling, and it is not recommended after recent rain which makes the rocks slippery.

From the ruined house follow the path west, passing some old fig trees to reach the stream-bed and then continuing alongside it. After passing a large pine tree a cairn in the bed of the *torrente* marks the place where the ascent begins. (A diversion west for 5 minutes to the deep pool of clear water below an immense rock tower is recommended before beginning the ascent.) Return to the cairn and start walking up the bed of the stream. After about 15 minutes a rock slab on the left of a pool has to be negotiated, which is not technically difficult but may be a little alarming. It can be crossed either low down near the water or higher up.

About 4 minutes after this turn left into a narrow branch, clearly marked by paint signs and cairns. This is an important junction as the right branch which looks easy becomes really difficult higher up. The left branch continues upwards with alternate sections of walking and easy scrambling. Finally the path tops out on to a flat area and after 10 minutes turns right to join the Mortitx-Lavanor track. Turn left and after going over the stile by the notice board ignore a right branch, then turn left by the large fruit storage sheds. Follow this road back past the tennis court to return to the Mortitx gate.

To find the way to the gorge from the top, look for the path on the right about 5 minutes after crossing the stile by the notice board.

15. LAVANOR AND THE COLL DES VENT

The area of Mortitx is of outstanding natural beauty and of great scientific interest for its flora and for its geology. Although this walk goes through wild and spectacular scenery it is entirely on a narrow road and is highly recommended. This road was improved in 1990 and although there are three sets of gates to prevent vehicular use, each has a pedestrian access stile. This route is in the centre of the area where black vultures live and it is essential that these rare and magnificent birds are not disturbed. Visitors are requested to keep to the road and only to go in small groups. Access is discouraged during the long breeding season from January to May and may not be allowed at all at weekends during this time.

Type of walk: Very easy on a narrow road, but rough ground at the end for 20 minutes.

Starting point:	Mortitx gates, K10.9, C710
Time:	4hr 30min
Distance:	11km
Highest point reached:	502m
Total height climbed:	400m
Grade:	C
Map:	Son Marc 1:25,000

There is room at the entrance gate for several small cars to park but this can be difficult at weekends. From the entrance gate, or the access on the right if it is locked, follow the main track round past the tennis courts. After passing some buildings the track swings right and heads towards the coast. Ignore a branch left and keep on the main track all the way. Orchards of peach trees and other fruit will be noticed on the left, although many of them have been uprooted. After going through the first gate, there is a shelter hut with a fire place on the right. The exit route from the Mortitx gorge may be noticed on the right among an open area of mature trees.

The track has been level up to now but soon begins to rise and then passes by a small reservoir fringed with reeds. It continues to rise to reach Lavanor, where there is a small house and a flat, cultivated area, conspicuous in the wilderness. After more uphill work the road dips down before rising to the Coll des Vent. From here there is a steep descent towards another flat field, and the road swings left alongside this to end by a ruined shelter. There were originally two gateways here, now fenced, with piled stones making a rough stile.

To reach the cliff edge and find a lunch spot involves some 15-20 minutes of rough walking, but is worth the effort.

16. A CIRCUIT OF THE PUIG CARAGOLER DE FEMENIA

This rocky massif lies between the well-known Puig Roig and the Puig Gros de Ternelles, in a wild and virtually uninhabited area north of the Pollensa-Lluc road. The route described is not as popular as the circuit of the Puig Roig but is extremely attractive and deserves to be better known. The views are extensive and varied. At first, the outlook is across the plain to the bay of Pollensa, then the eye is drawn to the steep and craggy Puig Gros de Ternelles. From the Coll Ciuro to the Coll des Pinetons there is a rocky wilderness sloping down to the sea. At the

Coll des Pinetons the whole of the north-eastern slopes of the Puig Roig come into view across a trackless valley. Finally, from the Coll dets Ases there is a view of Tomir bathed in the late afternoon light. In view of the current access restrictions at Mossa (see Walk 17) it may be advisable to choose a Sunday for this walk.

Type of walk: No steep gradients, but partly pathless and route-finding experience is essential. Not recommended in mist.

Starting point:	K14.2, Pollensa-Lluc road
Time:	4hr
Distance:	10km
Highest point reached:	676m
Total height climbed:	310m
Grade:	B+
Map:	Pollensa 1:25,000

The route begins at the entrance to Femenia Nou on the Pollensa-Lluc road. Although parking for one car may be found about 100m further on towards Lluc there is not much space anywhere else nearby. It is better if possible to arrange to be dropped off here and picked up at the end of the day. The main gate is usually locked, but there is an access stile on the left. In a short distance take a left fork and go through the gate behind Femenia Nou, continuing to Femenia Vell where the track appears to end. It does not end, but doubles back near the house to enter the pinewoods on the east side of Puig Caragoler. (Alternatively you can look out for a short cut on the left before reaching Femenia Vell and thus avoid setting off the farm dogs barking.)

This wide track ends at a spring, the Font d'en Quelota, where water gushes out of a rock into a stone trough which is roofed over and gated. A glass tumbler is provided inside! From the spring a rather narrow and overgrown path leads on to the Coll Ciuro, at first descending slightly and then contouring before rising towards the cliffs of Caragoler.

From the Coll Ciuro an old path goes left to circumnavigate the grassy hollow ahead. Go straight across here and pick up the path by a cairn on a large boulder. Although little used the path is marked by cairns and red paint. It contours at about the same height as the col, going through a gap in a wall and passing a ruined building. A few minutes after this building there is a choice of ways. The old way goes down to some old terraces near a spring, the Font d'en Castell, which is roofed. From above this can be recognised by the green damp area

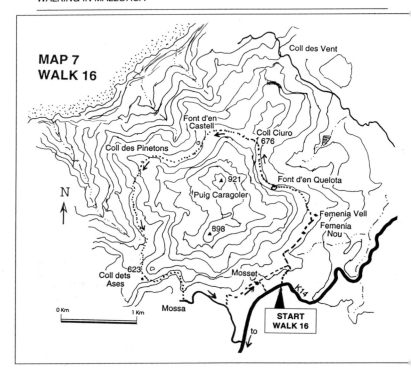

below it surrounded by a wall. To continue from the spring, descend slightly to cross the stream-bed and then up pathless ground towards the Coll des Pinetons.

The alternative way misses out the spring but avoids losing height. There are some cairns showing the best route, which crosses the same stream-bed at a higher level, and the two ways re-join before reaching the Coll des Pinetons. As this col is approached avoid the right branch to another small notch in the ridge.

At the Coll des Pinetons turn left and make a slightly rising traverse following a line of cairns. Then bear right, descending into a shallow *carritx*-filled valley. Follow the cairns for the easiest walking. The route divides to go either above or below a rocky outcrop, then re-joins,

90

traversing again before descending in the same direction. Further on a narrow rocky gully is descended, where traces of a carefully built mule track will be found. This leads into a hollow where there is a *sitja*. Leave the hollow by the stream-bed on the right. When a flat area is reached, turn left and then go up towards the Col dets Ases. The route is a bit vague here, although there are some cairns and traces of a very overgrown path.

Once on the col, the excellent path descending to Mossa is followed. From Mossa, follow the track towards the C710, in a few minutes turning left at an acute angle to go behind Mosset and join the Femenia Nou track. Turn right to reach the starting point.

K14.2 - Font d'en Quelota		30min
Font - Coll Ciuro		30min
Coll Ciuro - Coll des Pinetons	1hr	
Coll des Pinetons - Coll dets Ases	1hr	
Coll dets Ases - K14.2	1hr	

17. CIRCUIT OF THE PUIG ROIG

Note: at the time of going to press access through Mossa farm is only allowed on Sundays and the direct return from Coscona to Mossa is not being allowed, in the hope that this will change in the future, this walk, well-known to local walkers and others, is included in its original form.

The Puig Roig is the lowest of the 1,000m summits of Mallorca, but it is one of the most attractive mountains on the island with its encircling red cliffs. It is especially striking seen in evening light from the Soller-Lluc road and it is well worth stopping at the small *mirador* near Escorca. On this classic circular walk around the mountain, new views are constantly being revealed and give endless pleasure no matter how many times the walk is repeated. There are a number of excellent bivvy sites under overhanging rocks and local walkers used to start the walk in the late afternoon and sleep out there. The route also passes the interesting old cave houses of Coscona, built under overhanging rocks. These are still in occasional use.

The circuit of the mountain is a delightful excursion, far preferable than a climb to the top. The traverse of the mountain from south to north can be done, but is an arduous route over very rough ground.

Type of walk: On good but in places very stony paths. From Coscona to Mossa the path is less used and more difficult to follow.

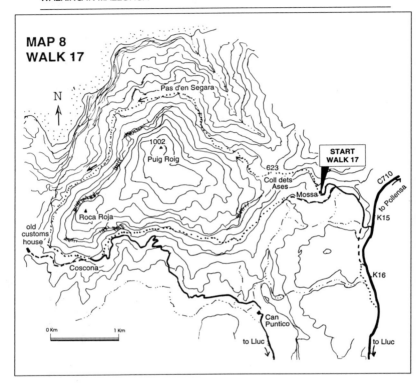

Starting point:	Mossa gates at K15.8 on C710
Time:	5hr 30min
Distance:	14km
Highest point reached:	c.700m
Total height climbed:	218m
Grade:	B+
Map:	Son Marc 1:25,000

At the time of going to press the return from Coscona is still prohibited, so it is best either to join a guided party or arrange to be dropped off at the entrance gate at K15.8 and picked up at Lluc at the end of the day. (Do not use the new entrance gate to Mossa at K15.3.) If you are walking the full round, then it is best to park at the Menut recreation area at K16.6 and walk along the road for 100m to find a path on the left which joins the farm track further on. Then return to Lluc along the Coscona track and return to the start by using ways described in Walk 22 or 24.

Follow the track to the finca, a large sheep farm, and go through the gate at the far side of the house. Cross the clearing straight ahead to find the beginning of the excellent mule track that leads up to the Coll dets Ases. This path slopes up the side of a very steep cliff and at one time had protective handrails, now disappeared. From the pass follow the path around the northern slopes towards the coast. At the most northerly point the path turns a corner, the Pas d'en Segara, then runs south-west, contouring below the cliffs. There are excellent views here of the old Torre de Lluc and the spectacular headland, the Morro de Sa Vaca. After crossing a stile by a sheepfold the ruined customs house comes into sight below. Go through a gap in the wall above the barracks. The path then traverses to Coscona where it joins the track from the customs house. (Alternatively follow the wall down to the ruined building and pick up the track there. There is a water tank with a spring behind it at this point.)

About 2 minutes or so after leaving the houses of Coscona, and just before the track bends to the left, look out for a narrow path beginning by a double-trunked olive tree growing at the edge of the road. (Ignore another path a few metres before this one.) This is the key point for finding the way back to Mossa. If you find the road is beginning to descend then you have gone too far and should return to find the start of this path.

At first the path is easy to follow with red paint marks and cairns, but encroaching vegetation sometimes obscures it. When the pinewood is reached, make for the terrace above the fig tree, then climb up onto the next terrace by a red paint mark. The path then contours some way to reach a clearing at the further edge of the woods. A large boulder with three paint marks indicates the place where a short descent is made to a terrace. Turn left along this terrace and go through an opening in a wall. Keep following the path along old olive terraces until the large circular platform of an old threshing floor is reached.

From the threshing floor the path rises slightly to go above an enclosure with an old building. Behind the building there is a spring in an underground tunnel, hidden by brambles. The path then crosses a stream-bed before dropping down by some old terraces and contours along one of these below a wall with a fence on top. Paint marks and cairns are then followed along a rather overgrown section, then down a slope of open ground to a gate at the corner of an oakwood. The path used to go all the way to Mossa inside the wood, but now a new road made for forestry operations is soon picked up and followed through the flat fields to reach Mossa.

Mossa gates - Mossa farm	30min
Mossa farm - Coll dets Ases	25min
Coll dets Ases - Pas d'en Segara	55min
Pas d'en Segara - Coscona	1hr 30min
Coscona - Mossa farm	1hr 55min
Mossa farm - Mossa gate	30min

18. PUIG DE MARIA

The Puig de Maria is a small but distinctive hill near Pollensa. There has been a chapel on the top since 1348, and in 1362 this was in charge of three women, the first female hermits in the history of the Baleares. At one time there was accommodation for as many as 70 people, and in recent years this was available to anyone. There was a large refectory and kitchens for the use of day visitors, for use of which a donation was requested. In 1988 the elderly nuns who had run the place for years decided the time had come to retire, and for a while the future was uncertain. However, it is now in private hands and the bar and restaurant services are once again available. (Not always; sometimes found to be closed.) Rooms are sometimes available but it is best to enquire locally.

Outside there are terraces and a natural garden from which there are extensive views. Many local people go up there on Sundays and on Easter Monday it is a place of pilgrimage to all Pollensa.

Type of walk: Very easy, but steadily uphill on a country lane which becomes a narrow but well-made mule track near the top.

Starting point:	Pollensa
Time:	1hr 30min
Distance:	3.5km
Total height climbed:	290m
Grade:	C
Map:	Pollensa 1:25,000

Start at the petrol station in Pollensa, in the wide road parallel to the main Palma road. Follow the signposted road 'Puig de Maria' across

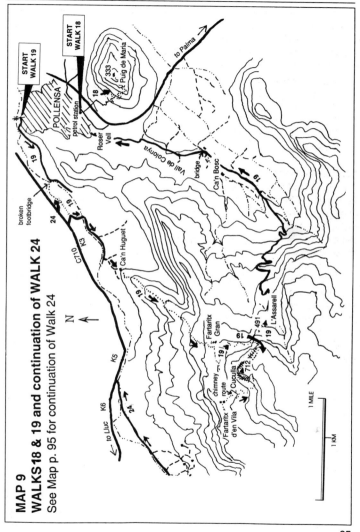

MAP 9
WALKS 18 & 19 and continuation of WALK 24
See Map p. 95 for continuation of Walk 24

START WALK 19

START WALK 18

to Palma

333 Puig de Maria

POLLENSA

18

Petrol station

Roser Vell

Vall de Colonya

bridge

Ca'n Bosc

19

broken footbridge

24

19

19

19

C710 K3

Ca'n Huguet

19

N

K5

L'Assarell

Fartaritx Gran

491

19

61

712

Cuculla

chimney route

19

Fartaritx d'en Vila

to Lluc K6

24

1 MILE

1 KM

the main road and straight up the narrow winding lane ahead. Turn sharp right at the first bend, then left past several terraced gardens and fields. At first the road is surfaced, but very narrow. (There is a turning space at the top but no parking.) From the end of the road a wide path with steps leads in 15 minutes to the walled terrace at the side of the chapel. Be sure to go through the gate at the left side of the chapel to reach the open ground behind, as well as exploring the buildings.

19. CUCULLA DE FARTARITX

This impressive peak, although of no great height, dominates the town of Pollensa and the Vall D'en Marc with its spectacular cliffs facing west, north and east. It is approached by a very interesting old mule track as far as a high farm on the Fartaritx plateau. An intermittent and narrow path now skirts the farm and leads to the summit plateau at a natural break in the cliffs. (An alternative walk involving a steep scramble up an interesting little chimney is also described.)

Type of walk: Level easy walking as far as Ca'n Huguet, then uphill steadily along a well-made mule track to the high plateau. After this the mountain path is less well defined but not difficult.

Starting point:	Pollensa
Time:	6hr 30min
Distance:	14km
Highest point reached:	712m
Total height climbed:	662m
Grade:	B+
Map:	Pollensa 1:50,000 or Pollensa 1:25,000 and Son Marc 1:25,000

Leave Pollensa by the Calle de la Huerta and turn left at the old unnamed road just before the bridge. After 1km a ruined footbridge will be seen on the right. Cross the stream-bed which is usually dry and go straight on along an old track, passing a large house on the left. When a good track is reached, turn left and follow this over a bridge, after which it swings sharp right. Keep straight on with the stream on your right. After about 700m the road turns sharp left. Almost immediately the main track bends left again, but at this point leave it and follow the minor track which forks right. Follow this track along as it passes between Ca'n Huguet on the right and a water tank on the left, after which it doubles back right behind the house.

At the old deserted house, above Ca'n Huguet, go up the steps, passing an old well on the right. Keep straight on, outside a wall, and into the oakwood by a wooden gate. Follow the track up through the woods where there are often several pigs foraging for acorns. The path goes through a gate at the top of the wood, then through a gap in a stone wall. Turn left here and go through a metal gate. After a further five or six minutes there is a sharp turn left along a track which becomes quite wide and appears to have obliterated the original mule track for a short distance. It leads in 10 minutes to a gate (new in 1989) where the old mule track is picked up again, winding upwards through an attractive natural garden of flowering shrubs. In about 45 minutes this leads to a high farmhouse, Fartaritx Gran, near a stream.

Turn right alongside the wall enclosing the fields. Where the wall turns left go up several zigzags and very soon leave the main path, which continues along the plateau, by a red paint sign and follow the wall uphill. A narrow trod can be followed up above the enclosed fields contouring towards some large oak trees. In the wood continue to contour along open easy ground with occasional cairns until after passing a *sitja* and a ruined shelter the path leads uphill towards the Cuculla. Below some pinnacles the path turns left then slopes up to the base of the cliffs. After turning a little corner a sloping rocky ledge, across which used to be a fence, leads up to reach the top of the cliffs at a natural break. Turn right and go up easy ground for about 400m to reach the top.

Alternative ascent: Grade A+

Instead of going round the outside of the Fartaritx Gran fields, where the wall turns at right angles, follow the main path which continues in the direction of Fartaritx d'en Vila, a ruined house completely hidden in a clump of trees. If you want to look at this, stay on the path which leads to a gate and then a flight of old stone steps. If not, bear left as you approach the trees, then make towards a large palm tree.

From the palm tree, it is easy to choose a way up into the wide upland valley of old neglected terraces backed by high cliffs. There may appear to be no way up these cliffs, but such a way can be found from the obvious corner up on the left. At the foot of the corner there is a large boulder covered with ivy. Go up past this on the right to arrive at the foot of the little chimney. There are no difficulties, although long legs are an advantage in one or two places. It is surmounted in about 10 minutes and a further 10 minutes of easy walking leads to the summit.

Descent:

It is possible to make a circular walk by descending to a high farm, L'Assarell, and walking back to Pollensa by the road in the Vall de Colonya, arriving in the town by the old church, Roser Vell. To do this, return to the prominent cairn at the cliff-edge some 400m south-east of the top. Follow the twisting path down the cliff, through the fence and past a little gully. Almost at once looking across to the right, a wall will be seen on a col. Descend and cross the intervening valley by any way that seems best and climb over the wall. Make for the farm below, choosing a way among the many animal tracks. Care should be taken not to disturb the many animals here. Once through the gate there is a surfaced road all the way back to Pollensa. At first this goes down quite steeply to the valley floor, then is level most of the way. Keep to the main track, taking a left turn over a bridge opposite a large house. If preferred, return by the same way used for the ascent.

Pollensa - Fartaritx	2hr 30min
Fartaritx - Cuculla	1hr
Cuculla - Assarell	45min
Assarell - Pollensa	2hr

20. PUIG DE CA

The Puig de Ca lies between Tomir and the Cuculla de Fartaritx, these three being the peaks which overlook the town of Pollensa on the south of the Vall d'en Marc. Although not as spectacular as the Cuculla, it has steep cliffs and provides an interesting walk. A particularly unusual feature is the old snow house with the curving roof, the only one of this type on the island.

Type of walk: Partly on good tracks and a well-made mule track and partly on pathless ground with some route-finding required. Rocky on the top but not difficult.

Starting point:	Ca'n Huguet
Time:	5hr 45min
Distance:	12km
Highest point reached:	878m
Total height climbed:	800m
Grade:	A
Map:	Pollensa 1:25,000 and Son Marc 1:25,000

Going from Pollensa towards Lluc, turn left at K2.7, cross the bridge

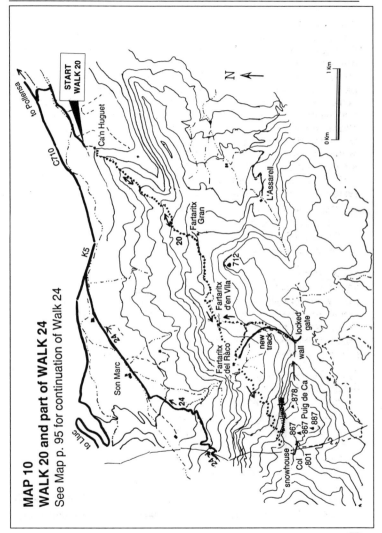

MAP 10
WALK 20 and part of WALK 24
See Map p. 95 for continuation of Walk 24

and follow the road to the right. Park somewhere along this lane which runs alongside the river. Go up the old mule track from Ca'n Huguet to Fartaritx Gran as for Walk 19.

Cross the stream and walk alongside the wall enclosing the fields. Where the wall turns left, go up a little zigzag and then keep on the path which continues in a westerly direction to the ruined house Fartaritx d'en Vila. There is a gate just before and below the house. Turn left up steps half-hidden among the trees and go between the old buildings. Behind the property turn right and continue along the track in the same direction as before. There is a locked gate to surmount at a boundary fence, after which it is better to avoid going too close to the next house, Fartaritx del Raco, where walkers are not welcome. It can be by-passed on the right.

Once this is passed, make towards the Coll del Puig de Ca, using traces of the old path where found. This must once have been an excellent mule track serving the snow house, but unfortunately it has fallen into almost total disrepair. Above the snow house the ground becomes steeper but the remains of the path are more evident. Go through the hole in the fence to reach the col, where a wide track leading south commences.

Follow the track to the boundary wall and then turn left into a shallow gully, making for a low crag at the top. There is an easy way up a sloping ledge and the west top is reached in a further few minutes. Double back to continue over the main top and along the ridge down to the Coll de Miner. Cross the wall across the col near the crag as there is a high locked gate on the col itself. Follow the new track (not shown on the published maps), but leave it where it bends left towards Fartaritx del Raco. Cut across the corner towards the ruined house, finding your own way rather than looking for the defunct path shown on the map. From Fartaritx d'en Vila, follow the path to Fartaritx Gran and return by the mule track to Ca'n Huguet.

Ca'n Huguet - Fartaritx Gran	1hr	15min
Fartaritx Gran - Coll del Puig de Ca	1hr	30min
Coll del Puig de Ca - Puig de Ca		45min
Puig de Ca - Coll de Miner		30min
Coll de Miner - Ca'n Huguet	1hr	45min

21. PUIG TOMIR

Tomir is a well-known and popular mountain, owing to its commanding position at the head of the Pollensa valley and its accessibility. It can be reached in 1 hour 30 minutes from the road end by a well-defined path and is one of the places where black vultures are sometimes sighted. For these reasons it is a mountain where other walkers are likely to be met, especially at weekends. Most people go up and down from Binifaldo, a short but enjoyable excursion. The views from the top are extensive and it is an interesting summit with a deep circular snow-pit. All the summit area is bare and rocky and there are steep crags on the northern side. This walk is an interesting circular route returning via Aucanella.

Type of walk: Mainly on rough and stony paths and including a short but very easy scramble. There are some route finding problems, especially at Aucanella where trees and scrub obscure the way.

Starting point:	Binifaldo
Time:	5hr
Distance:	7km
Highest point reached:	1,103m
Total height climbed:	638m
Grade:	A
Map:	Son Marc 1:25,000 and Selva 1:25,000.

To reach Binifaldo turn left (east) at K17.4 on the Pollensa-Lluc road, through an open gateway. Take the furthest left fork when three green gates are reached at Menut. (At weekends this gate is closed to traffic and this adds about 2km to the walk.)

The road ends at the Binifaldo bottling plant where there is a parking place. The walk starts between the gate to the plant and the forest fence. Follow the boundary fence up until a painted arrow marks a sharp right turn and the path begins to wind up through the trees. After leaving the woods there is a level section and then a rising traverse above a scree. After crossing a second and wider scree the path rises steeply to a little col. On the other side of this col it continues to rise steeply, keeping close against the rocks on the right. In the main the path is a good one with rock steps built up in the steeper places. It leads in a further 15 minutes from the col to a little rock slab about 4m high. Although this is very easily surmounted by means of a groove sloping up diagonally from right to left and well supplied with hand and footholds, it comes as a surprise to those unused to using their hands on a walk. The metal cable fixed to the rock in 1991 can be a real help

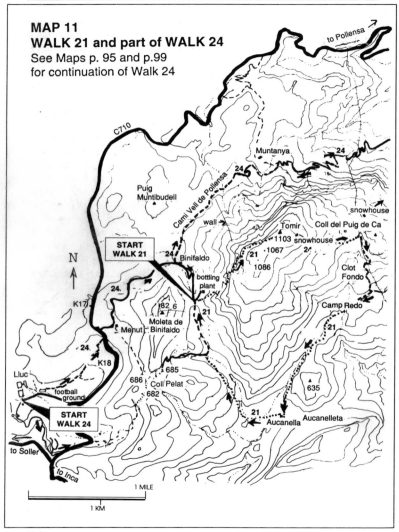

MAP 11
WALK 21 and part of WALK 24
See Maps p. 95 and p.99
for continuation of Walk 24

to Pollensa

C710

Muntanya

24

snowhouse

Puig
Muntibudell

Camí Vell de Pollensa

24

wall →

Tomir
1103
1067
1086

Coll del Puig de Ca

snowhouse

24

N

START
WALK 21

24

Binifaldo

bottling
plant

21

Clot
Fondo

Camp Redo

21

K17

24

82 6

Menut

Moleta de
Binifaldo

21

Lluc

24

K18

football
ground

686

685

Coll Pelat

682

635

21

21

Aucanella

Aucanelleta

to Soller

START
WALK 24

to Inca

1 MILE

1 KM

102

if the rocks are icy, thankfully a rare condition.

Above the slab the path continues upwards in a shallow valley which leads directly to the summit ridge. However, it is easier, being less loose and stony, to leave this valley in a few minutes by a cairned path on the right, only turning left towards the head of the valley when another line of cairns is reached. On arriving at a small col between two tops of the main ridge, turn left and follow the cairns up gently rising ground to the summit.

From the top go down east to reach the *casa de nieve* in 10 minutes, then continue down towards the Coll del Puig de Ca. In places the remains of the old track used by the snow-workers can be picked out. Aim slightly to the right of the col at first to avoid some steep ground, then towards the centre where a Land-Rover track will be found. Turn right along this and follow it down past a small hollow, the Clot Fondo, on the right. When another track is met turn right again to reach a flat plain known as the Camp Redo. From the turning circle at the end of the track a narrow path leads to a high wooden stile over a boundary wall and on through a narrow valley which skirts the south-east slopes of Tomir. There are occasional cairns on this path which leads to a sizable flat area containing the ruined house Aucanella. This was once a cultivated clearing but is now so overgrown with large trees and dense shrubs that it is difficult to find the way through. The best way is to turn left at the boundary fence and follow the path which rises slightly, and then turns right towards the house. Do not miss this turn or you will end up at Binibona, a long way off your route.

Leaving the house to start the ascent up to Binifaldo, follow the vestigial remains of the track which runs almost west for about 500m. Look out for the place where it turns north towards the Coll d'es Pedregaret. Once on this path it is easy to follow. After crossing the stream-bed it rises high on the left side of the valley where it is well marked by cairns. Higher up it goes into the forest, then crosses the stream to join a cart-track. This rises steadily to reach the col by the forest gate at Binifaldo.

Binifaldo - Tomir	1hr	30min
Tomir - Coll del Puig de Ca		45min
Coll - Camp Redo		30min
Camp Redo - Aucanella	1hr	
Aucanella - Binifaldo	1hr	15min

22. CAMEL ROCK

This well-known rock has been sculptured by natural forces to look almost exactly like a camel. If any member of your party is agile enough they can climb to the neck and pose for a photograph, emulating the postcards on sale in the shop at Lluc Monastery. The rock is partly hidden among trees on the rocky ridge between Lluc and the recreation area Es Pixarells and until the path was restored a few years ago it was quite difficult to find. The whole area is covered with oak trees and karstic rocks eroded into incredible shapes, with under shrubs of cistus, euphorbia and lentisc. The monastery at Lluc is an impressive building with a museum, art gallery, shops, restaurants, picnic areas and accommodation. The Menut and Binifaldo picnic area where the walk starts has ample parking and good facilities, but can be crowded on Sundays and holidays. The sign at the entrance says that firewood is on sale at weekends between certain times.

Type of walk: Easy and pleasant on good paths.

Starting point:	K16.6 on the C710
Time:	2hr 40min
Distance:	9km
Highest point reached:	600m
Total height climbed:	160m
Grade:	C
Map:	Son Marc 1:25,000 and Selva 1:25,000

Cross the road and take the signposted footpath directly opposite. This is marked with new wooden signposts and twists and turns through amazing rock formations as though through a maze. In about 10 minutes it joins a wide track (opposite a stone platform) which leads to another picnic area on the west side of the road. Follow the main track for about 20-25 minutes, then turn right on the branch track to Lluc. After a short rise, this track begins to descend towards the monastery. Immediately after passing a *sitja* and a stone bench, a narrow path on the left leads to Camel Rock. The path continues past the Camel to a rocky viewpoint. The climb up to the 'neck' is really a rock climb of about 7m and is not easy.

Return to the main path and descend to the valley floor at a new bridge by the football field. If you are visiting the monastery you return to this point afterwards; if you are starting the walk at Lluc then walk from the car park along the entrance road, turning first left then

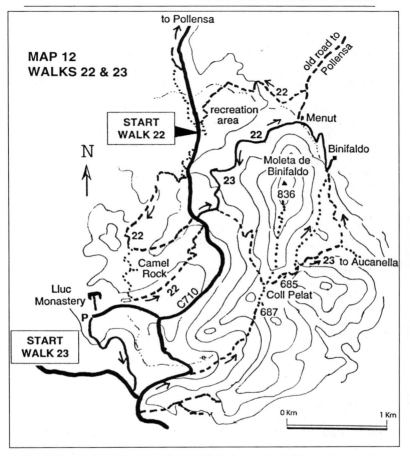

**MAP 12
WALKS 22 & 23**

to Pollensa

old road to Pollensa

recreation area

START WALK 22

22

Menut

22

Binifaldo

N

23

Moleta de Binifaldo
▲ 836

22

Camel Rock

23 to Aucanella

685 Coll Pelat

Lluc Monastery

C710

22

P

687

START WALK 23

0 Km   1 Km

immediately right. Cross the football field diagonally left to reach a good
track. This track is the beginning of the old road from Lluc to Pollensa
and is followed to reach the C710 at a gate. Turn left along the road
and after 100m turn right through an open gateway. When three green
gates are reached, take the road through the one on the far left. If it is
locked, as it may be at weekends, there is a pedestrian access gate.

This is a surfaced road leading to the Binifaldo bottling plant. After passing a water tank, look out for the old road where it branches left about 20m before reaching a large restored house, the headquarters of ICONA. Follow this old road for about 400m, then take a branch track on the left. In a little under 20 minutes this track passes a stone shelter, then bends left to meet a T-junction.Turn right here and follow it to a wooden gate near the main road. Do not cross the road but turn left and go up through the wood, where stone steps with a rustic hand-rail lead up into the Menut picnic site where the walk began.

23. BINIFALDO AND MENUT

Binifaldo and Menut are two publicly owned *fincas* in the mountains not far from the monastery of Lluc. They are managed and conserved by the Govern Balear in association with the Ministry of Agriculture and Fisheries. The houses at Binifaldo have been restored and are used for educational purposes. The house at Menut has a defensive tower and is used as a centre for forestry. The main road C710 passes through the Menut area and some excellent picnic areas have been provided, near to K17. There is also an area where camping is permitted, on application to the Conselleria in Palma.

This walk explores the area of the two fincas, which is very typical of the mountains of Mallorca. There are large areas of oak woodlands, formerly exploited for the production of charcoal, and pines growing higher up the slopes here and there, replacing the oaks. The bedrock here is a very permeable limestone with karstic erosion producing some very curious rock formations, such as the well-known Camel Rock, seen in Walk 22. The high rainfall combined with the rock type has produced a series of springs, of which one, the Font des Pedregaret, is exploited commercially at Binifaldo. One spring, La Font Ufana, is different from the others in that rainwater and melting snow from Tomir and Sa Moleta drain into a phreatic tube. This emerges in the woods at the side of the track in the Bosc Gran. It is said to flow all the year round.

A diversion up to the top of the Moleta de Binifaldo can be made from the Coll Pelat by following a fairly obvious path up the ridge, giving a slightly longer walk.

Type of walk: Easy on good tracks all the way. Some ups and downs, but nothing very steep.

Starting point:	Lluc car park
Time:	3hr 10min
Distance:	8km
Highest point reached:	687m
Total height climbed:	345m
Grade:	C
Map:	Selva 1:25,000 and Son Marc 1:25,000

From the monastery car park go south to the Restaurant de la Font Coberta. Turn left and follow the minor road up to join the C710 just below the road junction near the petrol station. Turn left and walk along the main road for about 500m to a hairpin bend. Just before this bend go through a gate with a private hunting sign. (If this is locked, access is made at the side of another gate about 50m further on.) Follow the main track up towards the Coll de Sa Font at 687m, ignoring branch tracks. High up, look out for a cairn on the right which shows the narrow path leading to the col. Go through a gap in the wall across the pass and follow the cairns across a large flat area (due north) until a new wide track is met at the Coll Pelat.

Ignore the left turn which goes downhill and keep straight on, still on level ground. (This area can be confusing as there are three cols very close together and the tracks are either not on the map at all or are not shown correctly.) From the Coll Pelat a diversion can be made up the ridge running north to the Moleta de Binifaldo, then returning the same way to the col. The level track leads to the third and unnamed col at 685m. Go through the opening in the wall and follow the forest track down into the Bosc Gran and the Aucanella valley. An alternative, which avoids the descent and subsequent ascent but is not so easy to find, is to go down the track for about 4-5 minutes and find the path on the left, just as the main track bends right. This pleasant path contours to the Coll de Pedregaret.

When the valley floor is reached, the track turns left and goes uphill to the Coll de Pedregaret, near the bottling plant. Go through the forest gate and follow the surfaced road down to the Binifaldo *finca*. There is a shelter here and a water supply. Continue down the road to meet a green metal gate that may be locked but has pedestrian access. Five minutes later turn left on the C710 and in 100m turn right on a wide track, by a wooden gate. This leads to Lluc and is part of the old road from Lluc to Pollensa. After passing a camping site the path goes across a football pitch to arrive at Lluc. Turn left amd then right along the road to reach the starting point.

| Lluc - Binifaldo | 2hr |
| Binifaldo - Lluc | 1hr 10min |

24. LLUC TO POLLENSA BY THE OLD ROAD
(See sketchmaps p95, 99 & 102)

The new road between Pollensa and Soller has resulted in the old road becoming a quiet and attractive byway through delightful countryside, making a pleasant and easy walk. The only snag is that some walking has to be done along the main road, the C710, from the junction at K5.4 to K2.7.

A party that can have the use of two cars might prefer to leave one at K5.4 before catching the Inca bus which leaves Pollensa at 09.15. A bus leaves Inca for Lluc at about 10.00 from outside the railway station, where it waits for the train to arrive from Palma. The bus journey from the flat plain up through the mountains to Lluc is worth every peseta, the scenery being most impressive.

Type of walk: Easy, along tracks, and mainly downhill. In midwinter it can be mainly in the shade.

Starting point:	Lluc monastery
Time:	4hr 45min
Distance:	20km
Highest point reached:	610m
Total height climbed:	100m
Grade:	C+
Map:	Inca 1:50,000 and Pollensa 1:50,000

From the monastery go out of the main entrance and turn left along the road. After about 200m turn left again between two stone gateposts, then almost immediately right through an iron gate. Go through the football ground and cross over to a stile at the far end on the left. The old road begins here and is at first horizontal, then rises in a series of bends to reach the C710 at a double wooden gate. Turn left along the main road and first right after c.100m at an open gateway with blue paint signs at K17.4. After a few minutes the road forks left, at the furthest left of three green gates. This road gently rises up to 610m, the highest point of the walk, before dropping down to Binifaldo. In about 30 minutes look out for a left turn, about 20m before reaching a large restored building, which is the headquarters of ICONA.

At this point we leave the tarmac road which services the Binifaldo bottling plant and return to the old unsurfaced road, crossing a little stream and going through a wooden gate. Twenty minutes later there is a double gate with a pedestrian access in a boundary wall. In a further 15 minutes take a right turn at a place where the main track goes sharp left, near a *finca* called La Montana. The old road we are following contours towards a stream-bed, then drops down fairly steeply to join another track from La Montana.

About 30 minutes later the track goes through a metal gate into a fairly level cultivated area, with carobs and almond trees, then descends gradually to another metal gate in a boundary wall with a 'private hunting' sign. Once through here it descends through a wooded area in a series of zigzags. In about half an hour Ca'n Cunat is reached at a green metal gate with round stone gateposts. Just past here the track swings sharp left opposite a wooden gate and in a further 10 minutes arrives at Ca'n Melsion. The old track then becomes much wider and continues to join the new road at an angle. This is at about K5.4 and there is a large tree in the angle between the two roads. (There used to be a sign on the tree, saying Las Creus.)

From the Las Creus junction it is unfortunately necessary to walk along the main road (except for a short stretch of about 700m at the start) to K2.7 (where a very small marker stone is partially obscured by grass). Turn right here and in a couple of minutes or so turn left along an overgrown grassy path at a point where the main track turns right. Ten minutes later, after passing a house with vociferous barking dogs, cross a stream-bed (usually dry) and turn left along a good road to reach Pollensa near the Roman Bridge. Turn right along the Calle de la Huerta, then left at the Banca Central to the square with the cockerel fountain, then right, left, and right and left again to get to the main square.

Lluc - Binifaldo	1 hr	
Binifaldo - Montana		35min
Montana - Ca'n Cunat	1hr	20min
Ca'n Cunat - K2.7	1hr	25min
K2.7 - Pollensa		25min

25. SES FIGUEROLES

The old farmhouse of Ses Figueroles can only be reached by mule track. The fig trees after which it is named grow on terraces surrounding

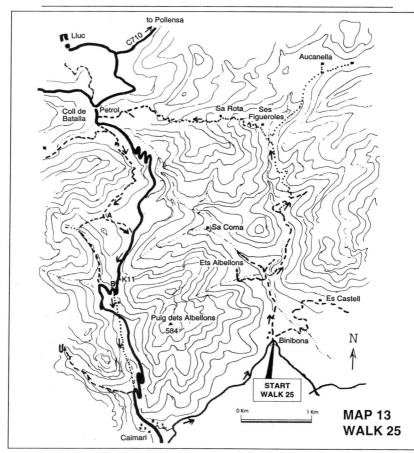

MAP 13
WALK 25

the house which is still in occasional use and has a modern solar panel on the roof. It lies in a narrow valley south of Aucanella and is approached by the same track from Binibona. On this circular walk an ascent is made to the Coll de Sa Batalla, then the newly restored 'Camí Vell' is followed down to Caimari, from where a country lane leads back to Binibona. (Large groups are advised to start at Caimari where there is more parking; parties with two cars can shorten the walk by leaving one car in Caimari.)

(An alternative to this circular walk is to go to the old house of Aucanella and back again the same way. This house, which is passed on Walk 21 to Tomir, is also only accessible by mule track. It makes an ideal picnic site, as does Aucanelleta which is 400m to the east over a 478m col. Instead of branching left to Ses Figueroles, take the right fork uphill. Rather overgrown, it is arduous at first until the edge of the old neglected fields is reached. Then walk along inside the wall and cross to an opening in the wall below the house.)

Type of walk: Varied terrain with forest tracks, country roads and mule tracks, overgrown in places.

Starting point:	Road end in Binibona
Time:	About 5hr 15min
Distance:	15km
Highest point reached:	625m
Total height climbed:	600m
Grade:	B
Map:	Selva 1:25,000

Park in Binibona where there is a small open space near the road end. Take the wide track on the left by a sign saying 'Ets Albellons, Agroturismo'. Two minutes after passing the gate to this house turn right to cross the stream-bed on a narrow path marked by a cairn. On the other side go through a gate made of an old bed and continue upwards to reach a wide forest track. Turn left and continue walking up the valley. Ten minutes after passing the second of two limekilns and having ignored a branch track right, look out for a small red paint mark denoting a short cut on the right. After rejoining the main track turn right and 2 minutes later find the continuation of the old path on the left, at the side of a large circular clearing.

The old mule track rises up out of the woods to cross a rocky shoulder, then vees into a stream-bed and up out again to a rocky cleft. The scenery is a wilderness of huge boulders and steep rocky bluffs, yet the main road up from Inca to Lluc is but a short distance above. The path descends gently to the valley of Ses Figueroles, passing through a gap in a boundary wall. A few minutes after this, go left through a gate in the fence at the point where the Aucanella path rises uphill.

When the house of Ses Figueroles is reached, double back left to a gate in a wall and fence, only about 30m from the house. Go through the gate and turn sharp right along the wall, then follow the path veering left into the pinewoods. This popular, much used path is easy to follow. After about 20 minutes' ascent it crosses the stream-bed into open ground and then follows the course of the original track which is mainly in good condition. Some abandoned terraces are reached, where there is a defunct well and a large ruined house, Sa Rota. After this the old path is not much in evidence but the way is marked by paint signs and cairns. On the 595m col between the Puig des Castellot and the Puig de Ses Covasses go through the gap in the wall. The path now winds about between rocks and *carritx*, gradually ascending towards a flat rocky shoulder on the slopes of Ses Covasses. Go through the gap in the wall and fence and then descend to reach a wide forest track. This leads to the Coll de Sa Batalla and comes out by the cafe at the side of the petrol station.

Turn left and cross the bridge, then turn right on the wide track which leads to Es Guix in about 10 minutes, passing on the way the track to Comafreda and Massanella. The restored track we are following down to Caimari is easy to follow. It rises to a prominent gap in the cliffs above the Salt de las Bella Dona and then descends gently to the main road. This must be followed now for about 1km, although if you do not mind some more uphill you can take the branch right at the point marked A on map 13 and go over into the Cometa Negra valley and rejoin the main road lower down. In this case turn left on the main road and leave it again at Point B. On the main route, the path is picked up again after passing the large house at K11, cutting across the road several times and continuing down the valley to reach it again on the outskirts of Caimari. In Caimari take the first left, the Carrer der Moritxo. Pass in front of the church and turn left and then right to find the Carrer de Binibona leading back to the start.

Binibona - Ses Figueroles	1hr	30min
Ses Figueroles - Coll de Sa Batalla	1hr	30min
Coll de Sa Batalla - Caimari	1hr	45min
Caimari - Binibona		30 min

The Central Mountains

26. LLUC TO COSCONA AND THE TORRE DE LLUC

Coscona is a fascinating place with a number of 'cave houses' built under a huge overhanging rock. They face south and have a very impressive view of the Puig Mayor. These houses can also be seen on the round of the Puig Roig, but the walk described here, although slightly longer, is a very much easier one. Before rising to Coscona the route crosses an absolutely flat plain which looks as though it once held a lake. Now there are cereal crops, olive trees and sheep with tinkling bells grazing among them. Impressive cliffs dominate this plain at the beginning of the walk, with the red walls of the Puig Roig in full view straight ahead. Further on the ruined barracks of an old customs house stand in a prominent position overlooking the deep cleft of the Torrente de Pareis. Although this makes a worthwhile objective in itself, the walk can be extended further on towards the old Torre de Lluc, perched on a headland overlooking the sea.

Access to this walk is restricted to Sundays only, as is the Puig Roig. The new parking restrictions at the entrance to Ca'n Pontico also add a considerable distance to the walk so that only the most active walkers stand a chance of reaching the Torre.

Type of walk: Very easy walking on a track which is level at first, then rises steadily up to Coscona. The surface is a kind of cinder track which is quite pleasant to walk on, but becomes stonier after Coscona. After the ruined customs house there is only a narrow and partially lost path, but the old Torre de Lluc is in sight all the way.

Starting point:	Lluc monastery
Time:	4hr 35min
Distance:	19km
Highest point reached:	560m
Total height climbed:	420m
Grade:	C (to customs house), B beyond
Map:	Inca 1:50,000 and Pollensa 1:50,000

At the front entrance of the monastery turn left along a road at the side of a restaurant. Go through a gate (which must be reclosed) then take

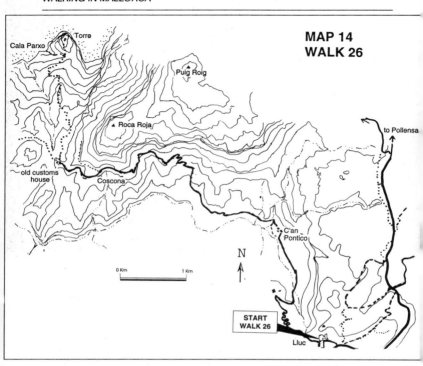

the first turn right. The road descends in a series of bends and leads to a heavily padlocked gate (where formerly parking was allowed).

Go through the pedestrian access gate and follow the level road to a large *finca* called Ca'n Pontico. (The barking dogs are chained.) The surfaced road becomes a cinder track at the back of the house and it is simply a matter of following it all the way to Coscona. There are several gates. Soon after passing a shallow covered water tank the track begins to rise in zigzags and occasional short cuts are worthwhile. About 1hr 15min from the start of the walk there is an open gateway with the word COSCONA chiselled out of a wooden board, but it is a further 25 minutes from this gateway to the cave houses.

After the cave houses, continue along the track which descends a

Cave house at Coscona

little then doubles back to a spring in a shallow valley before arriving at the ruined barracks. The ruins themselves are not exactly attractive, but the situation is a magnificent one. However, it is well worth the extra effort to follow the vestigial remains of the path which goes on to the old watch-tower near the sea. To do so, look for the red paint sign 'Morro Vaca' by the gap in the wall as you arrive at the barracks. Follow the line of the old path parallel to the wall, passing a pair of olive trees. Before the next large tree, turn right to find the traces of the old path, built up at the edges and marked by a few cairns. Keep to the left of the low hill ahead, then bear right to a small col and descend slightly to cross a stream-bed. Continue on fairly level ground and make towards a fence near two pine trees. Here will be found a gap in the fence with a red paint mark on one of the fence posts. A few yards to the left it is possible to pick up the old path marked by cairns as far as a little knoll, which is a really excellent viewpoint.

Locked gate - Coscona cave house	1hr	40min
Coscona - customs house		20min
Customs house - viewpoint		20min
Viewpoint - locked gate	2hr	15min

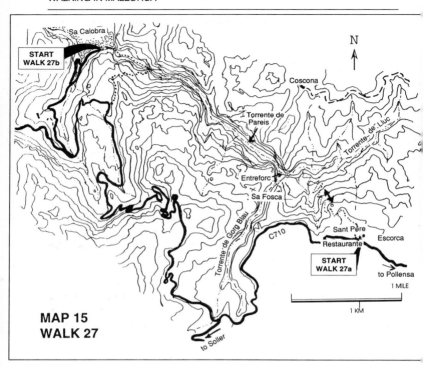

MAP 15
WALK 27

27. TORRENTE DE PAREIS

Pareis means 'twin' and this gorge has been cut by the action of the two streams Lluc and La Fosca, which meet at a place known as the Entreforc and continue as the Torrente de Pareis, the twin stream, to the sea at Sa Calobra.

The route is one of the most popular on the island, going through a narrow gorge between cliffs over 300m high. The scenery is wild and spectacular and the stream disgorges into the sea at a lovely bay with clear turquoise and deep blue water between rocky headlands. However, it is more of a scramble than a walk and is only recommended to those who are suitably experienced. In places the scrambling is more of a rock-climb and many people take a short line to safeguard the ascent or descent of the difficult places. Fixed ropes are sometimes found, but more often than not they have broken or worn out, although the pitons seem to remain in place. Recently some of the smooth boulders have been roughened to give a better grip. Although experienced climbers will have no trouble making a through descent of the whole gorge from Escorca to Sa Calobra, it is suggested that others take two bites at the cherry and make approaches from both top and bottom.

Logistics can be a problem for the through route, especially in winter. Some leave a car at Escorca and count on getting a lift back. In summer, the bus can be used from Soller to Escorca and a boat taken back to Puerto Soller from Sa Calobra (last boat 16.45). The whole descent takes from 3¹/2 to 5 hours, depending on conditions and the fitness and ability of the party.

It is essential to choose a day during a period of dry weather. After rain the rocks will be wet and slippery and there are deep pools which have to be waded or even swum across. Although high summer is usually recommended for this excursion, we have found that most winters provide suitable conditions most of the time.

27(a). ESCORCA TO THE ENTREFORC AND RETURN

This section is the easiest part of the gorge, but still takes you into very impressive places. It also allows time for a diversion to the entrance of the La Fosca cave system and to go beyond the Entreforc to the top of a large boulder section which is one of the more difficult places.

Starting point:	Restaurante Escorca
Time:	3-4hr
Distance:	c.6km
Total height climbed:	Descent from 650m to 180m and return
Grade:	B
Map:	Pollensa 1:50,000 and Inca 1:50,000

From the car park opposite the Restaurante Escorca, go through the new access gate signposted to the Torrente de Pareis. This bypasses the original way by the small thirteenth century church of Sant Pere. Follow the path down through the wood. After an iron gate, continue along the path in the same direction for 5 minutes, looking out for a sharp left turn. The old paint mark on an olive tree at this point is barely discernible, but there should be a cairn. If you come to a spectacular rock arch, you have gone too far and must go back. It might be considered worthwhile to miss this turn deliberately to enjoy the view.

From the sharp left turn the path goes down some steep rock, turning first left then right, after which it is easy to follow right down into the gorge in a series of bends. Low down, look out for a right turn some 20m after passing a fig tree. A narrow path leads through clumps of *carritx* into the bed of the Lluc stream. Note this point, which otherwise may be missed on the way back. Once in the stream-bed turn left and look out for another narrow path on the left which avoids some boulders and leads to the Entreforc. At the Entreforc is a stone marked as a crossroads, and pointing the way to Lluc, to Sa Calobra, to Sa Fosca and 'Millor no entri'. This latter points to the vertical rock wall and means 'better not go' in Mallorquin.

For the diversion to Sa Fosca, keep near the rock wall on the left where there is a trace of a path. After about 20 minutes the rock walls meet overhead and increasing darkness makes a return to the Entreforc advisable. (This is the entrance to a large and complex cave system requiring caving experience and equipment.)

From the Entreforc follow a narrow path on the right, indicated by red paint marks. This leads down into the gorge towards Sa Calobra. Twenty minutes later the top of some enormous blocks will be reached and it is recommended that a return is made from this point.

27(b). SA CALOBRA TO ENTREFORC AND RETURN

Sa Calobra is a tiny cove with a shingle beach between rocky cliffs and a small harbour where boats from Puerto Soller ply in the summer. It is a deservedly popular place but an early start will avoid the crowds who arrive by coach and boat. The drive down is spectacular with one hairpin bend after another and even a 'knot' where the road passes under itself. However, it is a wide, well-maintained road and the coaches are normally concentrated in the middle of the day.

All the difficulties of the gorge are in this section and it should only be attempted after a dry period. Sometimes bad flooding can occur after heavy rain and flash floods are not unknown. It is possible for the tunnel to be waist-deep in water, providing quite an alarming experience. Normally, the vast amphitheatre at the exit only has a trickle of water going out to sea and is even used for open-air concerts in the summer. The original way into the amphitheatre before the tunnel was constructed provides an 'escape route' should the tunnel be found in flood. Some old steps on the south side lead up a steep and narrow gully to a col. Going down, the left-hand branch leads down to the path near the car park. There are some stone steps still in place but with time and lack of maintenance these are likely to disappear.

Starting point:	Sa Calobra
Time:	5-6hr
Distance:	7km
Total height climbed:	180m
Grade:	A+
Map:	Pollensa 1:50,000 and Inca 1:50,000

(N.B. All lefts and rights in the following description are for anyone looking up the gorge.)

Go through the tunnel from the path at the end of the car park into the wide amphitheatre hidden behind the rocks. If the conditions are right for the walk there will be very little water disgorging onto the shingle beach. Start walking into the gorge and in about 10 minutes some easy boulders are surmounted on the left. Few of the many visitors venture beyond this point. Next, after stretches of easy walking interspersed with clambering over boulders, there is a narrow section leading to the first little difficulty. This is a large boulder with a pool at the bottom. The way up is by rather greasy holds on the right, finishing over a small chockstone. About 10 minutes later an enormous block almost fills the gorge, with a small boulder in front. The best way to tackle this is by the groove on the left wall.

An easier section of boulders and scree comes next, passing a side gully on the right, after which there is a varied stretch with two pitches easily climbed by sloping shelves on the left. The gorge then narrows again and is filled with a chaotic mass of huge blocks. On the right a red arrow indicates a fascinating through route between a giant block and the right-hand wall. After this only one more boulder gives a trifling difficulty before a path on the left avoids further problems and leads to the Entreforc.

If you are intending to continue up to Escorca, there are no further difficulties, but you need to look out for the exit from the Lluc stream on the right, leading up to the path.

Ascent: 2½-3hr   Descent: 2-2½hr

28. CALA TUENT AND SA COSTERA

Cala Tuent is a small bay which was the objective of an abortive 'urbanisation' project, of which there is little to be seen except a few isolated houses. Thankfully it seems the plans for a four-storey hotel

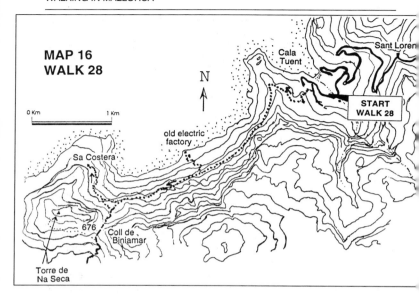

MAP 16
WALK 28

N

0 Km — 1 Km

Cala Tuent

Sant Loren

START WALK 28

old electric factory

Sa Costera

676

Coll de Biniamar

Torre de Na Seca

and other out of place projects have been abandoned, and although the bulldozed road has destroyed a traditional old mule track, it has its uses in leading to the start of this attractive walk. This road branches off from the spectacular La Calobra road and goes over a pass on which is the thirteenth century chapel of San Lorenzo. The path is part of a long established route from Soller to Sa Calobra, which is not easy to do unless transport can be organised at the beginning and end of the walk. (The route from the Mirador de Ses Barques to Sa Costera is decribed in Walk 47.)

The walk described here goes along a very pleasant corniche path overlooking the sea between two rocky headlands. The destination is a large ruined house called 'Sa Costera' where several large terraces make perfect picnic places and there is a spring hidden in a tunnel behind the house.

Type of walk: There is a rise up to 200m by a good path followed by the corniche path which has a few minor ups and downs before finally rising up to about 300m near the Coll de Biniamar. This path was
120

originally a well-made mule track and is still in good condition, although the vegetation is encroaching in places. The branch path out to Sa Costera is much more overgrown and rather rougher going. Although the measured map distance is only 10km, the actual distance must be rather more. There is a surprising amount of ascent involved too for a coastal contouring path.

Starting point:	Cala Tuent
Time:	4hr 40min
Distance:	10km
Highest point reached:	320m
Total height climbed:	370m
Grade:	C+
Map:	Soller 1:50,000 and Pollensa 1:50,000

Park at the side of a wide road immediately after crossing the bridge where the road swings round towards the sea. Walk along this road towards the restaurant (closed in winter) and take the first turn left, waymarked by a blue arrow painted on a rock and the words 'A La Costera'. The path leaves this track on the right after passing a concrete driveway and is marked by a cairn and another blue painted arrow. The old cobbled mule track is picked up behind a new building and leads to a large deserted house. In front of this is a sloping grassy terrace dotted with olive trees. The house itself is an interesting place with all sorts of old machinery such as olive presses. On arriving here, turn right across the terrace in front of the house, taking particular note of this point as it is easy to miss the left turn in descent.

Follow the path up to a gap in a stone wall, at which point a splendid view of the coast and the way ahead opens up. The corniche path begins here, descending at first then keeping fairly level for quite long stretches. At one point a flattish green field near a water tank and a small building will be noticed down by the sea. A cairn and a blue arrow marks the descent path to this spot, which could make an alternative walk. The remains of an abandoned hydro-electic factory and the conduit from the waterfall which powered it can be seen here.

When the path begins to rise up towards the Biniamar col, look out for a small cairn on the right just below a red arrow on a boulder. Turn right into a clearing, then leave the wide and obvious track to turn left up a narrow and rather overgrown path which cuts off a corner and an unnecessary ascent. It joins the main path from Biniamar by a wall with a red paint spot. Follow this path, mainly descending, to the Sa Costera

121

house, passing a branch path left which is signposted 'Torre' in red paint. Return the same way; the views are worth looking at in both directions.

Cala Tuent - Sa Costera	2hr 25min
Sa Costera - Cala Tuent	2hr 15min

29(a). MASSANELLA, NORMAL WAY

Massanella is the highest accessible peak in Mallorca since the Puig Mayor is prohibited. As such it is very popular and other walkers are often met, especially on Sundays when many local walkers take to the hills. Because of its height and situation the views are outstanding, so if possible choose a fine clear day for the ascent. The twin peaks at the top are visible from many places and make the mountain instantly recognisable. The old iron cross which used to mark the top has been replaced by a concrete trig point. Sometimes a summit book may be found in a sheltered place a few metres below the top. A freshwater spring, the Font de S'Avenc, not far below the summit, is approached by stone steps leading down into two caves. Water dripping down the rocks collects in a series of stone troughs in the lower cave. This is a very attractive place on a hot day.

N.B. A charge of 500 ptas per person is made at the gates of Comafreda. Sometimes passports or identity cards have been asked for.

Park near the petrol station on the Lluc-Inca road, avoiding the centre of the lay-by which is used by coaches stopping at the restaurant.

Type of walk: Quite strenuous, but mainly on reasonably good paths. In the upper part the paths are very stony in places and not always easy to follow.

Starting point:	Petrol station, Lluc
Time:	5hr 15min
Distance:	11km
Highest point reached:	1,352m
Total height climbed:	795m
Grade:	B+
Map:	Selva 1:25,000

Walk towards Inca and go through the green gates on the right immediately after crossing the bridge over the Torrent des Guix. Follow the unsurfaced track up to the *finca* Comafreda, doubling back up to the right about 250m from the start (where the road straight ahead

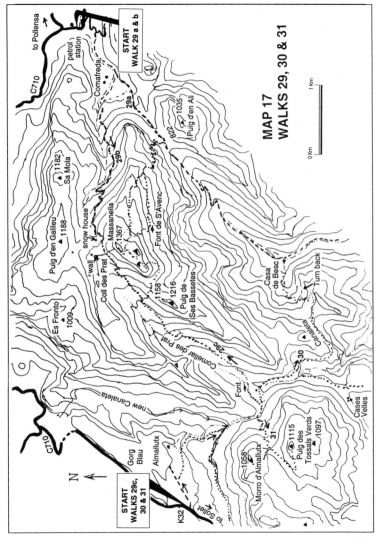

MAP 17
WALKS 29, 30 & 31

to Pollensa

C710

petrol station

Comafreda

START WALK 29 a & b

29a

▲822 (Puig d'en Ali) 1035

29b

▲1182 Sa Mola

▲1188 Puig d'en Galileu

snow house

"wall"

Massanella ▲1367

Font de S'Avenc

Coll des Prat

Es Fronto ▲1009

Casa de Besc

Turn back

▲1158
▲1216 Puig de Ses Basetes

Comellar des Prat

29c

new Canaleta

Canaleta

30

Font

31

Cases Velles

C710

START WALKS 29c, 30 & 31

Gorg Blau

Almallutx

K32

to Soller

Morro d'Almallutx 1058

▲1115 Puig des Tossals Verds 1097

N ←

0 Km   1 km

123

leads to the farm of Es Guix). Short cuts can be taken on the first section, but these are steep and can be muddy. They start just inside the entrance gate. After levelling out, the Comafreda track passes a locked gate with pedestrian access on the right. Beyond this is the cultivated area with the farmhouse set back on the right.

From here, bear left and take the path on the left-hand side of the wall which bounds the fields. The path follows the wall at first and then rises through the woods (paint marks renewed in winter 1991) to join a wide cross track at a large painted boulder. (This point may also be reached from the beginning of the cultivated area by following the blue arrows through the open gateway and along a wide track, ignoring right turns.)

Follow this track up left to the Coll de Sa Linea at 822m, where there is a large clearing. Turn sharp right at the two indication stones. A good path leads up fairly steeply in zigzags, arriving at an engraved stone marking a bifurcation in the path. The left-hand path is signposted 'Font y Puig' and the right-hand path 'Puig y Font'. Either route may be taken to the top by good well-marked paths, although the one to the right is the easiest to follow.

If the left-hand route is taken, a keen eye must be kept for paint marks and cairns as it is easy to wander off the route on one of the many natural ledges that look like paths. There is a large cairn marking a place where the path begins to rise towards an isolated alzine or evergreen oak. Marker stones have been cemented to the slabs to show the way. Above this a roughly horizontal section leads to the spring. From the spring the path continues horizontally for about 20m before leading up a rocky staircase to the sloping shelf that lies below the summit. On this shelf another indication stone points the way to the top, near which is an impressively deep pothole.

To descend, go down on to the shelf below the top and follow the path which is well marked and rejoins the route of ascent at the bifurcation with the engraved stone. In mist the direction from the top is south-east.

Lluc petrol station - Coll de Sa Linea	1hr	
Coll de Sa Linea - Font de S'Avenc	1hr	
Font de S'Avenc - Massanella summit		45min
Massanella summit - petrol station	2hr	30min

29(b). MASSANELLA BY THE COLL DES PRAT

The Coll des Prat is a high pass, 1,126m, to the north of Massanella. There used to be a very good track all the way up but it has fallen into disrepair since the old snow houses on the pass were abandoned. The pass was also used by pilgrims on the way from Soller to Lluc.

Type of walk: Quite strenuous. The scramble from the Coll des Prat to the summit is steep and exposed, requiring experience and a head for heights. (Note that this has been upgraded to A++ as several readers have found this route to be very difficult and some take a rope to safeguard the exposed part.)

Starting point:	Lluc petrol station
Time:	5hr
Distance:	12km
Highest point reached:	1,352m
Total height climbed:	795m
Grade:	A++
Map:	Selva 1:25,000

Follow the normal way up for about 40 minutes until the wide track is met by a large boulder with a red paint mark. Turn right here, passing a *sitja* on the left. Climb over a low wall at a barrier across the track and turn left to pass a spring. A good forest road leads up through the trees. When the trees thin out the old trail continues right up to the top of the pass. There is a little confusion around the ruined buildings and snow houses but it is very easy to reach the pass, across which is a wall. Turn left and go up to the foot of the crags on the left-hand side of the wall, looking for a gully which can be ascended fairly easily at first. Where this becomes steep traverse right until a way can be found up a steep but easy chimney, reaching the summit ridge about 70m to the right of the top. People have also been observed ascending a gully on the right-hand side of the wall, but this appears to be rather loose. Note that if this route does not appeal at this point, it is easy enough, but longer, to go over the Coll des Prat and then join the way up from Almallutx.

Descent can be made either by the direct route or by way of the Font de S'Avenc, which is recommended. From the top follow the path slightly east of south to the lip of the sloping shelf below the summit. An engraved stone points to the rocky staircase that leads down to the spring. The path from the spring is quite well marked, but surprisingly easy to lose, so keep looking for cairns and paint marks. This path leads to a junction with the more direct route from the summit, at a marker stone just above the 'Avenc de Cami'. The path down to the Coll de Sa Linea is now obvious. At this col turn left and in about 15 minutes turn right at a painted boulder and follow the path down through the woods to Comafreda.

Petrol station - Coll des Prat	2hr 15min
Coll des Prat - Massanella	50min
Massanella - Font de S'Avenc	30min
Font de S'Avenc - Coll de Sa Linea	50min
Coll de Sa Linea - petrol station	50min

29(c). MASSANELLA FROM ALMALLUTX

This interesting route makes use of an old track which is another part of the ancient Pilgrim's Way from Soller to Lluc. (This old route can be followed almost completely, except for a short distance near Cuber where the new *canaleta* must be used: Soller - Biniaraix - Coll de L'Ofre - Cuber - new *canaleta* - Coll des Coloms - Font des Prat - Coll des Prat - Comafreda - Coll de Sa Bataia - Lluc.) The first part over the Coll des Coloms is also used on several other walks and as far as the well-known covered spring, the Font des Massanella (or Font des Prat) with its crystal-clear water. The continuation of the route up the long Comellar des Prat, although a popular route for Mallorquins, is unknown to most British walkers.

If transport can be arranged from Lluc at the end of the day it makes an enjoyable excursion to descend Massanella by the normal way. Otherwise it is necessary to return by the same route. There is a point of difficulty on the way up to the col between Massanella and the Puig de Ses Bassetes, which some walkers may find too great. In this case a good alternative is to make for the Coll des Prat from which it is not much further to reach the top of Sa Mola, opposite Massanella to the north and west. Then either return to Almallutx or descend to Comafreda and Lluc by the way described for the ascent in 29(b), depending on transport arrangements.

Type of walk: A good path, well marked with red paint and cairns and at a reasonable gradient, leads all the way up to the Col des Prat. Paint signs and cairns on pathless ground lead to the col at 1,188m referred to above. The little rock step which must be surmounted here might be regarded as an easy rock climb. After that the route is rough and rocky but not difficult.

Starting point:	K32.2 on the C710
Time:	6hr 20min
Distance:	12km
Highest point reached:	1,352m
Total height climbed:	800m
Grade:	A++
Map:	Selva 1:25,000

From K32.2 go over the Coll des Coloms as for Walk 30 and continue to the Font de Massanella (marked as Font des Prat on the map). Just before reaching this a branch path right is marked with a red M for Massanella. This immediately crosses the stream-bed and continues away from it for 100m or so, rising slightly to the east side of the valley. It then bends left through the trees to follow the valley well above the stream-bed. (Alternatively go first to the spring, then cross the stream-bed immediately opposite and bear slightly right to join the path there.) The path is well defined and liberally endowed with paint marks and cairns. Higher up the path divides into two and then rejoins. Take the right branch which passes below some large rocky outcrops of a coarse conglomerate. Look out for the painted boulder with the words 'Lluc' and 'Massanella', the latter pointing up to the pass between the latter and the Puig de Ses Bassetes. The rock step to the col is surmounted by stepping up on adequate but sloping footholds for two or three moves until a large and comforting 'jug-handle' can be gripped with the right hand. A few easier moves and it is done. Once on the col the only difficulty is in deciding the way through the rocky wilderness ahead. There are no more paint marks and few cairns, which in any case are difficult to see amongst the rocks.

Rock-climbers may like to turn left and go straight up the steep ridge leading to the top. Walkers should make a very slightly rising traverse across easy ground to the foot of a rocky spur about 300m away. Look out for the easiest ways up sloping ledges and gullies until it is possible to go back left to join the ridge above the steep section. Follow the ridge up to the top. There is quite a prominent cairn on the first top, then the twin top can be visited before crossing over easy ground to the main top with the trig point.

K32 - Font des Massanella	1hr 10min
Font des Massanella - col	1hr 20min

Col - top	1hr 30min
Descent to petrol station	2hr 20 min

30. CANALETA DE MASSANELLA FROM THE GORG BLAU

This old *canaleta* carries water from the Font des Prat, high up in the mountains, to the village of Mancor de la Vall, on the edge of the plain to the north of Inca. The project was carried out by a local man, Montserrat Fontanet, after it had been declared an impossible feat by various prestigious foreign engineers. It still functions as well as it did when it was built 240 years ago. Before modernisation in 1983 when the water was piped, it used to flow in an open channel and was even more attractive. One of the snags of the pipeline being buried is that wild pigs which forage in the woods keep digging up the earth, making walking more difficult. Access to the water is provided by taps at intervals along the pipeline, signposted 'Agua potable'. In dry weather when the reservoirs are low, hardly a trickle comes out of the taps, so don't count on being able to quench your thirst here.

Type of walk: Not strenuous, but somewhat exposed on the aqueduct.

Starting point:	K32.2 on C710
Time:	4hr 20min
Distance:	12km
Highest point reached:	795m
Total height climbed:	315m
Grade:	B
Map:	Selva 1:25,000 and Soller 1:25,000

Park near the Gorg Blau at K31.8 and walk up the road to the Almallutx gate, then follow the route up to the Coll des Coloms as in Walk 31. Follow the path down over the pass and after about 10 minutes go through a gateway. Go straight on to reach the Font des Prat, or Font de Massanella, in a further 5 minutes. Alternatively, take the first narrow path on the left by a *sitja* to the old Es Prat farmhouse, from where there are good views, then bear right to reach the spring. The spring, situated in an open glade, is covered over and gated. Cross the stream and follow down the left bank for about 300m to an open meadow. Large clumps of the summer snowflake, *Leucojum aestivum*, flourish here in late winter and early spring, in pools of water fed by the stream.

The *canaleta* begins here, with the pipeline buried by earth and stones in between the stone walls that used to bound the open channel. In about 5 minutes an arched aqueduct carries it across a ravine, then it continues along the side of a wooded hill. Soon it goes round a corner by means of a tunnel, then drops down slightly to a wooded col at 692m, between Es Castellot and Mitjana. After this it falls, gently at first then more rapidly, to the long and narrow Massanella valley. Continue following the pipeline as far as the place where it is crossed by a wall and begins to plunge steeply down the hillside. Return by the same route to the starting point. (Before reaching this turning point several cairns may be noticed, marking a path which goes down into the forest on the left. This can be followed on a longer walk starting at Mancor de la Vall, Walk 34.)

K32 - Coll des Coloms	50min
Coll des Coloms - Font des Prat	15min
Font des Prat - wall	1hr 10min
Wall - Coll des Coloms	1hr 15min
Coll des Coloms - K32	50min

N.B. 1. The Coll des Coloms is shown wrongly on the IGN maps as being between Morro de Almallutx and the Tossals Verds.

2. Mancor del Vall is also known as Mancor del Valle and Mancor de la Vall.

31. MORRO D'ALMALLUTX

The Morro d'Almallutx is one of the peaks of the Tossals group which lies south of the Gorg Blau and east of Cuber. It is the easiest top to reach and has splendid views of Massanella and the east side of the Puig Mayor with its impressive cliffs. One of the other tops, the Puig des Tossals Verds at 1,115m may also be climbed from the col between the two peaks. A cairned path leads SW at first, then doubles back NE along a ridge.

On this col at 954m are the remains of an old *casa de sa neu* and a hut where the snow collectors lived.

Type of walk: Some route-finding because of trees limiting vision. Pathless and rough at the top, but not difficult ground.

Starting point:	K32 on C710
Time:	3hr 20min
Distance:	8km
Highest point reached:	1,058m
Total height climbed:	433m
Grade:	B
Map:	Selva 1:25,000 and Soller 1:25,000

Park near the Gorg Blau at K31.8 on the Pollensa-Soller road. Walk up the road towards Soller to the first gate on the left at K32.2: this is the entry to the *finca* Almallutx and there is a 'no entry' sign on the gate. The track leads down to the valley floor and makes a sharp bend to the right before going through a gateway. A cairn on the right marks the beginning of a good path leading up through the woods, a little indistinct at first. This path passes several *sitjes* before leaving the woods for more open ground. Turn right to re-enter the woods almost opposite to an old bread-oven, which at first sight looks like a very large cairn.

Soon the path crosses a modern aqueduct along which water is pumped from the Gorg Blau to Cuber in a deep open channel. The path now goes through a narrow valley, rising slightly to the Coll des Coloms, reached shortly after passing the second of two gateways. Where the path starts to level out, an enormous pointed rock can be glimpsed through the trees high up on the right. Keep the position of this in mind, in case you lose the path in the trees, which is very easily done. About 20m after the main path starts to descend, turn right at a marker stone bearing the numbers 802,092.

This path used to be a good one as it once served the needs of the snow house on the col above, but is now partly obscured by fallen trees. There are some cairns and some red paint marks. An old limekiln is passed. After passing a large boulder, the path crosses the valley to the left. Make for the left-hand side of the large rock pinnacle noted from below, after which the col is easily reached. Turn right and go up by easy rocks, almost bare of vegetation, to the top of the Morro.

K32 - Coll des Coloms	50min
Coll des Coloms - Morro d'Almallutx	1hr
Morro d'Almallutx - K32	1hr 30min

(N.B. the Coll des Coloms is shown wrongly on the IGN maps as being between Morro d'Almallutx and the Tossals Verds.)

32. CANALETA DE MASSANELLA FROM MANCOR DEL VALL

This very interesting circular walk makes use of country roads, old mule paths, the *canaleta* path, and forest paths and tracks. The scenery is varied and it is a good walk for seeing wild flowers. The descent down the Massanella valley goes through a very narrow and wild gorge between vertical rock walls, gradually giving way to olive terraces and almond orchards. The walk starts from the small village of Mancor del Vall (aka Mancor del Valle/Mancor de la Vall) which is 5km north-east of Inca.

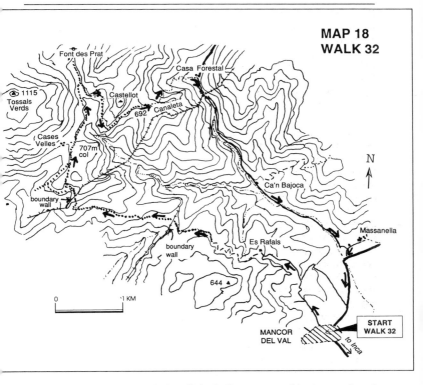

Type of walk: A very varied walk including easy walking on surfaced roads, good tracks, overgrown paths and easy but spectacular walking along the *canaleta* with some exposure. Descent is by a well-graded forest path to the Massanella valley and the wide easy track downwards. The ascent is nowhere very steep, but there are some route-finding problems especially on the overgrown part. This section would be improved if more walkers did this walk. (They have and it is.)

Starting point:	Mancor del Vall
Time:	5hr 50min
Distance:	16km
Highest point reached:	approx. 750m

Total height climbed:	510m
Grade:	A
Map:	Selva 1:25,000

There are some wide roads where a car can be left on the east side of Mancor. Follow the Carrer Mayor to the Placa de Dalt and turn right into the Carrer Bartolomeu Reus. This road bends sharp left at a restaurant and begins to go uphill. After crossing a stream-bed there is a branch track left. Ignore this and go straight ahead on the main right-hand branch. Five minutes further on the road swings right and there is a *camino particular* notice (which applies to cars). A footpath misses out the first bend on this road. In a further 5 minutes there is an unlocked gate across the road. Continuing uphill a large *finca*, Es Rafals, comes into view. Before reaching it there is a covered well on the left of the road. The surfaced road ends at the house, but a good track continues through a gate on the left of the house.

Keep following this track until it turns right through a wall. Go straight on at this point on a less well-used track which descends slightly to an oakwood. In a few minutes this track approaches an obvious boundary wall, very high and with a fence on top. The old 1:25,000 map (1962) shows two tracks continuing on the other side of this wall which don't appear to exist, and the new map shows no paths beyond this point. The way to continue is to follow the red paint spots roughly parallel to the wall and leading to a gateway.

On the other side of the wall an excellently made path continues, sometimes contouring and sometimes rising gently. Occasional cairns and red paint marks are useful as vegetation has obscured the way in places. After almost 2km this path turns a corner and rises in a few bends to a gap in another boundary wall. The next objective is a low col across an intervening valley. Fires have destroyed the path in this area, so either strike due north to the higher of two cols seen ahead, or bear left to the lower col and join the good path coming up from the Tossals *rifugio*. When the col is reached make for a gap in the wall and on the other side follow a faint path down slightly to join a better path rising up from the Tossals Verds house. Turn right and follow this path up to the 707m col. This is a large flat area with a rough shelter on the left, and an old well, the Font de Sa Basola, up on the right. Keep straight on roughly in the centre of the flat area. The path keeps to the right of a line of bushes and then enters the wood on the left through a gateway. This path is now a well-built one contouring into the valley head below a pipeline. When the stream is reached, cross it and scramble up the bank to find the *canaleta* path.

Follow the *canaleta* to the right along the viaduct and round the head of a side valley, through the tunnel, then round another corner and on to a wooded col at 692m. Approximately 20 minutes after the tunnel and shortly after the *canaleta* begins to descend from the col, look out for a narrow path leading into the oak forest on the left. This is a key point and it is well cairned.

The excellent path beginning here can be followed easily down through the trees, being very well constructed as well as marked by blue painted arrows and a number of cairns. It is narrow at first but becomes wider after passing two *sitjes* and leads down to a clearing with a forest house (*casa forestal*). (At the time of writing this was being refurbished as another mountain hut). At this point it joins another track coming down from the Pas de N'Arbona. Turn right and follow the main track down the Massanella valley, passing a house called Ca'n Bajoca, where there is a wooden stile at the side of a locked gate. Lower down, the track bends sharp left, then goes through a gate near the property of Massanella. Turn sharp right here, as indicated by a white arrow painted on a tree. The road then bends left to arrive at a T-junction. Turn right here and walk the short distance along the road to Mancor and the starting point of the walk.

Mancor - Es Rafals		40min
Es Rafals - boundary wall		35min
Boundary wall - 707m col	1hr	30min
707m col - *canaleta*		25min
Canaleta - descent path		40min
Descent path - Forest house		40min
Forest house - Massanella	1hr	
Massanella - Mancor		20min

33. CIRCUIT OF THE TOSSALS GROUP

The four peaks of the Tossals group are in the reservoir area south of the Gorg Blau and east of the Embalse de Cuber. This walk follows various pipelines and goes through some interesting country. A torch is advisable for some of the tunnel sections. The Tossals Verds house which is passed on the walk is the first of a network of mountain huts planned to provide accommodation throughout the Tramuntana. Since

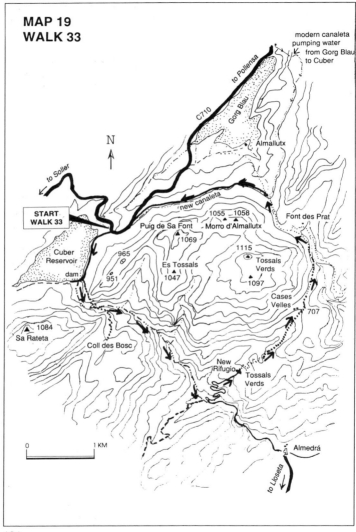

MAP 19
WALK 33

modern canaleta
pumping water
from Gorg Blau
to Cuber

to Pollensa

C710

Gorg Blau

Almallutx

N

to Soller

new canaleta

START
WALK 33

Puig de Sa Font
1055 – 1058
Morro d'Almallutx

Font des Prat

1069

Cuber
Reservoir

965

1115

Tossals
Verds

dam

951

Es Tossals
1047

1097

Cases
Velles
707

1084
Sa Rateta

Coll des Bosc

New
Rifugio

Tossals
Verds

Almedrá

to Lloseta

0   1 KM

it opened in April 1995 it has already proved popular, with accommodation for a maximum of 30 in dormitory rooms and a restaurant service and bar.

Type of walk: Fairly rough walking most of the way, especially the downhill section from Cuber. An easy middle section on a surfaced road up to the Tossals Verds house, then an old path, now restored and easy to follow.

Starting point:	Cuber reservoir
Time:	4hr 45min
Distance:	12km
Highest point reached:	822m
Total height climbed:	467m
Grade:	B
Map:	Soller 1:25,000 & Selva 1:25,000

From the parking place at the entrance to the Cuber reservoir walk through the access gate and along the road towards the dam. Just before reaching the dam take the stony track descending into the gorge below. In 5 minutes either go straight on along the main track, or branch right by a large boulder with a paint sign to go through the first tunnel. At first it is very rough and stony but the walking becomes easier after crossing the stream. Later there is another rough section where the path has been washed away and is badly overgrown with brambles and other vegetation. The path then accompanies the waterpipe's four tunnels, taking 3, 5, 4 and 3 minutes to negotiate. If preferred the old *canaleta* can be followed on the outside of the cliff instead of going through the last two tunnels, where the old *canaleta* or open water channel can be seen, still with water flowing along it.

After the last tunnel the wide track gives easy walking and leads down to an upland plateau above Almedra. Follow the main track downwards, ignoring an apparent left turn which leads only to a pipeline. About 5 minutes after this, take a left fork which leads in another 5 minutes to a yellow gate with a green stile on the left. There is a tarmac road from Almedra on the other side. Turn left here and follow this road up through olive terraces to the new *rifugio,* Tossals Verds, mentioned above. The tarmac road ends here. Go up through the house gates and another gate at the left-hand side of the house. A well-laid mule track marked with blue paint signs will now be found leading by twists and turns up to a shallow valley, almost a plateau. Some ruins marked as 'Cases Velles' on the map, will be seen high up on the left. The path then follows a new pipeline which lies in the old *canaleta*, to arrive at a col at 707m, quite near the ruined house. There is a rough shelter on the left here, made of tree branches and tarpaulins, and also an old well, the Font de sa Basola, on the right.

Keep straight on roughly in the centre of the flat area. The path keeps to the right of a line of bushes at first and then enters the wood through a gateway on the left. This is a good path keeping below a pipeline. Before the stream is reached the old Canaleta de Massanella will be seen on the other side of the valley, being carried round the hillside on an arched aqueduct. Just before reaching the stream, scramble up a dark smooth slab to reach the pipeline and follow this along, crossing the stream near a *sitja*. Follow the track up to the Coll des Coloms and down the other side. When the new aqueduct is reached turn left and follow it all the way back to Cuber. It joins the main road about 5 minutes before the reservoir.

Cuber - yellow gates	1hr 40min
Yellow gates - Tossals Verds	35min
Tossals Verds - Cases Velles	45min
Cases Velles - Coll des Coloms	50min
Coll des Coloms - Cuber	55min

34. SA RATETA AND L'OFRE

L'Ofre is best seen from Soller, from where it is usually climbed, as a distinctive triangular peak. The walk described here starts and finishes at the Embalse de Cuber (pron. *em-bal-say day coo-bair*), a large reservoir where sometimes ospreys may be seen fishing. Many other birds too may be seen, including red kites and black vultures. This route is a high ridge walk from Sa Rateta to L'Ofre, returning by the Cuber valley.

Type of walk: Not too strenuous, thanks to the high starting point at Cuber, but rough rocky ground and quite difficult route-finding on the ascent of Sa Rateta. Easy return route along a cart track.

Starting point:	Cuber gates at K34 on C710
Time:	4hr 20min
Distance:	8km
Highest point reached:	1,091m
Total height climbed:	561m
Grade:	B+
Map:	Soller 1:25,000

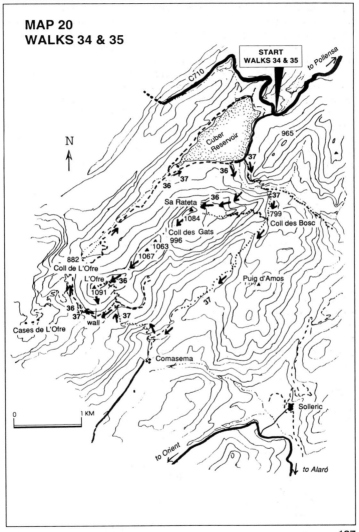

**MAP 20
WALKS 34 & 35**

START
WALKS 34 & 35

to Pollensa

C710

N

Cuber
Reservoir

965

37

36

37

36

36

37

799

Sa Rateta

1084

Coll des Bosc

Coll des Gats
996

1063

1067

882
Coll de L'Ofre

L'Ofre

36

1091

Puig d'Amos

37

36

37

37

Cases de L'Ofre

wall

Comasema

Solleric

0   1 KM

to Orient

to Alaró

Park by the locked entrance gate to Cuber. Go through the pedestrian access gate and walk along the road to the dam. It is best to study the next part of the route while approaching the dam. Looking straight ahead a narrow scree-filled gully with a sharp right-angled bend in it can be seen, falling away into the gorge below the dam. The aim is to reach this gully at the 'elbow'. The easiest way is to continue along the road past the dam for some 50m or so, then turn off left. Cross over a rocky spur and then contour round the shallow valley, rising towards a cluster of evergreen oaks. When the 'elbow' is reached, a broken wall and fence is crossed and from this point a series of cairns leading up the gully will be found. This ascent is quite easy but steepens a little higher up. Exit from the gully is by a conspicuous pine tree seen on the skyline. On the other side of this skyline ridge is a hidden valley. Cairns continue to mark the route which progresses upwards at an easy angle, making use of natural ledges of rock and scree. It emerges finally on a plateau at the head of the valley.

Swing round to the right and make for the top of Sa Rateta, across rocky but easy ground. There is a summit book started by a group of Mallorquin walkers in 1983. (This was missing in 1990.) From the top the ridge continues horizontally at first towards the south-west and then drops down quite steeply to the Coll des Gats at 996m with traces of a path. There is an unusual and conspicuous patch of short grass on this col, rare in Mallorca. Going up the next ridge from here, the steep crag ahead is avoided by making for an obvious shelf on the left. Then easy rocks lead round behind the steep ground to rejoin the ridge. Continue over the double top of the Puig de na Franquesa (1,063m, 1,067m) and descend to the 965m col before L'Ofre. (There is a way down into the Cuber valley from this col if a shorter walk or an escape route is wanted.) The L'Ofre ridge is gained by easy slabs to the left of the pylon, and a cairned path followed to the top.

To descend, go back along the ridge for about 50m to a small shoulder and find the path down to the south, towards the Coll D'en Poma, marked by red paint. This path has many variations, but the main one arrives on flattish ground about 50m east of the wall which runs south from the foot of the rocks. Turn right along the cart track and go through the gap in the wall. Follow this track round to the Coll de L'Ofre where there is a large cairn. The wide track leads back along the Cuber valley to the starting point. A short cut through the trees is signposted on the left quite near the beginning of the descent from the col.

Massanella from Sa Rateta

Cuber entrance - Sa Rateta	1hr 30min
Sa Rateta - L'Ofre	1hr 15min
L'Ofre - Coll de L'Ofre	35min
Coll de L'Ofre - Cuber entrance	1hr

35. CUBER AND COMASEMA CIRCULAR WALK

The Cuber reservoir is the starting point for several walks, and the wide track leading past it to the Coll de L'Ofre is well known. The Comasema valley on the other side of the Sa Rateta - L'Ofre ridge is less well known and this circular walk links the two by little-used paths, giving an interesting round with splendid views. There are two telescopes at two viewpoints along this walk, slightly off the track but worth the short detours. One is just before going through the gap in the wall on the wide track south of L'Ofre. The other is on a gently sloping shelf overlooking Soller, 200m or so south of the Coll de L'Ofre.

Type of walk: Mainly easy on fairly level wide tracks, but some ups and downs on rough and stony paths.

Starting point:	Cuber
Time:	5hr 40min
Distance:	12km
Highest point reached:	888m
Total height climbed:	530m
Grade:	B
Map:	Soller 1:25,000

Walk along to the reservoir and just before the dam turn left and follow the track down the valley with the pipeline. Five minutes later either turn right opposite a paint sign on a boulder and go through the tunnel or keep straight on along the upper track which goes over a shoulder and then zigzags down. Cross the stream-bed and turn left, following the concrete wall of the pipeline on the right. In a little under 5 minutes look out for a cairn (at times demolished but always rebuilt!) and a painted red arrow showing the way up onto a cobbled track which goes up parallel to the pipeline at first. This old track, once part of the ancient Pilgrim's Way to Lluc, twists and turns and eventually turns right up a rock slope to the Coll des Bosc, at the head of the Comasema valley. The Coll des Bosc can be a slightly confusing place because visibility is hampered by the trees. First of all a false col is reached, then the path rises again. When the true col is reached there are several

Comasema. A typical old Mallorquin manor house

prominent cairns, and the more obvious path turns right to go up Sa Rateta (good alternative ascent route). At this point turn left through trees and shrubs to find a broad clearing.

The easy but rather stony old track beginning at the clearing leads down through the woods into the Comasema valley, passing after 15 minutes an old spring on the right, the Font de sa Cisternata (not good water). The path continues down through the woods passing signs of charcoal-burning activities and an animal shelter before reaching a gateway at the edge of the woods.

Some 20 minutes after the gateway and about 200m before reaching the large buildings of Comasema, turn right between two stone walls into a dry stream-bed. Paint signs on the right-hand wall include a blue arrow showing the way to Soller, and a yellow one pointing back to Cuber. It is quite likely that these are completely obscured by brambles, but there is only one such stream-bed.

This is the beginning of an ancient track, again part of the Pilgrim's Way, which leads up a steep hillside, Es Barrancons, by a winding route on the right of the gully. Well graded, but partly obscured by vegetation and damaged by fire, this emerges onto a flat shelf below a wood, a good viewpoint. Go through a metal gate into the woodland and turn left to follow the main path, with some blue paint signs and cairns. Turn sharp right after going through a broken down wall and follow the path at the side of this wall up towards a flat circular area. Look out for occasional cairns, but in general keep straight on up a kind of ridge to reach a wide forest track at a bend. Turn left and follow this along to the south side of L'Ofre. After going through a gap in a wall, near where a path goes up to L'Ofre's summit, the track swings round and arrives at the Coll de L'Ofre.

From here there is an easy walk back to Cuber and the start of the walk. A short cut is signposted on the left of the track on the way down from the col.

Cuber - Coll des Bosc	1hr 10min
Coll des Bosc - Es Barrancons	1hr 15min
Es Barrancons - Coll de L'Ofre	1hr 45min
Coll de L'Ofre - Cuber	1hr 30min

36. PUIG DE S'ALCADENA

The massif of S'Alcadena is on the east of the Alaró-Orient road, opposite the Castell d'Alaró, Walk 37. Quite different in character from the walk up to the castle, which is easy and popular, this walk is rough and does not attract many people. It is a striking mountain from all directions, being defended on all sides by vertical cliffs. These cliffs are in places 200m high and extend for several kilometres and have been used for climbing competitions. This walk utilises the one line of weakness on the east side. The approach is by a private road through the grounds of the *finca* Son Cadena where the owner is likely to be met. It is necessary to ask permission to continue.

Type of walk: Although a good path is used most of the way, this has fallen away at one point in a fairly steep gully. Some walkers have been forced to retreat at this point.

Starting point:	K18, Alaró-Orient road
Time:	4hr 10min
Distance:	8km
Highest point reached:	813m
Total height climbed	607m
Grade:	B+
Map:	Alaró 1:25,000 and Inca 1:25,000

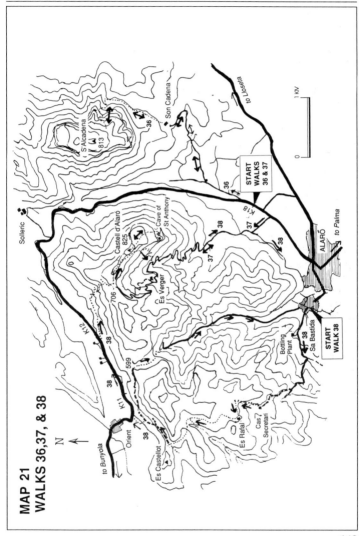

MAP 21
WALKS 36,37, & 38

A car may be left on the grass verge near the K18 stone. Walk towards Orient and almost immediately take a right fork where the main road bends left. Take the second right down a narrow lane with a stone barn on the corner and then cross the Sollerich stream by a ford (no water, normally). The gates of the *finca* Son Cadena are soon reached and the track followed up to the farm buildings. At the house turn right through a gate, then left round the back of the house. Turn right up a well-laid cobbled track which leads through olive terraces to the east side of the mountain and eventually through a gate.

Go through the gate, turn left and then almost immediately right. This path continues to contour along the eastern slopes through cultivated terraces and then into a wood of evergreen oaks and pines. After going through another gateway with a boulder at the right-hand side the path begins to rise more steeply and there are some cairns. Soon a very old gate between high stone gateposts topped with wooden beams is reached; this is the only access to the normal way up the mountain.

The route now goes up a wide gully by a well-constructed path. The only difficulty is at the point where this has collapsed and steep ground has to be crossed with some care. After emerging on a shoulder the path ascends gradually to the south to end at a *sitja*. From this *sitja* go straight on along a continuing and waymarked path which slowly contours round the top of the cliffs until it turns up fairly steeply towards the top. A shorter way is to go straight up from the *sitja* but this is rough, vegetated and steep and not recommended.

K18 - Son Cadena		40min
Son Cadena - path end	1hr	10min
Path end - summit		40min
Summit - Son Cadena	1hr	
Son Cadena - K18		40min

37. CASTELL D'ALARÓ

The Puig d'Alaró is one of the two 'sugar loaf' mountains seen on the west side of the Palma-Inca road. The other is S'Alcadena, Walk 36. The castle formerly covered almost the entire top of the mountain and the approaches to it are well defended by steep cliffs. The only way up is by a steep cobbled path with steps and ramps leading to the gated entrance. The remains are still very impressive and the views extensive. On the topmost point of the hill is a small bar-restaurant in the style of an alpine hut, offering coffee, food, wine and accommodation at reasonable prices (closed on Tuesdays).

An optional extension to the walk is a visit to the Cave of Saint Anthony, a large cave with a sloping floor reached in about 30 minutes from the top. This lies out at the end of a ridge running south-east then south and culminating in an old defensive tower with steep drops almost all round.

A narrow road runs up to a col at 706m, passing the restaurant Es Pouet on the way. Good traditional food is served here and it is very popular at weekends, which are best avoided.

Type of walk: Easy walking up a narrow road and a good path. The extension to the cave is over more difficult terrain; the path is not very easy to follow and the going is quite rough at the end.

Starting point:	K18 on the Alaró-Orient road
Time:	3hr 30min (add 1hr for the cave)
Distance:	9km
Highest point reached:	825m
Total height climbed:	600m
Grade:	C (B to the cave)
Map:	Alaró 1:25,000

A car may be left on the wide grassy verge near the K18 stone on the road from Alaró to Orient. Turn back towards Alaró and take the road signposted 'Castillo, Es Pouet' which is about 200m from K18. (Alternatively drive up this road for a short distance to park on waste ground on the left.) Walk up the road, taking advantage of the short cuts. The first one begins by an enormous boulder after going through a gateway. There are three short cuts which make use of an old mule track, winding up through terraces of olive trees. The third short cut bypasses an alternative path used on the descent.

After passing the restaurant Es Pouet the main track keeps to the left, or an alternative on the right with more bends can be used. Both lead to the col where there is a large open space used as a car park. The path to the castle goes up on the left of a wall and is signposted with a yellow painted arrow. This well-built path joins another path used on the descent and the gatehouse of the castle is reached 5 minutes later. Allow a few minutes for looking round here before continuing to the top.

To find the cave, go past the outbuildings and follow a rather confusing path through the woodlands, looking out for cairns and paintmarks. A descent of the order of 100m or more is called for, but

Castell d'Alaró from the east

this is fairly gradual. The entrance to the cave is well hidden and unlikely to be seen until the old tower perched on the end of the ridge is reached. From the tower, look back along the path and the dark hole that leads into the cave will be seen. Go inside, and light shining through another hole shows the way. If the floor is dry it is safe to explore thoroughly, but remember there is a steep drop below. This is not a place to take small children.

Retrace your steps back to the top and continue down past the castle to the path junction met on the way up. Turn left and follow the path down to join the road. It is signposted 'Alaró a pie'. On the way down a branch path leads back to Es Pouet if you are in need of refreshment. If you are going straight down, there are two short cuts to find.

K18 - summit	2hr
Summit - cave, and return	1hr
Summit - K18	1hr 30min

146

38(a). ALARÓ-ORIENT CIRCULAR WALK

The walk to the Castell d'Alaró from Alaró is well known and deservedly popular. Less well known is the approach from Orient, a very attractive old village situated in a peaceful valley. The 'surprise view' of Orient on this circular walk is really outstanding and the whole walk is full of interest. Alaró is an old town with narrow streets, many of them one way. Approaching from the Palma or the Inca direction, follow the town centre signs until a way out on the west side of the town can be found. There is a place to park by some new houses just outside the old quarter of Sa Bastida.

Type of walk: All the walking is easy on lanes, tracks and good paths, except for a short distance between Cas Secretari and Es Rafal. The pull up to the Coll de S'Era is quite steep but on a surfaced road.

Starting point:	Sa Bastida, Alaró
Time:	5hr 20min
Distance:	13km
Highest point reached:	825m
Total height climbed:	626m
Grade:	C+
Map:	Alaró 1:25,000

Leave Sa Bastida by the Carrer de Son Borras. In 10 minutes the road passes the bottling plant of the Bastida spring. Follow the narrow but surfaced road up through the woods to the Coll de S'Era, ignoring a number of branch tracks on both sides. Approaching the cols is a sign 'Camino cortado a 200m' indicating the locked gate on the col which prevents unauthorised traffic. On the far side of the col is a valley filled with olive terraces, the Clot des Guix (483m). Go to the side of a new metal gate, then take the first turning right about 2 minutes further on, bypassing another locked metal gate. The track ends at a house, Cas Secretari, but a path continues at the right-hand side of it, passing a spring. A rough path now leads upwards to the top of the terraces, keeping near the right side. A vertical metal stile gives access to the top terrace, where the path turns left and leads easily to a ruined house, Es Rafal, going through a metal gate with a sign saying it is to be kept closed. Before reaching the house and less than 20m from this gate turn right at the far side of a low wall. Follow the path alongside this wall and go through an open gateway into a wood. When the path bifurcates take the left-hand branch which runs parallel to the wall. Go

147

Approaching the Castell d'Alaró

through a gap in a wall and keep following the woodland path which is well marked.

After crossing a low wall on the Pas de S'Estalot the path descends into a side valley, then turns left and contours to arrive at a pass at 572m on the east of Es Castellot. On this pass the path turns at right angles between two rock walls which frame an outstanding view of Orient and the hills beyond. Follow the wide track down and after 10 minutes turn down left at a fork. Continue along this track until a gate is seen on the left. Painted signs to Santa Maria point back the way you have come. Go through this and follow the track down through the orchards into Orient, joining the tarmac road at K10.5. (Note that the gate at K10.6 is locked.) Turn right and follow the road past the Hermitage hotel. Less than 300m from here turn right through a gate into the olive terraces. Turn left and follow the path, at first parallel to the road, then sloping uphill towards a wooded gully. The path enters the wood and rises up in zigzags to reach a large sloping area used as a picnic place and, regrettably, as a car park, the Pla d'es Pouet. From here the descent can be made either by the narrow road on the right via the Es Verger restaurant, or preferably by following the path to the castle and the footpath down from there (see walk 37). If you have left a car at Sa Bastida, then keep following the road which hugs the bottom of the hill and leads into the old part of Alaró and Sa Bastida.

Alaró - Cas Secretari	1hr
Cas Secretari - Pas de S'Estalot	50min
Pas de S'Estalot - Orient	15min
Orient - Castle	1hr 30min
Castle - Alaró	1hr 45min

38(b). ALARÓ-ORIENT CIRCULAR WALK: SHORT VERSION

This route does not include the Castell d'Alaró, but is a most enjoyable excursion in quiet and little-known countryside.

Starting point:	Sa Bastida
Time:	3hr 15min
Distance:	10km
Highest point reached:	599m
Total height climbed:	422m
Grade:	C+
Map:	Alaró 1:25,000

Follow route 38(a) as far as the gate by which there are signs pointing back to Santa Maria and where the path descends through the orchards to Orient. Continue along the track which rises steadily and then in zigzags through the woodlands until there is a sudden view of the Orient valley, near a hunter's shelter. The track turns right here and keeps to the right of flattish ground, before going into woodlands again and descending into a narrow valley by an old mule track which is stepped in places and quite delightful. The path joins a cart track which goes steadily down the valley to reach the houses of Sa Bastida where the walk began.

39. PUIG DES JOU

This peak is also known as Ses Heures, but 'Jou' means yoke and as the peak is yoked to the main Alfabia ridge by the Coll des Jou it seems an apt name. The col is easily reached from Orient by good tracks made in past times by the charcoal burners. Thereafter a delightful and

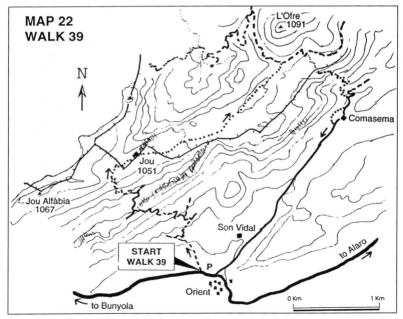

easy scramble leads to the peak of 1,051m which is a superb viewpoint. The return is by the Comasema valley. Note that the walk can only be done in the direction described because of a locked gate between Comasema and Orient which allows walkers to get out but not in to the property.

Type of walk: Mostly on good tracks and paths, but the crossing from Jou to the Es Barrancons path is on pathless, rocky ground and needs an eye for picking the best route. To find the start of the walk drive through the village to a triangular field on the outskirts, where there is parking by some large trees.

Starting Point:	Orient
Time:	5hr 25min
Distance:	12km (approx)
Highest point reached:	1,051m
Total height climbed:	665m
Grade:	A
Map:	Alaró 1:25,000 and Soller 1:25,000

Cross the bridge and go over a wooden stile next to the gate on the right. The track crosses the field and after 10 minutes another stile is reached leading into an olive grove by a large carob tree. Follow the wide track up through the terraces ignoring a path left and a branch track right, where the route goes left behind a *caseta*. Higher up olives give way to oaks, and about an hour from the start a branch left is ignored and the track levels out at a small clearing known as the Pla des Porxo. Remains of charcoal workers' activities are everywhere, including an old *caseta* which in 1996 was being extended and restored. The wide track ends here and a red arrow points the way to a continuing path on the left. A few minutes later the way is confirmed by another arrow and the words 'Coll des Jou' painted on a rock. The way becomes a narrow path, twisting and turning between the rocks and trees, on a surface softened by leaves. Through the trees there are occasional glimpses of the Penyals d'Honor above the flat fields and orchards of the Orient valley. Higher up a wall is crossed and the angle eases before the col is reached. L'Ofre is seen towering over the tiny cultivated valley of the Cases de L'Ofre.

At first sight the Puig des Jou appears intimidating with formidable crags overlooking the sloping valley below the col. In reality there are no difficulties and some small cairns, beginning near an old wall, show

151

the way up to a sloping grassy ledge on the west side of the ridge. This leads in 10 minutes to a breach in the rocks giving access to the Orient side. Ten minutes' easy scrambling now leads to the top.

The next objective is the shoulder to the right of L'Ofre. Start to descend in a roughly ENE direction, following occasional cairns. This is where a good eye for picking the best route comes in useful. Veer east and find a gap in the boundary wall, then gradually descend to a valley floor and into a stream-bed. Where this swings right, leave it and start ascending at a gentle gradient to reach traces of a path at the left-hand side of a cliff. This is the Pas de Na Maria, a path built in the fifteenth century and used to transport sacred relics from Soller to the Castle of Alaró. Now little used there are few cairns, but it is not difficult to find a way which rises and then contours along the Soller side of a broad ridge. After crossing the tops of a couple of side valleys it goes over to the Orient side, before dropping down and then rising slightly to a gap in a stone wall. On the other side of this gap stands a telescope with a coin slot. Above it is the wide forest piste which runs from the Coll de L'Ofre to a spring, the Font de s'Aritja.

Walk north along the track and in about 7 minutes, after a bend left, look for the blue paint spot which marks the start of the descent path, Es Barrancons. After about 5 minutes turn left at a cross-path, then ignore the path veering left and keep straight on to find the metal gate in the wall at the escarpment edge. The old zigzag mule track winds down from here to the main valley of Comasema. A bad fire a few years ago contributed to the deterioration of this path which is also badly overgrown. Try to pick out and follow the old built-up path wherever possible, as the taking of short cuts is only causing further erosion.

When the main track in the valley is reached, turn right and follow the signposted diversion which avoids the lovely old house of Comasema. The locked gate, where there are many signs forbidding entry, is surmounted by metal rungs cemented into the right-hand gatepost. A fireman's pole is provided to aid descent.

Orient - Coll des Jou	1hr 45min
Coll des Jou - Puig	20min
Puig - L'Ofre track	1hr 40min
L'Ofre track - Orient	1hr 40min

40. PENYALS D'HONOR

The Penyals d'Honor are the high tops of a limestone escarpment overlooking the narrow valley which links Bunyola with Orient. The main top at 819m is tree-girt and rather difficult to reach, but on the lower 809m top there is a small *mirador* with panoramic views over the south of the island, including the bay of Palma and the high peaks of Galatxo, Es Puntals and Teix. Across the valley to the north are close views of the steep slopes of the long Alfabia ridge. Although the area is mainly wooded there are open views too. Ca's Garriguer is a well-equipped picnic place with barbecues belonging to the council of Bunyola and is kept in excellent condition. Permission to camp may be obtained by writing to the *Ajuntament*. This area can be reached by a long drivable track from Bunyola and is sometimes crowded at weekends and holidays.

40(a). FROM THE COLL D'HONOR

Type of walk: Mainly easy on good tracks and paths.

Starting point:	On the col where there is limited parking
Time:	3hr 25min or 3hr 50min
Distance:	12km
Highest point reached:	809m
Total height climbed:	407m
Grade:	C+
Map:	Alaró 1:25,000

Approaching from Bunyola the Coll is reached shortly after K6. Descend the Orient side for about 50m and follow the wide path easily up to the Coll des Pico. After a short descent another path is reached at a T-junction and a right turn taken. The path rises quite steeply for a short distance below a rock wall. When a branch path is seen, marked by a cairn at the foot of a large pine tree, keep straight on; the path on the right is the return route. Going straight on the path rises slightly at first and then descends to join a wide cart track. Turn right and follow this as it contours the south-eastern slopes of the upland area. Ignore a branch track right opposite a new water tank. Immediately after this the main track swings right and is joined by a track coming up from the valley. Keep on the main track which swings north to reach the Ca's Garriguer picnic area.

At this point there is a choice of two ways. The longer and more

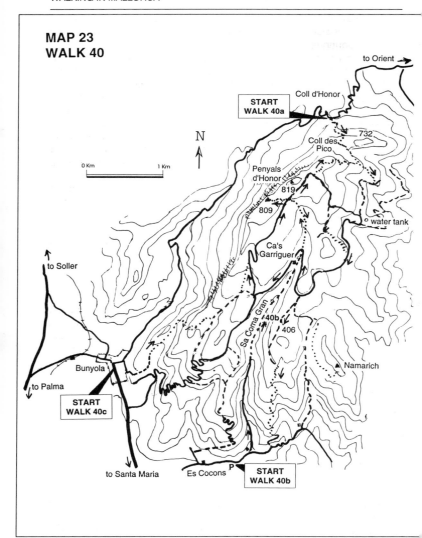

MAP 23
WALK 40

to Orient

Coll d'Honor

START WALK 40a

732

Coll des Pico

N

Penyals d'Honor

0 Km — 1 Km

819

809

water tank

Ca's Garriguer

to Soller

Sa Coma Gran

40b

406

to Palma

Bunyola

Namarich

START WALK 40c

to Santa Maria

Es Cocons

P

START WALK 40b

gradual way is to follow the main track SW for about 1km, then turn right and immediately right again where there is a signpost to the Penyals d'Honor. Continue gently uphill on the wide easy track for about 30 minutes until another signpost shows the way to the top by a path on the left. The second way of reaching this point is much shorter but also steeper. This is to go directly up the wide track leading north from the hairpin bend in the road at Ca's Garriguer. After about 1km this becomes a narrow path but is easy to follow and joins the main track exactly opposite the signpost to the top.

The top is easily reached in about 10 minutes. Return the same way and turn left on the main track, following it until it makes a sharp bend to the right. Just after the bend a cairn shows the beginning of the descent path. This twists and turns through the trees and would be difficult to follow were it not for the frequent cairns and paint marks. At one point it goes near enough the escarpment edge for an open view across the Orient valley. The path leads down to the junction by the pine tree passed on the outward route. Turn left and retrace your steps back to the Coll d'Honor, not forgetting to take the left fork where you turned right near the start of the walk.

40(b). FROM ES COCONS

This is a longer walk with 660m of ascent. To reach the start from Bunyola, go past the cemetery on the Santa Maria road and turn first left along a narrow lane. Pass the hamlet of Es Cocons where there is a tree in the centre of a small open area and continue to a wide parking area on the right, after passing two houses on the left, Ca'n Oliver and Ca'n Fiol.

Type of walk: Mainly easy on good tracks and paths.

Starting point:	Es Cocons
Time:	4hr 30min
Distance:	13km
Highest point reached:	809m
Total height climbed:	660m
Grade:	C+
Map:	Alaró 1:25,000

Walk east along the lane for about 3 minutes, then go straight on where the lane turns sharp right by a corner of a house. There is a small almond grove on the left. Follow this track all the way up the Coma

155

Gran, passing a 'cave house' below steep crags in the narrow section. Higher up, the valley widens again and is cultivated. Above, the track goes through a gate into the oakwood and continues to rise to Ca's Garriguer. Cross the wide road here and continue up the same valley. The path narrows and steepens a little as it curves left to reach a wide track near a signpost to the Penyals.

Follow the path to the top and then return to this point. Turn left and follow the track uphill at first, then swinging right and descending. Just before a sharp bend right take the narrow path on the left, descending through the woods to meet a cross-track in about 20 minutes. Turn right and in less than 10 minutes reach another cross-track. Turn right and follow this along the eastern slopes of the massif for about 50 minutes until it begins to swing north towards Ca's Garriguer. At this point take a left turn and after about 4 minutes go straight on at a branch path left (which is the route to Namarich). A good path rises gently at first and then descends the ridge between Sa Coma Gran and the Coma d'en Buscante. When the valley is reached by the iron gates of Ca'n Bergantet, turn right to return to the starting point.

40(c). FROM BUNYOLA

This walk uses a newly restored path, the Cami des Grau, starting in the old town of Bunyola which can be reached by train from either Soller or Palma.

Type of walk: Easy, on good tracks and paths.

Starting point:	Bunyola
Time:	3hr 30min
Distance:	10km
Highest point reached:	809m
Total height climbed:	609m
Grade:	C+
Map:	Alaró 1:25,000

The Canaleta de Massanella (Walk 30)

Cornadors from near Coll de L'Offre (Walk 44) (Author)
Descent from the Portell de sa Costa (Walk 45) (Author)

From the station walk up into the town and turn left at the signpost to Orient. Go up the steps of the Carrer de Sant Bartomeu to reach the Carrer d'Orient and turn right. At the Carrer de la Commuña turn left up more steps at the top of which is found a cart track. Follow this for about 200m until some sliding iron gates are seen on the left. The Cami des Grau begins at this point. Turn left and after a short distance ignore a right fork, continuing up the restored path which is easy to follow. After rising steadily and passing several sites, labelled for parties of visiting schoolchildren, the path zigzags up a steep section. Look out for a signpost indicating a short diversion left to a *mirador*.

Ten minutes later the path joins another track by a large limekiln and turns left up a narrow valley with more kilns. At a cross-track where there is a red paint mark on a tree go straight on up the narrow Comellar d'en Cupi. The path rises and then joins a major track. Turn left and follow this up past a double bend and on for a further kilometre, where a signpost points the way up a winding path to the summit.

To vary the descent route, go down to the signpost and straight on across the wide track to descend the upper part of the Coma Gran. On reaching the wide road at the hairpin bend by Ca's Garriguer turn right and after about 1km go straight on at a junction, passing a new water tank on the left. After 3-4 minutes the route used on the ascent is reached at the tree with the red paint mark. Turn left and follow the Cami des Grau back to Bunyola. For a slight variation at the end, descend the steps of the Carrer de la Lluna to reach the main square by the church. From here it is a little under 10 minutes to the station.

41. MIRADOR LEANDRO XIMENIS AND PAS DE SA FESA

Leandro Ximenis was a well-known Mallorquin mountaineer and this *mirador* was erected in his memory by the Fomento del Turismo. The situation on the top of Sa Gubia is a magnificent one with panoramic views in all directions. Gubia (named on the map as Alqueria) is a hill of 609m some 2km west of Bunyola whose cliffs provide some of the best rock climbing in the area. Gubia means gouge, and from the south the cliffs which tower over the orchards look as though a giant has gouged out a deep groove in the solid rock. The Pas de'Sa Fesa is a narrow cleft in the rocks, giving an easy but fascinating passage down steep ground leading into the valley of Biniforani, a quiet place filled with olives, lemons and almonds. This walk is well known and popular, so weekends are best avoided.

157

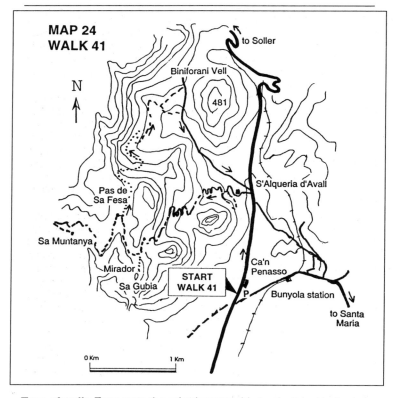

MAP 24
WALK 41

N

to Soller

Biniforani Vell

481

Pas de
Sa Fesa

S'Alqueria d'Avall

Sa Muntanya

Mirador

Sa Gubia

Ca'n
Penasso

**START
WALK 41**

P

Bunyola station

to Santa
Maria

0 Km   1 Km

Type of walk: Easy up to the *mirador* on a wide track almost to the top.
The descent is quite steep but not difficult and the walk finishes on a
narrow country lane.

Starting point:	Ca'n Penasso
Time:	4hr 30min
Distance:	10km
Highest point reached:	609m
Total height climbed:	440m
Grade:	B
Map:	Alaró 1:25,000

Walk along the main road north to the gates of S'Alqueria, a large manorial house on the left. The large black dog chained to the wall cannot reach walkers as long as they keep close to the wall on the left. Follow the zigzags of this wide easy track all the way up to a col at 539m. On this col is a stone marker indicating the stepped path which leads easily to the *mirador*.

From the top return to the wide track by the marker stone and turn left. This track continues to a property called Sa Montanya, but is left at the point where it makes a sharp left turn near a shelter, the Porxo des Pouet. Take a wide but somewhat indistinct path leading north from here and rising slightly to a col at 534m. Cross the open flat area to the left when the cairn which marks the top of the narrow cleft of Sa Fesa will easily be found. There is a tree at the top and, part way down, a decrepit gate. At the bottom there is a flat platform below a vertical wall.

The steep and narrow path slopes down to the right until a thrush-hunting station is reached, when it goes back left to pass several more of these structures. It leads to a wall with a wooden step down and then on to a wide cart track. Turn left and follow a winding route up into the valley, aided by some red paint marks. After a level section running north there is a right turn down some zigzags with unusual cypress hedges. Turn right down the road from Biniforani Vell. After passing an orchard of lemon trees the valley narrows and the track runs alongside a stream before joining the main road near S'Alqueria d'Avall.

There only remains to walk back along the main road to Ca'n Penasso. This can be avoided of course in both directions by taking the longer meandering route past the station and through the countryside. The walk can also be done by taking the train to Bunyola.

42. CUBER AND ES BARRANC

Mallorca has no natural lakes, but the two reservoirs built to augment Palma's water supplies provide satisfactory alternatives. The largest of them, Cuber, occupies a natural basin below the steep buttresses of the highest mountain, Puig Major, looking doubly impressive reflected in the still water. This can be a good place for birds, red kites for example, sometimes an osprey and black vultures quite frequently.

This easy, classic walk through the mountains, mainly downhill, is carried out with the aid of the C710 bus which runs from Soller over to Pollensa.

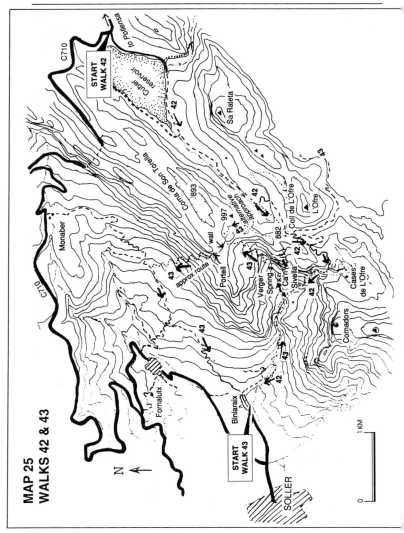

MAP 25
WALKS 42 & 43

There is a natural picnic place on a gently sloping grassy shelf overlooking the Soller valley, very near the Coll de L'Ofre. The descent by the Pilgrim Steps goes down an impressive gorge below the steep rock walls of Cornadors, with typical Mallorquin terraces growing ancient olive trees.

Type of walk: Very easy, along a wide track at first, over the Coll de L'Ofre, then down the excellent built up mule track known as the Pilgrim Steps down to the hamlet of Biniaraix.

Starting point:	Cuber gates, C710
Time:	3hr 45min
Distance:	13km
Highest point reached:	882m
Total height climbed:	Ascent 130m, descent c.800m
Grade:	C+
Map:	Soller 1:25,000

Go through the entrance gate and follow the road along past the dam. Just at the end of the lake there is a mountain shelter with a fireplace in one corner, but no other comforts. There are locked gates along this road, which is used by the people who work at the L'Ofre farm and drive up from Soller each day, but pedestrian access is provided for walkers, who are requested to keep to the paths.

Where the track bends left near some trees, walkers are directed to the obvious short cut by a pleasant path up through some woodland, leading up to the Coll de L'Ofre where there is a large cairn. On the other side of the col turn right at a junction and follow the descending track towards the Cases de L'Ofre. Short cut paths are shown by red paint signs. At the last bend before the Cases the way for walkers has been diverted so as to avoid the farm and this is well signposted, with steps leading down into the *barranc*. Walking down the *barranc* is like walking down a stone staircase but with spectacular views at every turn. About halfway down you will notice a path junction by a house with a walled garden, which is the way up to the Verger spring and the Portell de Sa Costa, Walk 43.

Once in Biniaraix turn left through the village and follow the road back to Soller.

Cuber - Coll de L'Ofre	1hr 10min
Coll de L'Ofre - Cases de L'Ofre	25min

Cases de L'Ofre - Biniaraix   1hr 40min
Biniaraix - Soller   30 min

43. PORTELL DE SA COSTA

The 'Portell' is a gateway on the high ridge of the Serra de Torrelles where there is a sudden and magnificent view of the Soller valley and the coast with its circular harbour. The Verger spring is an attractive place to visit, especially after recent rain when little waterfalls cascade over mossy rocks, but this is a difficult route. An easier approach to the Portell is from the Coll de L'Ofre, either from Cuber (see Walk 42) or by the *barranc*. If the *barranc* is used, then take the right fork at the junction described below and at the Cases de L'Ofre turn left and follow the track to the col.

Type of walk: A steep and stony descent. Ascent by the Verger spring is very strenuous with loose scree.

Starting point:	Soller
Time:	6hr 20min
Distance:	11km
Highest point reached:	c.900m
Total height climbed:	c.860m
Grade:	A+
Map	Soller 1:25,000

Leave the main square in Soller, the Plaza de la Constitució, by the road to Biniaraix. Go through this village to the public washplace at the end and there turn right on the narrow track signposted to the 'Barranc'. The path crosses the stream, which is usually dry, and then goes up by the old stepped path, part of a centuries old Pilgrim's Route to the monastery at Lluc. After going through a narrow section of the gorge and passing a small house, a path junction will be reached at the corner of another house. (Both the left and right-hand ways from here look impossible, although the path on the right, leading to the Cases de L'Ofre, is actually very easy all the way up and can be used as an alternative approach.)

To go up by the Verger spring route turn left here and in 10 minutes Ca'n Sivella will be reached. This is a house in a most attractive situation having a terrace with a round stone table. From the terrace there is a marvellous view of Soller framed by the walls of the *barranc*. With your back to the house, the path goes up straight ahead and crosses the stream. Keep following the path which goes up through old terraces, watching out for a right turn indicated by a faint silver arrow and the words 'Es Verger'. Soon after this fork right along a horizontal path, indicated by another painted arrow. The Verger spring will be reached about 20 minutes after leaving Ca'n Sivella.

The difficult part begins after this, with only traces of paths up loose stones and scree and several patches of brambles and other thorny vegetation. The best way is mainly on the right-hand side, although sometimes clambering up large boulders in the centre makes a good alternative. Eventually easier ground is reached after passing some pine trees, although before this you may well wish you had opted for the easier way up the *barranc*. When a wall is seen across the top of the slope ahead, make for a gap near the middle. A few yards on the other side of the gap there is a view down the Torrella valley and on the left the Portell de Sa Costa will be seen.

Turn left to reach the portal. Just through the opening is another gateway below which is a rather fine rock pinnacle. Here is a good place to rest and admire the view before starting the descent, because although there is an excellent and well-graded path all the way down, it is rather stony and care is needed. At first there are some tight bends, then wider sweeps. There are a few places where a fallen tree or minor rock fall has blocked the way. If the path is lost, it is best to backtrack and find it again. After about 1hr of descent, the path goes left and slightly uphill to reach a small knoll. Continue over this in the same direction and in 2-3 minutes a green paint sign saying SOLLER with an arrow will be seen.

After about another half hour the path arrives at an old stepped track between walls, but there is a little confusion here and it may be necessary to cast about to find it. There are some weekend houses in the woods here, fenced off both from the mountainside and a dirt road. If this dirt road is accidentally reached, turn left and the stepped path will be found by the entrance gate to Ca'n Xarpa. Follow the old path down past a spring to reach the Monaber road, and then turn left to return to Biniaraix by the public washplace at the top end of the village.

Soller - Biniaraix		30min
Biniaraix - Ca'n Sivella	1hr	
Ca'n Sivella - Verger spring		20min
Verger spring - Portell	1hr	50min
Portell - road	1hr	30min

Road - Biniaraix	40min
Biniaraix - Soller	30min

Alternative starts

From the Coll de L'Ofre pick up a narrow path on the west side which leads slightly east of north towards an unnamed top with spot heights of 966m and 997m overlooking the high Torelles valley and almost 1km from the col. (This top is named as Loma, 966m on the older maps.) The path veers round this on the east side and then turns towards the west to reach the Portell de Sa Costa. It crosses some flattish ground between the upper slopes of the Verger spring route to the south-west and the Torelles valley on the north-east. Allow about 40 minutes from the Coll de L'Ofre to the Portell de Sa Costa. If using the bus from Soller along the C710, from the Cuber entrance gate to the col it is about 1hr 10min. From Biniaraix to the col allow about 2hr 50min.

44. CORNADORS

(See note at end of preface.)

Cornadors overlooks the *barranc* of Biniaraix, up which go the well-known Pilgrim Steps, a wonderful old cobbled track originally going all the way from Soller to Lluc. There is a viewpoint near the top, the Mirador de L'Ofre, from which the mountain of L'Ofre is seen to great advantage. The view of the almost vertical face of Cornadors from the path is possibly even more striking than the view from the *mirador* itself. The walk up the *barranc* contends for the most popular walk on the island, so weekends are best avoided. The gorge itself is outstandingly attractive with hundreds of tiny terraces accommodating olives and oranges, flanked by steep rock walls on either side.

There is some confusion about the height of Cornadors on the maps and in various books. The *mirador* is undoubtedly on the 957m top, which has a precipitous north face towering over the *barranc*. The name 'Cornadors' means horns, and there is another steep-sided top at 809m which also overlooks the *barranc* and must be the other 'horn'. However, the name Cornadors on the map is nowhere near either of these. The 1,014m top on the Alfàbia ridge is now named as Sementer Gran, so is not the other top of Cornadors, as previously assumed.

The Mirador de L'Ofre is maintained by the Fomento del Turismo, as is the mountain hut near the top of Cornadors on its southern side. This has a sound roof and stone benches.

It is a moot point whether this walk is better done as described or in the reverse direction. For those who elect for the latter, some notes are included in the text to indicate key points. The attraction of ending at Biniaraix is that you can look forward to a glass of freshly squeezed orange juice at a bar on the main street.

Type of walk: Almost entirely on cart tracks and well-made paths. No difficulties, but quite a long and strenuous ascent.

Starting point:	Soller railway station
Time:	5hr 40min
Distance:	16km
Highest point reached:	957m
Total height climbed:	900m
Grade:	C+
Map:	Soller 1:25,000

From the railway station, face downhill towards the church and turn first right along a narrow street, passing the Hotel Guia. Take the first right again, second left, then first right again. Keep along this road, the Calle de Pablo Noguerra, until the cemetery is passed on the right. After passing the cemetery take a left fork, then in 2 minutes a right fork which crosses the stream by a bridge. A minute or so later take a sharp left turn. After this it is a question of keeping to the main track, marked here and there with small red paint marks. The track is well maintained and leads up through an area of old olive terraces and some weekend houses. Higher up it enters a forest of evergreen oaks where *sitjes* and lime-ovens abound.

After about an hour and a half go through a gate to meet another track at a T-junction and turn right. (There is a blue painted sign here pointing down to Soller, useful if reversing the walk.) After 5 minutes or so go through a metal gate and take a right fork. The farmhouse S'Arrom is now in sight on a plateau high above. The track swings left, then goes up a narrow gully in a series of tight bends. Watch out for the steps leading to a pedestrian access gate, as the double gates across the track are locked. When S'Arrom is reached, follow the track past the farm to the left, then right again past the house to the south. At a sharp bend left the track starts rising gently uphill to the north-east. (The engraved stones which used to show short cuts in this area have disappeared; it is best to follow the main track.) This becomes a narrow path which climbs in zigzags up a sloping shelf to a col, where a high fence is crossed by a stile. The *rifugio* is in sight here and is reached in

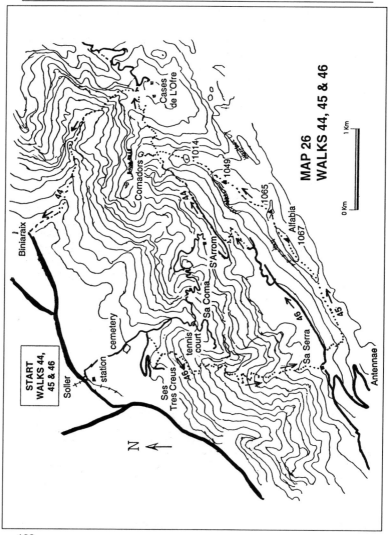

MAP 26
WALKS 44, 45 & 46

0 Km   1 Km

START WALKS 44, 45 & 46

Soller

station

cemetery

Biniaraix

Ses Tres Creus

tennis court

Sa Coma

S'Arrom

Cornadors

Cases de L'Ofre

1014

1049

1065

1067

Alfabia

Sa Serra

Antennae

N

44

45

46

a further 15 minutes, turning left at the 917m col due south of the top of Cornadors.

From the shelter it is only a few minutes to the top and over the other side to reach the impressively situated *mirador*. To continue the walk, return past the shelter to the col. Turn left here and follow the path down into the *barranc*. This has been diverted to avoid the houses on the tiny green plateau of L'Ofre and the old way is fenced off. A new path leads down to join the old route by a new bridge in the *barranc*. About 50 minutes after starting the descent, the path arrives at a corner of a wall, where there is a painted arrow pointing up. In reverse, look out for this junction as the other branch goes up to the Verger spring (Walk 43).

Continue down the main track which goes through a narrow and shady section and crosses the stream several times by bridges and stepping-stones. Not that there is much need for these as there is rarely any water in the stream-bed. Near Biniaraix the path joins another track at a gate with a 'No entry' sign and another sign which reads 'L'Ofre, Lluc a peu' (L'Ofre, Lluc on foot). Turn left to arrive at the small village by the old public washplace. Follow the road through or take the stepped street on the right, rejoin the road and follow it back to Soller. To return to the station from the main square, go up the hill to the right of the church.

Soller station - S'Arrom	2hr	
S'Arrom - Cornadors	1hr	
Cornadors - Cases de L'Ofre		35min
Cases de L'Ofre - Biniaraix	1hr	35min
Biniaraix - Soller station		30min

45. THE ALFÀBIA RIDGE

(See note at end of preface.)

The long high ridge of Alfàbia dominates the Soller valley and represents a constant challenge to walkers based in the area. The ridge is over 4km long with several tops over 1,000m, the highest being 1,067m. Although the southernmost top is despoiled by TV and radio masts, all the rest of the ridge is wild and pathless, and being difficult ground to walk on is rarely visited. The views are extensive and the glimpses down into the quiet Orient valley on the east are especially charming.

Type of walk: Steep but easy at first, then rough and slow along the ridge over tilted and dissected limestone pavement.

Starting point:	Soller railway station
Time:	8hr
Distance:	20km
Highest point reached:	1,067m
Total height climbed:	1,076m
Grade:	A+
Map:	Soller 1:25,000 and Alaró 1:25,000

Follow Walk 44 as far as S'Arrom and continue along the cart track past the farm towards the south-west until, about 250m after a sharp hairpin bend to the left, a red arrow is seen, pointing to a path leading up into the oak woods. Follow the path with the aid of red and orange paint marks, over a wall by a ladder stile and on until you come to a *sitja*. Turn right along a track just above it, then right again along another wider track where there is an orange arrow painted on a rock. This track bends left at a junction, then curves back right below a steep rock wall. A few minutes later the track arrives at a broad shelf with few trees. This now curves to the left and joins a track leading towards some gateposts. Turn right and follow this along the plateau towards the radio masts.

At a bend, where the track crosses a stream-bed and just before reaching the access road to the masts, turn up left towards the lowest point on the ridge. The stone walls seen on the way up are the remains of an old snow house. Progress along the crest of the ridge is difficult and slow, and the new bulldozed track on the Orient side is now fenced off. After crossing a col natural ledges may be found leading easily up towards a gap in a wall on the way up to the main Alfàbia top. There is a trig point on the first top and about 15 minutes later a wooden cross on a secondary top. Although the broad rock ridge is easier than the southern part, the going is still quite hard and it may be quite a relief to reach the final top of the ridge, Sementer Gran at 1,014m. After this it is 20 minutes or less to join the path near the *rifugio* on the Cornadors walk.

Turn left here and return to S'Arrom, or turn right to descend by the *barranc* to Biniaraix.

Soller - S'Arrom	2hr	
S'Arrom - 978m col below masts	1hr	15min
978m col - Alfàbia	1hr	
Alfàbia - Cornadors col	1hr	15min
Cornadors col - S'Arrom		45min
S'Arrom - Soller	1hr	45min

Alternative start

Follow the S'Arrom track until it turns left by a large house on the left with a tennis court on the right. Take the narrow track on the right through an open gateway and passing above the tennis court. Follow this lane up into a sloping valley, the Coma des Negret, passing several small houses. When the last house is passed the track becomes narrower and old steps in zigzags lead high up into a corner below an impressive steep wall. Ignore the left turn into the wood and follow the path making a rising traverse to the right. This leads to a restored *caseta* in a magnificent situation looking across the Soller valley to Mitx Dia, the western outpost of the Puig Mayor.

The path continues up to a small col bounded by a wall with a fence, which can be surmounted without too much difficulty. On the other side of the wall turn left and follow a pleasant woodland path up for about 10 minutes and go through or over an old gate. A continuous but sometimes overgrown path twists and turns up towards the Alfàbia ridge, the antennae on the southernmost top being visible from time to time. Occasional cairns are a help where the path is obscured by vegetation or falling trees. This path leads to the plateau below the ridge quite near a farm building shown on the map. At this point refer to the main description for the continuation of the route up to the ridge. See also Walk 46 for another start to this walk.

46. CIRCUIT OF S'ARROM
(See note at end of preface.)

Although this walk reaches no mountain tops, it is interesting and something of a challenge in route-finding. There is a diversion to a curious *mirador* with a battlemented wall. The easy middle section gives wonderful views from a broad shelf below the Alfàbia ridge. The ascent route can be used as an alternative start for the Alfàbia ridge, Walk 45.

Type of walk: The ascent is quite strenuous and if your route-finding is poor can become even arduous.

Starting point:	Soller station
Time:	6hr
Distance:	14km
Highest point reached:	870m
Total height climbed:	840m
Grade:	B+
Map:	Soller 1:25,000 and Alaró 1:25,000

From the front entrance of the station in Soller turn right along the narrow street in front of the Hotel Guia. Turn first right, second left, then right again and keep straight on up the hill along Pablo Noguerra street. After passing the cemetery turn right towards Ses Tres Creus and continue past the left turn which leads to S'Arrom. About 50m past this turn go left on to an old stepped mule track. This winds up through terraces in a tortuous way, but with some waymarks, joining a gentle ridge above the Tres Creus at a cross-path by a barn. If preferred this point can also be reached by keeping on the road to the Three Crosses, going down on the road behind and taking a left fork at the first bend, almost immediately doubling back left again.

The path up the ridge is a well-made mule track and leads up past a small restored *caseta*, often occupied at weekends and holidays. Shortly after this is a beautifully painted heraldic shield on a boulder. After this the path continues to rise in zigzags, occasionally making traverses to the right before passing another small house. When a boundary wall is reached the path rises in sharp bends, then goes through an opening in this wall. About 10 minutes later it goes through a gate in another wall, after which the path becomes overgrown and difficult to follow. After some 40 minutes the path levels off near some big pine trees, the radio masts come into sight and there is some relief from the vegetation. The path arrives on a kind of ridge which connects a rocky spur with the main Alfàbia massif. Follow this ridge up towards the masts. Before the last rise up to the high plateau the path veers left to go through a gap in a wall and fence. A built-up section of path then makes the final climb to arrive on the shelf behind the large old farmhouse of Sa Serra.

Go to the left of the house and follow the fence to the gate, then follow the farm road to reach the wide track on the plateau. Turn left and follow this to the north along the high plain, the Pla de Ses Jovanelles. After about 2km the track rises slightly and goes towards a gateway. Turn left before reaching this and keep on the track which swings over a flat shoulder and then descends into woodland. After dwindling to a narrow path it leads to a stile over a wall below a steep crag. This path then descends to the main S'Arrom-Cornadors track, at a cairn and a red arrow showing the way up.

Turn left and follow the main track down past the high farm of S'Arrom, which is the Cornadors walk in reverse. About 10 minutes after descending the tight bends below S'Arrom, look out on the left for the branch path to the Torre-Mirador, a worthwhile detour. Return the same way to the track which is easy to follow all the way. After going through a gate on a col there is a rather tedious descent with about 20 hairpin bends before the angle eases off and you come to the sharp bend right near the tennis court. From this point it is approximately 40 minutes down to the station in Soller.

47. SA COSTERA

Sa Costera is an abandoned property in a delightful situation on a headland overlooking the bay to the south of Cala Tuent, from where it can also be reached as in Walk 28. If backpacking or with arranged transport it is enjoyable to walk right through from Soller to Sa Calobra, and an overnight stop can be made at Balitx d'Avall. This is a 300 year old house with a round defensive tower much older than the main buildings. Under the Agroturismo scheme this offers dinner, bed and breakfast at reasonable prices. If you are only out for the day you can still call in for a glass of freshly squeezed orange juice and a glimpse of the interior with antique farm tools on display.

Hard walkers who like a challenge may like to reach the old Torre de Na Seca by branching off left from near the Coll de Biniamar then descending on the north side towards Sa Costera. The way is rough with much thorny vegetation and having done it once the author recommends spending the extra time enjoying the scenery at Sa Costera.

Type of walk: Mainly easy on good tracks but quite long.

Starting point:	Mirador des Barques
Time:	5hr 15min
Distance:	16km
Highest point reached:	439m and 376m
Total height climbed:	710m
Grade:	B
Map:	Soller 1:25,000

Leave the large parking area at the *mirador* by the stepped path going north. It rises over a small hill to join a concrete road which is followed to the left to join a wide track. This then contours through a broad grassy field of olive trees to the first farm, Balitx de Dalt. Just before reaching the farm turn right through a gateway and continue as far as a sharp bend left. Leave the road here and go down the old stone steps straight ahead. These lead to Balitx d'en Mig, once a fine house but now ruinous.

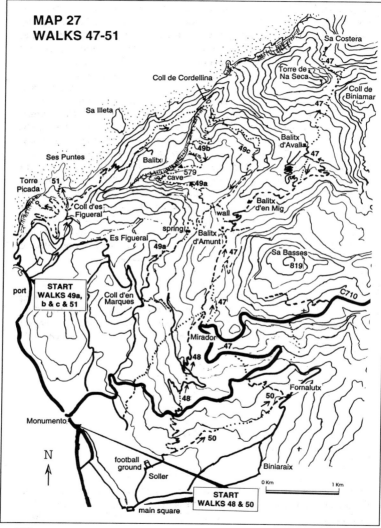

MAP 27
WALKS 47-51

Sa Costera

47

Torre de
Na Seca

Coll de Cordellina

Coll de
Biniamar

47

Sa Illeta

Balitx
d'Avall

47

49b

49c

Ses Puntes

Balitx

579

cave

49a

Torre
Picada

51

Coll d'es
Figueral

Balitx
d'en Mig

wall

spring

Balitx
d'Amunt

Es Figueral

49a

47

Sa Basses
819

port

START
WALKS 49a,
b & c & 51

Coll d'en
Marques

47

C710

Mirador

47

48

48

Fornalutx

50

Monumento

50

N

football
ground

Soller

Biniaraix

0 Km   1 Km

START
WALKS 48 & 50

main square

On the way a spring of beautiful clear water is passed, the Font d'en Mig, believed to date from 1567. Roughly 15 minutes after the ruined farm and shortly after going over a new cattle grid there is a branch track left which leads in 20m to a continuation of the old path signposted 'Tuent'. However, it makes a better walk to save this for the return and continue for now down the main farm track to Balitx d'Avall.

After the not-to-be-missed orange juice stop, the wide track continues up to the Coll de Biniamar and in fact has been widened in connection with the building of a pipeline to take water from Sa Costera to Palma. There is no need to use this, however, as the old mule track has been restored and is a much more enjoyable alternative. The start is found on the right shortly after crossing a stream-bed and rejoins the main track some 10 minutes or so below the Coll de Biniamar. Once on the col start descending the other side but in less than 5 minutes turn left along a narrow path and go through a gate. Although narrow this is easy to follow in spite of being a little overgrown. The path which comes from the Cala Tuent direction is joined and the old house reached in less than half an hour. There are many places to picnic and enjoy the scenery before returning. On the way back, the old stepped path is found about 5 minutes after passing Balitx d'Avall.

48. MIRADOR DE SES BARQUES

This *mirador* on the C710 is well known as a viewpoint for passing motorists and also as a starting point for the walk to Sa Costera, Cala Tuent and Sa Calobra. With a bar serving freshly squeezed orange juice and a panoramic view over the point it makes a worthwhile destination for a walk from Soller.

Type of walk: Easy, on footpaths and tracks.

Starting point:	Main square in Soller
Time:	3hr 30min
Distance:	11km
Highest point reached:	380m
Total height climbed:	400m
Grade:	C
Map:	Soller 1:25,000

From the main square in Soller take the Biniaraix road and turn left at the second turn, the Calle de Sa Victoria. Fork right just before a bridge and continue to the football field. Turn right along the narrow lane between the football field and the stream, then left at the end and then first right. At a house called the Villa Alegre take a left fork. (The right branch leads to Binibassi.) Either stick to the track which rises very gently or take the steps which cut a straight line up through the olive terraces. The track leads to the Capelleta, an unattrative rustic structure built in 1917. Next to it is a monastery, a larger and plainer building.

When the main road is reached cross it and continue up the old road on the other side. After a few tight bends this narrow road makes a big sweep to the left and then back right. A short cut at the side of a wall avoids this but is very narrow and after rain the vegetation is water-laden. If you take the second short cut, then turn right and immediately left when the main track is rejoined. If you go the long way round, out right and back left, then look out for this turn after a slight descent. Keep following the narrow lane up, now through more open ground where the olive trees are replaced by pines. When a T-junction is met at a metal gate turn right to reach the *mirador*. (Note: recently a new gate has sometimes been locked across this track. Unless a pedestrian access has been made, it will be necessary to continue along the Balitx track for about 500m, then double back right on a waymarked path to reach the *mirador*.)

To descend return to this junction and turn left, then immediately right down a narrow path at the side of a fence. The path is indistinct here and crossed by other more well-defined tracks, but some blue paint signs are a help. After about 20 minutes a narrow lane is reached. Cross it, ignoring the sign to the Port on the right. Some 10-15 minutes after passing a spring turn left by a large house. This path is not signposted but is found a few yards past the house at the point where the main track bends right and goes down through a rubbish dump. A group of Umbrella pines will be noticed straight ahead. The downward path passes Ca'n Nou and then reaches the C710. The continuation of the old path is found by turning left uphill for a few metres and then right down a lane signposted Ca'n Brisbal. The footpath is found behind the gate to the house. Turn right and continue downhill to a T-junction. Either turn right to reach the C710 then left to the Monumento, or left to return to the town centre after passing the football field.

49. BALITX

Although only 579m high Balitx is an impressive mountain with two rocky ridges extending one to the north and the other to the south-west. Together these ridges form a continuous wall of crags overlooking the sea and the little island Sa Illeta. The south face too has some steep crags overlooking the Es Figueral valley and there are not many ways up to the top without some rock-climbing.

49(a). ASCENT FROM THE COLL D'EN MARQUES

This is the easiest route to the top and recommended before attempting the more difficult route from the Coll de Cordellina.

Starting point:	Tram terminus, Soller Port
Time:	5hr 40min
Distance:	15km
Highest point reached:	579m
Total height climbed:	579m
Grade:	B+
Map:	Soller 1:25,000

From the sea-front walk up the road by Es Figueral and on to the Coll d'en Marques. Turn left up the narrow lane which begins on the col (at K1.7) and follow it uphill passing several restored houses. The road is a private one, going through several gates, which are normally closed but not locked. (Cars must not be taken up here.) The road stops by the last gate and a path continues along a terrace above a *caseta* to reach some stone steps leading up to an old stile made from tree branches. From the spring and water tank on the other side of the stream a wide track leads up to the 398m col SW of Balitx. Do not go through the gate on the col but turn left, passing a large flat area on which are several abandoned cars. Continue up the rough track for about 5 minutes, looking out for a narrow path on the left just after a sharp bend right.

A good path rises up from here and then makes an undulating traverse above the cliffs towards the SW ridge. Just before reaching the ridge and about 20m to the right of a prominent dead tree there is an interesting cave, the Cova des Migdia, so called because at midday the entrance is fully illuminated by the sun. Steps have been built down into it. There is more than one dead tree and the entrance is partly screened by other trees, so it is easy to miss it. Continue to the top of Balitx along the rocks of the SW ridge or by traces of rough path alongside it. A return by the same way is recommended.

49(b). FROM THE COLL DE CORDELLINA

This circular route is quite challenging because the route-finding is difficult but the outstanding views from the top are ample reward for the effort required.

Starting point:	Tram terminus, Soller Port
Time:	6hr 40min
Distance:	15km
Highest point reached:	579m
Total height climbed:	610m
Grade:	A
Map:	Soller 1:25,000

Follow the well-known route 49(c) to the Coll de Cordellina. From this col, start descending towards the valley but then pick up a line of cairns which starts at the foot of a little rock spur. These lead up into the valley on the east side of the north ridge, at first keeping high above the stream-bed. Later this is crossed and after rising in zigzags the path appears to end at the foot of a steep rock wall. Keep going through the *carritx* grass which is hiding the path for a further few minutes to reach an old *sitja*, which should be reached about 40 minutes after leaving the Coll de Cordellina. Looking upwards from here a large cave can be seen high up on the right. Aiming just slightly to the left of this large cave, pick a way up reasonable ground until another *sitja* is reached. Remains of a built-up mule track are found near here and lead up to a sloping shelf which is part of the north ridge. Turn left and follow an animal path up through a little wood to a notch in the ridge from which there is an exciting view down to Sa Illeta and Torre Picada. The path now turns left to avoid the crag which blocks the direct way to the top. Soon a sharp right turn leads to the broad east ridge along which cairns (and the signs that many agile donkeys have passed this way) show the way to the top. A plastic box containing a summit book is hidden near the trig point.

To descend follow the SW ridge for roughly 20 minutes until a prominent dead tree is seen ahead. This is before the angle steepens but is not easy to find, even for those who have previously reconnoitred from the south. With luck you may find the large cave and the path which leads eastwards from it along the sloping shelf not far from the cliff edge. This leads to a wide bulldozed track which is followed right, past the flat area with old cars to reach the 398m col. Turn right here to reach the spring by the water tank. Go left to cross the stream, over a stile and along a terrace to reach the narrow private road leading down to the Coll d'en Marques and so back to the port.

Port - Coll de Cordellina	1hr 50min
Coll de Cordellina - Balitx	2hr
Balitx - 398m col	1hr
398m col - port	1hr 50min

49(c). THE CIRCUIT OF BALITX

A long and interesting walk with varied scenery. From the Coll d'es Figueral there is an excellent corniche track about 200m above the sea, with panoramic views of the coast, the rocky islet Sa Illeta and an impressive overhanging tower, the Penyal Bernat. The return route goes inland with views of the Torre de Na Seca, Coll de Biniamar, Puig Mayor, the Torrent des Llores and the farmlands of Balitx in the valley below. From Balitx part of a very old path, which was the original way from Soller to Sa Calobra, is used for the return to Soller.

Type of walk: Easy at first along a corniche track, followed by rough descents and ascents involving some scrambling and route-finding.

Starting point:	Puerto Soller
Time:	6hr 15min
Distance:	13km
Highest point reached:	407m
Total height climbed:	c.490m
Grade:	A+
Map:	1:25,000 Soller

From the quay walk south to the Sa Figuera road and turn left at this double street on the left (true right) side of the river. Follow it up to the Carrer de Belgique. At the first sharp bend in this new road go straight on through an open gateway and continue on up a narrow and fairly steep lane which leads directly to the Coll d'es Figueral. At the col follow a narrow lane which makes a sharp bend to the right and winds slightly uphill before beginning to contour in a north-easterly direction above the coast. Some height is gained in a series of bends and some steps make a short cut at one point.

Shortly after passing a new concrete road on the right, leading to the property of S'Illeta de Ca'n Cordo, a high locked gate is met. Just before the gate a way has been made (by many feet) bypassing it on the left. Cross this terrace below the gate to go through a gap in another wall. A few metres after the gap ignore a branch path on the left and continue horizontally along the terrace. The path is not obvious at the beginning but soon becomes a wide well-made path, very easy to follow although a few trees have fallen across it.

This excellent path gives good views of the Sa Illeta island, and after sweeping round a corner even more dramatic views of the cliffs. Although this path ends at a *sitja*, a continuation marked by cairns leads up to the crags below the Coll de Cordellina. The route, which is cairned, has been built up in one place to aid rounding the steep rock face. This is not difficult but is quite steep and requires some care. After this it descends slightly and then rises in zigzags to the Coll de Cordellina, between an impressive rock pillar of 277m and Balitx.

Climb over the stile on the col and then turn left as indicated by red paint marks on the rock. The next objective is a small col, the Pas de H'Eura (the Pass of the Ivy) at c.350m, seen on the opposite ridge across a small intervening valley. Two sticks to the right of a big tree mark the spot. One way to get there is to follow the narrow path down to the valley floor, then up again on the other side with the aid of cairns and paint marks. A larger cairn marks the place where the route goes up a diagonal rake across a prominent yellow wall, at first sloping from right to left and then back from left to right. It is a great help to pick out this cairn from the Coll de Cordellina with the aid of binoculars. It may be shorter, but no easier, to go straight down bearing slightly right from the Cordellina pass to the bottom of a little rocky outcrop and then contour round to reach the vital cairn at the foot of the yellow wall. Whichever way is chosen, this is difficult ground with loose stones and prickly vegetation. After scrambling up to the 'pass', which is really just a step on the ridge, cairns continue to mark the way for another 50m when a real path will be found among some olive terraces.

All this area has changed almost beyond recognition with the bulldozing of a wide track in connection with the pipeline taking water from Sa Costera to Palma. The easiest thing to do is to follow this, but those with eagle eyes might like to try and find the traces of the old cobbled mule track before they disappear entirely. The track goes between the barn on the right and two large boulders making natural shelters on the left. After rising slightly it goes through a gate and curves right towards the valley head at 398m, reaching a junction just before the col. (To return to the port, keep on this track to the col where a locked gate is easily surmounted. Follow the track down to a spring and turn left to cross the stream. Go over a stile and cross a terrace to reach a narrow private road leading down to the Coll d'en Marques.)

To continue this walk take the left turn at the above junction and follow the track which descends slightly to join the main Balitx valley track. Turn right along this track towards Balitx d'Amunt and then turn left away from the farm after going over a cattle grid. After about 1km and as the *mirador* is approached a path is signposted on the left and should be followed if this is your destination. Otherwise bear right along the main track and at a junction by a painted boulder, turn right down a narrow path at the side of a fence. (Note that the track going straight on here leads to the *mirador* but a new gate across it is sometimes locked.) This path is not easy to follow at first although there are several paint marks, but in a few minutes a small house will be noticed and the descending track found just below this, at the side of a wall with a fence on top. There are blue arrows painted on the wall and the path descends at the side of some olive terraces. Go through two gates and in a few more minutes arrive at a road, where there is a red arrow on the wall pointing to the right and the word 'Port'. (To find a way to the port, follow the lane as far as a sign which reads 'Cami cortado a 200m' and at this point look for a narrow path on the left, indistinct at first, leading down to the Coll d'en Marques.)

Instead, turn left and then immediately right to pick up the continuation of the old track. Some 10 minutes later a small spring of drinkable water is passed and in a further 5 minutes a cart track is joined, by a yellow painted arrow. After a further few minutes the track passes a large house, and starts to bend right. Turn left along a footpath at this point and follow it down until it is cut by the C710. Find it again by turning left, then immediately right, at a sign which says 'Ca'n Bisbal'. The track is surfaced as far as this house, then the old path continues down towards Soller. In 10 minutes or less turn right at another road junction, where the sign on the path you have just left says 'Camino Viejo de Balitx - Tuent - Sa Calobra'. Go down to a T-junction and turn right. Follow this road to join the C710 at Sa Taulera and turn left to the Monumento, where the tram or bus can be picked up to either Soller or Puerto Soller.

Puerto Soller - Coll d'es Figueral		25min
Figueral - Cordellina	1hr	30min
Cordellina - Balitx de Dalt	2hr	30min
Balitx de Dalt - Ses Barques		20min
Ses Barques - Monumento	1hr	30min

50. FORNALUTX

The village of Fornalutx is one of the most attractive in Mallorca. It is very old, with picturesque buildings in narrow stepped streets and well worth allowing several hours to look round.

The excursion begins among typical Soller houses, then follows a narrow path up to Binibassi with its splendid fourteenth century mansion and where the oranges are reputed to be the best in Spain. The path leads through olive terraces to Fornalutx, in the centre of which is a small square with a fountain. One of the shops in the square sells a small booklet in English describing the old customs and way of life as remembered by one of the older inhabitants.

The Monumento, where the walk begins, is a prominent landmark between Soller and Puerto Soller, at the junction of the C710 with the road linking the port and the town. The tram (or bus) stops here.

Type of walk: Easy, on country lanes and easy paths.

Starting point:	Monumento
Time:	2hr
Distance:	8km
Highest point reached:	150m
Total height climbed:	130m
Grade:	C
Map:	Soller 1:25,000

From the Monumento walk towards Soller on the old road and turn left along Calle Rvdo. Miguel Rosello, towards the church of Nuestra Señora de la Victoria. Turn right at the church, then continue straight on at an off-set crossroads where the road bends to the left. Bend right a little further on and continue to the far corner of the football field. Turn left here along the narrow road between the football field and the river. When the bridge is reached, don't cross it but continue to follow the track which bends left then right. At the next junction, go straight on, ignoring both the left fork and the path turning sharp right.

Ten minutes later turn left up a narrow path which begins by a large carob tree at a bend in the road. A blue painted arrow points the way. After a few minutes take a right turn at a path junction and in a further few minutes Binibassi will be reached. A stepped path begins on the left, between two of the buildings and by a channel of water flowing from the Binibassi spring. Blue and red arrows are painted on the wall and the way goes through a gate with a 'no dogs' sign. After about 10 minutes turn right and go through a wall at a place marked by cairns. This path descends through olive terraces to arrive in Fornalutx by the cemetery. Continue into the centre of the village past the sports field to reach the main square.

Leave Fornalutx by the main road towards Soller but after a few minutes turn left along a narrow lane signposted to Biniaraix. This leads to the top end of the little village near the public washplace. There are two ways through Biniaraix, one a road and the other a stepped lane, where unsuspecting tourists sometimes get into difficulties with cars. Return to Soller by the road.

Monumento - Binibassi	50min
Binibassi - Fornalutx	20min
Fornalutx - Biniaraix	20min
Biniaraix - Soller	30min

51. SES PUNTES AND TORRE PICADA

Ses Puntes are two rocky points jutting out into the sea on the wild coastline north of Soller. There are views of some impressive cliffs and the small island of Sa Illeta. An idyllic place for picnics or fishing, regrettably somewhat spoilt by litter. The Torre Picada is one of the old coastal watch towers, at present closed to visitors. The area surrounding it is a natural rock garden on the edge of the cliffs, with beautiful pink flowers of sage-leaved cistus, rosemary, asphodels and many other plants.

This walk may easily be extended by continuing along the road from the Coll d'es Figueral towards the small island of Sa Illeta and returning the same way.

Type of walk: Short and easy, mainly on lanes and tracks, but the narrow path from the Coll d'es Figueral down to the sea is a little steep and stony.

Starting point:	Tram terminus, Puerto Soller
Time:	1hr 50min
Distance:	5km
Highest point reached:	151m
Total height climbed:	255m
Grade:	C
Map:	Soller 1:25,000

From the bus and tram stop walk south along the sea-front as far as the Sa Figuera road, a double street with the river in the centre. Turn left here, on the left (or true right) side of the river and follow the road up to the Carrer de Belgique. At the first very sharp bend of this new road go straight on through an open gateway and up a narrow lane which leads directly to the Coll d'es Figueral.

At the col go through a gateway and take the track directly in front descending through woodland towards the sea. It leads in 10 minutes to an old limekiln by a stream-bed. Either follow the stream down, or turn right and then first left down a narrow path marked by a cairn. This way leads to a little col behind the Grossa Punta.

To reach the Torre, retrace your steps up to the Coll d'es Figueral and turn right to follow the wide track which leads directly to it. If preferred there is a short cut up through the woods from here which rejoins the main track at a junction with an olive tree in the middle of the road.

The return route to Puerto Soller can be varied. One way is to go back down the track to the junction with the olive tree and turn right. This wide track descends very gradually in big bends. A cairn marks the place where a short cut can be taken to avoid a long descent and re-ascent. When the bottom stretch of road is reached turn right, passing a locked gate which keeps traffic out but allows walkers through.

Another way to reach this point is to go directly south from the tower, following a red earth path that meets the wide track 200m from the locked gate. Keep straight on past a conspicuous round building and the Atalaya Club. Follow this road down through the built up area and past the restaurant El Pescador to the sea-front, then turn left to reach the starting point.

Tram stop - Coll d'es Figueral	30min
Col d'es Figueral - Ses Puntes	15min
Ses Puntes - Torre Picada	35min
Torre Picada - Tram stop	30min

52. THE LIGHTHOUSE AND PUNTA DE SOLLER

The aim of this excursion is to reach two spectacular viewpoints on the very edge of the cliffs. There are excellent views of mountains and sea. Although only a short distance from the busy resort of Puerto Soller, this area is tranquil and quite wild. In early spring there are hundreds of bright yellow-green euphorbias.

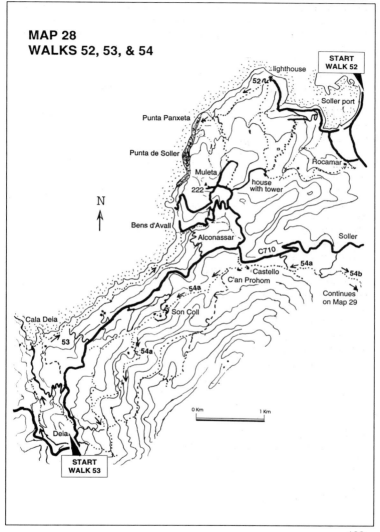

MAP 28
WALKS 52, 53, & 54

Type of walk: Short and easy. Tarmac road to the lighthouse, then a broad track and finally a short distance on a rough and rocky path.

Starting point:	Tram terminus, Puerto Soller
Time:	3hr
Distance:	6km
Highest point reached:	124m
Total height gained:	224m
Grade:	C+
Map:	Soller 1:25,000

Walk south along the sea-front and cross the river by the footbridge. Follow the road which climbs steadily uphill right round the harbour to the lighthouse, overlooking the sea all the way. The track begins between the lighthouse on the right and an abandoned military building on the left. Two locked chains prevent the gate being opened and access is by ducking between them. Ignore two forks to the left and after 20 minutes a ruined limekiln will be reached. At this point there is a large fallen tree across the track, which has now become a narrow path. Continue along this for several minutes, horizontally at first and then beginning to descend slightly. Here numerous fallen trees have obscured the way and there are several variations marked by small cairns. Leave the path and cross this area diagonally to the right, where a little search will reveal a very ruinous limekiln overgrown by trees. The path may be picked up again before it descends in zigzags to a dry stream bed, which is reached only 10 minutes after passing the first kiln.

Ten minutes further on the path goes through a gap in a low wall, then rises to a viewpoint on the cliff edge near an impressive overhanging rock. The continuation is marked by cairns and goes up from here, partly on rocky slabs, to reach a higher viewpoint with good views both north and south along the coast. The end of the route is marked by a small red paint sign on a rock, a cross surrounded by a circle.

Return is by the same way, but it can be varied by following the 'blue arrow' path back from the lighthouse to the junction by the house with a tower, then descending by the Rocamar mule track.

Puerto Soller - lighthouse	45min
Lighthouse - Punta de Soller	45min
Punta de Soller - Puerto Soller	1hr 30 min

Punta Panxeta. (Photo: Kevin Parker)

53. DEIÀ COASTAL WALK

The stretch of coast between Cala Deià and Alconassar is particularly attractive with an undulating path giving lovely views of the sea. Given as a linear walk, linked by the bus service between Deià and Soller or the port, it is easy to combine with Walk 54, the Cami del Castello, to make a much longer route. Cala Deià is a gem, with a cluster of old fishermen's shelters, a few boats and a beach cafe in season. The village itself is also most photogenic and a stroll up to the central hill is recommended before starting the walk.

Type of walk: Mainly easy, but care is needed where erosion has destroyed the original path. Diversions are sometimes necessary, but most are marked with paint signs. All the stiles at boundary fences are in place.

Starting point:	Bus stop in Deià
Time:	4hr 25min
Distance:	12km
Total height climbed:	About 300m
Grade:	B
Map:	See sketch map 28

From the bus stop in Deià walk in the Palma direction to the sharp bend right in the main road. Turn right down the shallow steps and continue downhill, taking a right fork after a few minutes. When the lane ends a signposted footpath continues in the same direction. After about 5-6 minutes turn right by a white painted sign. This path, the Cami des Rabasso, has recently been restored. The surfaced road to the beach is reached after crossing the stream-bed and the tiny cove reached by turning left along this.

The coastal path begins up a flight of steps about 20m from the road end. Ignore a left branch after about 5 minutes, but 2 minutes later turn left where the stepped path swings right. The coastal path immediately turns right along a terrace, then crosses a low wall and turns left downhill at the side of this wall. One minute later it turns right again and continues to an attractive headland among the pine trees, overlooking the sea and the prominent white rocks of Cala Deià.

Continue along the path, passing a *mirador* with a protective handrail. After passing two stiles there are notices forbidding camping and picnics, not far from a large circular stone table with surrounding seat. This is a useful landmark, indicating a fork left downhill to another stile. A few minutes later, after going below a stone enclosure, the path has fallen away and a diversion must be made up to a slightly higher level. Some boats are passed and the path again disappears, with another diversion inland to a headland with almond trees.

Round the corner here is a gully where erosional features make it advisable to go high and avoid the steepest places, reaching a terrace well marked with cairns. At the end of this terrace, by a large cairn, take the lower path to reach the next stile and a terrace quite low down near the sea. Next, go uphill by a fallen tree, cross a headland among boulders and heather and then go steeply upwards between terraces of olive trees. This part is well marked and leads in about 15 minutes to a path which contours left above a steep cliff and leads to another stile. The path then dips into and out of a stream-bed and goes over another stile into a lane. Turn left and one minute later when the lane ends find the continuation of the path on the right. Four minutes later this reaches a concrete road near some houses. Continue steeply uphill, but keep a sharp look-out (after roughly 5-6 minutes) for a place to cross the stream-bed. This is not obvious, but you will see metal pegs hammered into the stone walls to make it easier. At this point you find yourself on a wide road near the Bens d'Avall restaurant (expensive; closed in winter).

Follow the road up for 1.5km to join the road over the Muleta. Turn left, then right, to reach the cross-track near Muleta Gran, a large house with a square tower. Turn right and go through the gate towards the house, following a path to the right and then between the buildings to the back where a mule track leads down to the back of the Rocamar hotel. (An alternative ending is to turn right on the Muleta road and return to Soller by the Castello path as in Walk 54.)

54(a). SOLLER TO DEIÀ BY THE CAMI DEL CASTELLO
(See maps p184 & 192)

Between Soller and Deià some of the high tops of the Tramuntana are only about 2km from the sea. This linear walk explores the delightful area between the mountains and the sea, using old tracks and paths, not all of which are shown on the maps. There are some lovely views of the coast and there is time to look round the attractive village of Deià.

In winter an early start is recommended as the bus returns from Deià at 15.45 and the next one is at 19.45. In summer the times are 17.00 and 20.15.

Type of walk: Fairly easy, mainly on good paths. There is a fairly steep

187

uphill section towards the end, and attention to route-finding is necessary in places. For an alternative start for this walk see 54(b).

Starting point:	Soller, petrol station on bypass road
Time:	3hr 30min
Distance:	11km
Highest point reached:	c.400m
Total height climbed:	400m
Grade:	B
Map:	Soller 1:25,000

Begin by the petrol station on the Soller to Puerto Soller bypass road. Go up the road opposite which bends right and in a few minutes go straight on along a narrow path at a point where the main track bends sharp left. The path crosses a stream-bed then rises up an impressive flight of old steps that crosses over the rail track near a tunnel. A few minutes later a branch path will be noticed on the left, but keep straight on here. Ten minutes later the path inexplicably becomes a surfaced road for a few metres, then reverts to a path. Five minutes later go through a gate, and another 5 minutes after that ignore a right turn. Five minutes later still go through another gate to arrive at a crossroads. An engraved stone here shows the way to Deià is straight on, and another points back to Soller. The path now bends right and after about 80m there is a right fork on to another path. This path traverses along terraces just outside the boundary wall of the Ca'n Carabasseta estate. When the Castello is reached there are some large signs explaining that the path has been restored by the Govern Balear and the School of Stonemasons. Go straight on through the gate following the newly engraved signs past the old hermitage to the large farm Ca'n Prohom.

A signpost on a corner of the building points the way to Deià. The track curves round a large threshing floor and leads to a field gate. Do not go through this gate, and do not turn into the field just before it, but carefully open up the fence on the right of the gate to gain access to a narrow path next to the wall. After about 200m the path goes through a gate to enter a wood and continues in the same direction. Half an hour later the path is cut by a new road near some houses but continues on the other side. (Shortly after crossing this road a short diversion on the right can be made to a spring, reached by a signposted path in 25m. The water in this spring is not flowing strongly and may need sterilising tablets.) Continue along the main path and after passing a row of houses look out for a path junction, ignoring the first set of steps leading only to

Stone steps and water irrigation channel at La Trapa
(Walk 61) (Author)
Typical flowers of Mallorca: below left - Bermuda Buttercups
below right - Cistus Albidus

terraces, but taking a sharp left turn up the second flight of stone steps, where there are several cairns. (The path which goes straight on leads down to the main road near Lluc-Alcari and the walk can be shortened in this way.)

This path rises up to about 400m, levelling out after about 15 minutes and passing a *caseta*, or small fieldhouse. (A severe landslip in 1996 seriously damaged the path just before reaching the *caseta* but with the passage of time a path has developed through it.) Go through a gate here and follow the path up through cultivated terraces in a wide upland valley. At first the path goes straight on at the side of a fence, then sweeps back left and goes up a series of ramps connecting the terraces. The route here seems to change from time to time, but aim to join a wide track in the woods at the top of the terraces. Turn right and follow it through a gate, contouring to reach a small flat area on a broad shoulder before descending towards a red and crumbling cliff.

After passing this cliff the track makes a left turn and goes through a gateway into an area of open terraces where the rooftops of Deià are visible ahead. In 1990 this area was levelled and in 1996 a new house was completed. At one time the gate was locked, but the owner has told friends that the intention is for it to be unlocked, so all should be well. After going through this gate turn left and keep roughly on the same level along a terrace just above a pipeline to reach a *caseta* which has been restored and extended. Go through the wooden gate or over the fence by the makeshift stile of two stones and carry on, slightly uphill and still following the pipeline, towards the valley head along a faint path with some cairns. Look out for a cairn indicating a right turn away from the pipeline. There is a confusion of paths here and the main thing is to keep roughly on the same level passing below another *caseta*. The aim is to reach a wooden gate in a stone wall. Follow the path along to reach an old stone track leading to a red dirt road. This descends to pass a large hotel, La Residencia, before arriving in the village by a phone box. (N.B. If reversing this walk, look out for the left fork from the red dirt road onto the old stone track.)

Soller - Ca'n Prohom	1hr 15min
Ca'n Prohom - Deià	2hr 15min

54(b). PUERTO SOLLER TO SOLLER BY THE CAMI DEL CASTELLO

This delightful and undemanding walk is ideal for a hot day. It makes use of an old cobbled track not marked on the maps to go up onto the Muleta plateau with excellent sea views. A level easy track leads through fields of olives and joins the Castello track near Ca'n Prohom. The descent by the old Cami del Castello path gives excellent views over Soller to Mitx Dia, L'Ofre, Cornadors and Alfàbia. A cold refreshing drink in the square and a return to the port by the old-fashioned tram make an attractive finish to this walk.

Type of walk: Easy, along reasonably well defined paths and tracks and with no steep gradients.

Starting point:	Tram terminus, Puerto Soller
Time:	3hr 45min
Distance:	10km
Highest point reached:	260m
Total height climbed:	275m
Grade:	C
Map:	Soller 1:25,000

From the tram terminus in Puerto Soller walk south along the sea-front and over the footbridge. Turn left at the first road by the Bar Las Delicias and continue along to the Hotel Rocamar, a big place easily seen from the road to the port from Soller. Turn right up to the hotel then left in front of it until the track ends in a rough parking area about 150m past the hotel. On the right will be found an old mule track doubling back up behind the hotel. Follow this up first through woods and then some olive terraces, passing through several gates which need to be kept closed because of livestock. Some red and green painted arrows and yellow paint marks show the way. A little stream is crossed by a bridge and the path then contours back into a gully.

After about 35 minutes a small farm is reached. There is a huge olive tree in the middle of the track and a blue arrow on the wall to the right of the tree shows the continuation of the track. Five minutes later bear right, go through a gate and cross a stream-bed. The track now goes up through olive terraces, and becomes a little indistinct. In fact there are two ways here. Either go right then back left parallel to a wall, or straight on across rocky ground.

A wooden signpost to Deià on one of the trees points to a gate. Go through this gate and keep close to the wall to reach a group of buildings, one of them very large and with a tower. The path curves right behind the end house and then goes through a double wooden gate. There is a sign on the pigsty here pointing back to Puerto Soller. A blue arrow on the corner of the tower points towards a green metal gate. Go through this gate and turn left at a crossroads, through a gateway marked with a red arrow.

The track now winds between olive terraces, making several sharp bends, to reach a T-junction at an open gateway. Turn left here and follow the road round to reach the main Deià road. Turn left towards Soller and in about 100m turn right again up a cart track signposted to Ca'n Prohom. This is a private road but at the second bend on the left is a public footpath marked by an engraved stone. A second engraved stone shows the way up to an old hermitage, the Castello, where the path joins one coming up from Soller. At this point there are notices

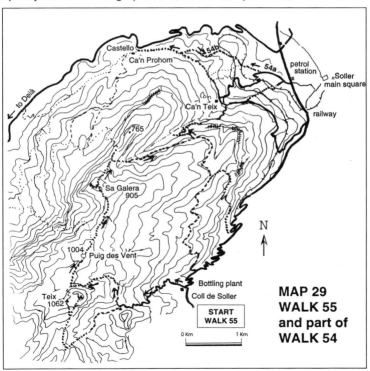

MAP 29
WALK 55
and part of
WALK 54

explaining that this old path has been restored by the Govern Balear and the School of Stonemasons.

If this approach is being used as an alternative start to the Soller-Deià walk, turn right to reach Ca'n Prohom. To continue the walk to Soller, turn left along the path outside the wall of the Ca'n Carabasseta estate. In about 20 minutes go straight on at a cross-track where there are more engraved signs to Soller and Deià. Five minutes later ignore a left turn and in another 5 minutes bear left where the track appears to go into a field. The path then goes through a gate outside a boundary wall. Further on the track has been surfaced, but soon reverts to the old cobbled track with steps. It crosses the railway track and then descends to cross a stream-bed. Keep straight on and follow the road round to reach the main road opposite the petrol station. Go down the narrow street ahead and after several twists and turns the main square will be reached.

Puerto Soller - Castello	1hr 45min
Castello - Soller	2hr

55. TEIX AND SA GALERA

Note: Recently access to Teix from the Coll de Soller has been restricted by the farmer due to ever-increasing numbers. If you would like to use this route, then asking your hotel to phone for permission the day before is recommended, especially if you are going to the expense of taking a taxi.

Teix is a popular mountain, easily ascended from either Valldemossa or the Coll de Soller, but Sa Galera is rarely visited. The views are extensive and this is a long and interesting walk. From Teix the blue Mediterranean can be seen on both sides of the island, with the main chain of the Tramuntana stretching out on the other side of the col and beyond it the central plain and the hills of the east. Sa Galera itself is an outstanding natural *mirador*, giving almost a bird's-eye view of Deià and the coast between Deià and Puerto Soller. A high level ridge including the Puig des Vent connects Teix with Sa Galera. There is evidence that this stony, arid area was at one time cultivated and possibly even inhabited during the summer months, with some terracing, buildings that were once roofed and even a threshing floor at an altitude of almost 1,000m.

A taxi or a lift is needed to reach the starting point on the Coll de Soller as there is no bus service over the col. A taxi is not too expensive, especially if four people share; certainly cheaper than hiring a car for the day.

Alternatively, a bus can be taken from Puerto Soller to Valldemossa and the Pla de la Serp reached by one of several possible routes. These are described in a note at the end.

Type of walk: A large part of the route is trackless and it is not recommended in mist. Route-finding on the descent from Sa Galera is not easy, as there only seems to be one way down the line of encircling cliffs.

Starting point:	Coll de Soller
Time:	6hr 30min
Distance:	12km
Highest point reached:	1,062m
Total height climbed:	622m up, 938m down
Grade:	A+
Map:	Alaró 1:25,000 and Soller 1:25,000

The walk begins at a bend in the road a little below the col on the Soller side where a surfaced road leads to the Cases d'es Teix and a water bottling plant. After passing in front of the bottling plant bear right and go through an iron gate, behind which are chained dogs. Follow the stony track which leads up through the oakwoods to the Cases del Rey D.Jaime, passing a spring on the right. Many remains of *sitjes* will be noticed in the woods. The three houses lie on a little plateau. Go through the iron gate with a 'please close' notice in five languages and turn sharp right by the fence. The path now contours in a roughly northerly direction for about 600m, when it turns to the west and rises up at the side of a stream. On the whole it is easy to follow, but look out for a place where it doubles back left at a water trough. Oaks give way to pines and open ground is reached before the path leads to a small plateau on the north side of Teix. This is the Pla de la Serp, where there is a spring with good drinking water in a stone trough.

A good path marked by cairns leads from the spring to the top of Teix by way of a small col between Teix and Teixoch. (Teix has the trig point: Teixoch to the north is the same height; older maps had it one metre higher.)

Return to the Font de la Serp by the same path. (The direction is north, should the clouds descend.) From the spring cross the little plain and go up on to the ridge beyond. Several ways can be found, starting

193

near a ruined building at the foot of the Puig des Vent. Once up on the high ground, which is very stony and arid, the way is marked by paint spots and a few cairns. The route passes a ruined hut, some enclosures and a threshing floor in a very windy spot.

Either go over the top of the Puig des Vent, marked as Cañizo on some maps (1,004m), or keep on the east side of it. A slight descent leads to a gap in a stone wall, after which the ridge narrows a little and the walking becomes easier over solid rocks instead of loose stones. Continue along the ridge until the subsidiary ridge leading out west to Sa Galera is reached. This is almost at a right angle to the main ridge and some cairns will be found marking the way to the white column of the trig point.

A wide tree-filled valley, the Coma de S'Ombra, goes down from Sa Galera in a north-easterly direction. The stream in the centre of this valley is known as the Torrent des Cinc Ponts (five bridges). The descent makes use of some old and rather disused tracks here. Start the descent by first following a narrow path marked by cairns and beginning almost at the summit. This leads down left (north-east) to the col at c.750m between Galera and the Puig d'es Moro. There is a wall running along the col parallel to the ridge, with a fenced-off opening, on the other side of which is a good view down to the coast. This is an alternative way down, to Ca'n Prohom and Soller or Puerto Soller, described later.

To continue the descent turn right at the col and go down in roughly the centre of the valley floor on a poorly defined path with a few cairns. About 10 minutes after leaving the col a *sitja* and a ruined building will be reached. Continue down for a further 5 minutes to reach a much larger *sitja* and 3 old shelters. From this point a well-made but overgrown cart track leads down the valley on its right-hand side. Follow this to the right for about 25 minutes, looking out for a cairn where the main track bends to the right. Turn left at this cairn down a track which zigzags down towards the valley floor. Avoid two turnings off this track, the first leading up the valley and the second heading downwards. After a further few minutes the track becomes less well defined whilst heading up the valley, but continue to follow its line and it soon leads to a broken-down brushwood fence. Step over this and turn immediately right down the valley until another little path is found. This zigzags steeply down to a small enclosure, which has a stile made of branches on the far side (a sort of goat-pen?). After a further short descent, there is a post in the middle of the path which may once have been an indicator. The track left crosses the stream and leads to some terraces, but we turn right, keeping on the right-hand side of the stream and passing between two small buildings, after which the path improves. Rising slightly the path goes through a gate with an access stile and a 'private hunting' sign.

A very attractive path now leads below an impressive overhanging cliff, the Cingle de Ca'n Canals, then down through terraces of olives. Some curious buildings will be seen further down, built under overhanging rocks. It is now a question of following the main track down towards Soller. This becomes a drivable road from the 'cave houses' and winds back and forth between terraces. Go through a gate by a water tank, to meet a wide track at a T-junction. Turn right and after about 100m go left through an old gate into a wood. After about 30 minutes an old stepped path is joined, the Cami de Rocafort. Turn left and after crossing the railway twice join a tarmac road. Turn right, then left, to reach the petrol station on the Soller road, 10 minutes from the town centre.

Coll de Soller - Cases de Rey D.Jaime	1hr
Cases - Teix	1hr
Teix - Sa Galera	1hr 30min
Sa Galera - Cingle de Ca'n Canals	1hr 40min
Cingle de Ca'n Canals - Soller	1hr 20min

Alternative start from Valldemossa
This is the recommended way because it includes the Camino del Archiduque, but it adds 4km and c.90m of ascent to the route. (See Walk 57 for Cairats valley approach.)

From the new car park and bus stop in Valldemossa go up through the urbanisation or by the steps at the side of the school to reach the start of the path at the road end. This goes towards a conspicuous group of umbrella pines, but branches left before reaching them at a rock painted with a yellow 'U'. The track is an old charcoal burners' route zigzagging up through the woods of evergreen oaks, going through a couple of ruined gates. Forty-five minutes after the start of the walk a red spot marks a short cut on the right which rejoins the track about 10 minutes later. Almost immediately go through a boundary wall to reach a flattish area of fairly open ground, the Pla d'es Pouet. There is a multitude of paths and tracks in this area where it is very easy to take the wrong one.

Ignore the first tracks going both left and right, and keep straight on across the clearing for about 80m until you reach a fork. Take the left fork across a *sitja* and in 5 minutes reach another clearing at the end of which is the polluted Es Pouet well. Three paths begin near here. One goes left to the Mirador de Ses Puntes (the way of return on Walk 57). One on the right goes to the Pla d'es Aritges and is a shorter way to Teix but misses out the spectacular archduke's path. Take the middle way which leads up to the Coll de S'Estret. There are some stone seats here and some red paint signs to Deià and Teix. Turn right and follow the path leading steeply up to reach the magnificent wide track built by the archduke. This continues along the very edge of the steep cliffs overlooking Deià, passing Puig Caragoli, a splendid high viewpoint on the cliff top, and on to the plain of Ses Aritges.

Turn left at a prominent cairn, prevously signposted Al TEIX. The path goes up steeply at first, then in 10 minutes crosses a boundary wall with a large ICONA sign. Cross the Pla de Sa Serp towards the spring, the Font de Sa Serp, which is reached on the ascent from the Coll de Soller. Before reaching this point you can look out for sheep tracks to use as short cuts up to the col between Teix and Teixoch.

Alternative descent to Ca'n Prohom and Puerto Soller

At the col between Sa Galera and the Puig d'es Moro, go over the wooden branches blocking the gateway.* Turn right by the wall and in 10m find the beginning of the descent path on the left, marked by cairns. The path is easy to follow with cairns and paintmarks, except occasionally where a fallen tree has obscured it. There are sections where it contours and others where it zigzags down between impressive cliffs. Eventually it reaches a flat area of the forest and becomes a wide track. Two minutes after passing a *porxo* or shelter it goes through a wall and meets a wide cross-track at an angle. Turn right here and about 15 minutes later note a rising path on the left at the side of a *sitja*. This branch leads to Deià. Two hundred metres further on go through a gate and follow the wide track down to Ca'n Prohom. Follow Walk 54(a) to Soller, or reverse the first part to arrive at the port by the Rocamar hotel.

56. PUNTA DE SA FOREDADA

A pleasant coastal walk from near Valldemossa to a spectacular prominent rocky peninsula pierced with a large natural hole, La Foredada. This can easily be seen from the coastal road near Deià or

---

* There are signs at this gateway indicating walkers are not welcome.

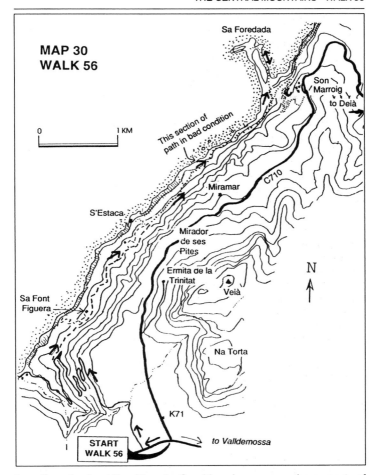

**MAP 30
WALK 56**

Sa Foredada

Son
Marroig
to Deià

This section of
path in bad condition

0   1 KM

Miramar

C710

S'Estaca

Mirador
de ses
Pites

Ermita de la
Trinitat

Veià

N

Sa Font
Figuera

Na Torta

K71

START
WALK 56

to Valldemossa

from the *mirador* at Son Marroig. Son Marroig was once the property of
the archduke Luis Salvador, and is now a museum worth visiting if time
is available. (There is a snack bar on the *mirador* which closes at 17.30.)

If possible, it is best to use a car to Son Marroig, at K66 on the
C710, then take the bus to K71.3, which is the junction with the Esporles

road just outside Valldemossa, so as not to be limited by the bus time at the end of the day. It is quite feasible to do the walk by taking the 09.30 bus from Puerto Soller and returning from Son Marroig at about 15.35 (15.30 bus from Valldemossa [check]). However, this does not leave much time for full enjoyment of the most interesting part of the walk. Taking a taxi from Valldemossa to the Font Figuera gate is well worth considering and also has the advantage of cutting out the road walking section.

Another option would be to drive to the Port of Valldemossa then walk to the last headland where the path disappears. Returning the same way gives a very easy walk of about 3hr. Another day or half day could then be spent walking down to La Foredada and back from the *mirador*. In this case permission should be sought at the house. The way down is over a vertical metal stile at the side of a double gate and thereafter is obvious.

Type of walk: Very easy, except for a 1km stretch near La Foredada. The path has disintegrated here and some care is required, whether clambering over boulders or negotiating the narrow remains of the path. It is this section only which gives the walk a B+ grade. (Since this was written a better path has developed.)

Starting point:	K71.3 near Valldemossa
Time:	5hr 10min
Distance:	12km
Total height climbed:	Descent 380m, ascent 300m
Grade:	B+
Map:	Soller 1:50,000

From the Deià-Esporles road junction walk towards Esporles, then turn first right towards the Port de Valldemossa. This pleasant narrow road descends in zigzags with some entrancing views of the cliffs and the little marina. At K4 turn right along a good cart track starting at a double bend. There is a double metal gate with pedestrian access on the left and the sign on the gate reads 'S'Estaca FONT FIGUERA'. This good level track leads at first through pinewoods and then more open ground with views of the sea. The houses of S'Estaca and Font Figuera are passed, going through another locked gate with pedestrian access.

Further on, the road goes down left towards a chained gateway, but the old track continues in the same direction, by a red sign saying 'Fora' and an arrow. The wide track soon ends at a stile, but a narrow path continues, contouring into a re-entrant and then passing a *sitja* and bending left to arrive at a pine-covered headland. There is a picnic place where a stone table has been built between two large rocks. This potentially attractive place has been ruined by an extraordinary amount of litter.

It is at this point that the path deteriorates. Find a way down on to the rocks near sea level, and then make your way along boulders and the remains of the old path until this improves just before the col between the Foredada peninsula and the main coastline. If you are not tied to catching a bus, then you will be able to enjoy the easy walk out to the Foredada. There is a sort of shelter with a roof of pine branches built into the rock near where the track crosses a narrow neck before the final climb to the rock. This is a steep but short little scramble and on the top a path can be found leading to the white column over the hole. (The descent to the hole involves rock-climbing and should not be attempted.)

K71.3 - Font Figuera gate	1hr 15min
Font Figuera gate - picnic table	1hr
Picnic table - Foredada path	1hr 15min
Foredada path - Foredada	40min
Foredada - Son Marroig	1hr

57. THE ARCHDUKE'S WALK AND TEIX

The archduke Luis Salvador (Ludwig Salvator is the original form of his name) of Hapsburgo-Lorena came to Mallorca on a visit in 1867 and liked it so much he later came to the island to live, settling at the *finca* of Miramar, near Valldemossa. He was a great benefactor of the island and a very early conservationist; he restored old buildings and did not allow trees and shrubs to be cut down on his properties. He made a marvellous garden at Miramar with native Mallorquin plants and wrote a treatise on the island which dealt with almost every aspect including natural history, economy, language and folklore. One of his properties was Son Moragues, which was bought by ICONA in 1979 and turned over to public use. It is a centre for nature conservation and very carefully managed, with strict rules to protect plants and animals and guard against fire.

One of the archduke's achievements of great benefit to walkers was the construction of excellent paths on the Son Moragues estate, in spectacular situations along the edges of high cliffs looking down to

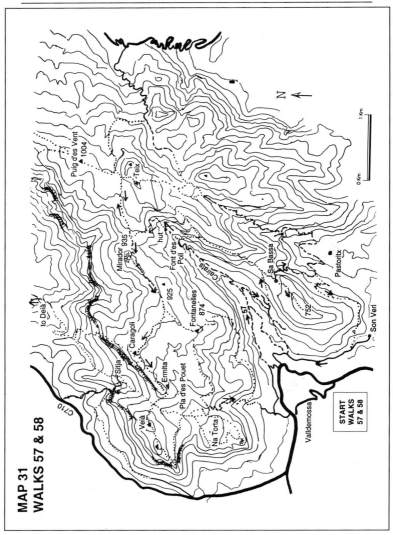

MAP 31
WALKS 57 & 58

Deià and the coast. Luis Salvador had these built so that he could walk or ride here and enjoy the views without danger or difficulty. To follow in his footsteps is an enjoyable and exhilarating experience and provides one of the best walks on the island. The route described here is quite long and strenuous, but it could easily be split into two or even three shorter walks to allow more time for appreciation of the scenery. One suggestion is to spend a day on the ascent of Teix by the Serra des Cairats, described later, and devote another day to the round walk excluding Teix.

A further interest in this area is the open-air museum provided by ICONA in the Cairats valley, where there is a restored limekiln, a snow house and a *sitja* with logs piled up as though ready for charcoaling. All these and more are described in a little booklet with many illustrations. (See bibliography.)

ICONA have also provided an attractive picnic place at the Font d'es Poll or Poplars' Well, with wooden tables and seats. A little higher up is a hut where overnight stops can be made. It is equipped with tables and benches and has an enormous fireplace across one corner. The walls are decorated with coloured posters showing plants and animals. This hut was originally the living quarters of the *nevaters* or snow collectors. The *casa de sa neu* nearby is an enormous pit 24m x 8m.

Incidentally the name Teix means yew in Catalan, and there are a number of yew trees, quite rare today in Mallorca, growing on the slopes of the mountain.

Starting point:	Son Gual, Valldemossa
Time:	6hr 10min
Distance:	16km
Highest point reached:	1,062m
Total height climbed:	790m
Grade:	B+
Map:	Esporles 1:25,000 and Alaró 1:25,000

Park in the main car park on the outskirts of Valldemossa. Walk along the main road towards Palma and take the first wide street on the left and then turn first right. Alternatively continue along the main road for a further 100m and turn left up some old stone steps. From Son Gual, the large house with the tower, walk along a road called Luis Vives, parallel to the main road at first. After passing some new houses the track goes through a gateway into the Cairats valley. It is joined by another track from Sa Coma after crossing a cattle grid in the valley bottom. Further up the Son Moragues estate is entered by a stile next to a locked gate. There is an information board and higher up signposts to the points of interest.

The track rises quite steeply before reaching the Font d'es Poll and 10 minutes further on arrives at the shelter. The road ends by the snow-pit and the walk then continues along the archduke's path. The signpost (sometimes missing) for Teix is reached in about 20 minutes. This path leaves the archduke's path on the right and after 10 minutes crosses a boundary wall by a stile. It leads easily in another 10 minutes up to a small plain, the Pla de Sa Serp, where there is a spring. Before reaching the spring a branch path marked by red paint signs slants up right to the col between Teix and Teixoch, then to the top of Teix with its two iron crosses. Return to the archduke's path to continue the walk.

The next point of interest is a *mirador* on the edge of the cliffs overlooking Deià. The path then crosses a flat area, the Pla dets Aritges, where it becomes a little indistinct (Aritges = smilax, the plant with vicious backward-pointing thorns.) The direction here is almost due west. Forty minutes from the junction with the Teix path there is a branch left which can be followed over Fontanelles and down to Es Pouet to shorten the walk. However, the main path is now especially attractive. It swings towards the Puig Caragoli, a high point with a branch path leading up to it and an excellent viewpoint. After this the path continues along the edge of the cliffs before descending towards a wooded pass, the Coll de S'Estret de Son Gallart. There are some stone seats here in the form of a 'V' and plentiful signs of the thrush-hunter's activities.

There is a path leading down to Deià here on the right, while on the left a path descends to the Pla d'es Pouet, another way of shortening the walk. It is easy to shorten the walk inadvertently here, so if intending to continue to Veià, then make sure to cross the col and find the path leading uphill. Keep straight on at another cross-path, looking for the cairns and paint marks leading up to an old stone shelter near the top. This is another of Luis Salvador's buildings. From the top continue along the wooded ridge, passing a trig point. This path is another of the archduke's constructions and easy to follow in spite of being somewhat overgrown by trees. The path leads to the Mirador de Ses Puntes, another impressive viewpoint on the edge of a 400m drop down to the flat plain of Valldemossa.

From the *mirador* turn left along a path which passes an old bread-oven and several *sitjes* on the way to Es Pouet. At Es Pouet go straight on past the polluted well and in 5 minutes a clearing on level ground will be reached. Go straight on again and through a gap in a stone wall. When a cross-track is met, go straight on down a short cut and rejoin the main track a few minutes later. The whole area is riddled with paths, but the route is now an old charcoal-burners' track at a reasonable gradient. Many *sitjes* will be noticed in the forest. Look out for the red paint signs and continue down the track to the forest gate, taking advantage of the short cuts if preferred. At a wider track turn right and continue downhill to Son Gual and Valldemossa.

Son Gual - ICONA shelter	1hr	
ICONA shelter - Teix	1hr	
Teix - Estret de Son Gallart	2hr	
Estret - Veià		20min
Veià - Mirador de Ses Puntes		30min
Mirador - Es Pouet		20min
Es Pouet - Son Gual	1hr	

Variation: Teix by the Serra des Cairats

This alternative way up Teix is highly recommended. It begins at the Font des Polls and is signposted 'Serra des Cairats'. A wide and well-made track leads to a steep and narrow wooded valley which is surmounted in zigzags. Take a left turn where the main track goes straight on about 15-20 minutes after the start. In a further 20 minutes the track ends at a *sitja*. After this there is no path but cairns show the way up through the wood in a northerly direction to reach a wall. This is crossed by a broken fence at the point where the wall with the fence on top meets a higher wall. The way continues at right angles to the wall up stony ground. When the trees thin out and the angle eases the route continues up the right-hand side of a ridge on bare and solid rock. Cairns show the way to a gap in another wall, and when this is reached the top of Teix with its iron crosses can be seen and is easily reached.

To descend, follow the paint marks down towards Teixoch and then down to the Pla de Sa Serp. (To go to the spring, take a right branch before reaching the plain.) Follow the path across the plain and over a slight rise before descending to a wall. This is crossed by a stile constructed from a forked tree. In a further 10 minutes the archduke's path is met at a wooden signpost. Turn left to descend the Cairats valley, reaching the snow house and then the shelter in about 20 minutes. A further 10 minutes and the track arrives at the Font des

Polls.

Valldemossa - Font des Polls	1hr 10min
Font des Polls - Teix	1hr 15min
Teix - junction on path	30min
Junction on path - Valldemossa	1hr

·Note: Still another variation for those who are already familiar with this one is to go up to Sa Bassa, as in Walk 58, then find the interesting path which follows (vaguely) the cliff edge to join the Serra des Cairats route at the double bend about 15 minutes above the Font des Polls.

58. SA MOLETA DE PASTORITX

This steep-sided wooded hill lies to the east of Valldemossa. It is of particular interest for the abundance of sites used by the charcoal burners. These include *sitjes*, some of them very large and prominent by reason of the bright green moss growing in a perfect circle and at least three bread-ovens in excellent repair. Although there are some panoramic views, both of Valldemossa and the peaceful valley of Pastoritx, these are only seen occasionally because of the trees. Another point of interest is the spring, the Font de Sa Predio, passed on the descent. A kind of chapel with a double arch dated 1591 has been built above it. The walk includes a complete circuit of the hill as well as an ascent and is an excellent choice when shelter is required, whether from the hot sun or a cold wind. Park in the main car park on the west side of Valldemossa, or in the urbanisation near Sa Coma.

Type of walk: Terrain very varied, along country lanes and tracks, easy woodland paths, and a descent of a very stony disused cart track which is quite steep. Attention must be paid to route-finding as trees frequently obscure the next objective.

Starting point:	Valldemossa
Time:	4hr
Distance:	10km
Highest point:	752m
Total height climbed:	460m
Grade:	B
Map:	Esporles 1:25,000

Walk out of Valldemossa either by the bypass road towards Palma, or by going down the main street, past the post office, then bearing left to a road with a no exit sign 'Calle sin salida'. This joins the bypass road by some steps.

Turn left at the first sharp bend and follow the narrow road behind the large house Sa Coma. Turn left through a wooden gate with a pictorial 'no dogs' sign. After 1km turn right along the main Cairats valley track which comes in on the left. Approximately 150m after passing a small building turn right again. Follow this track (SW) for a little over 600m and then turn left at a T-junction. Almost immediately leave the wide track where it bends left and go straight on to some stone steps up a wall. Follow the narrow path at the foot of the wall which encloses a wood on the right and after a few minutes climb this wall by some stone steps. The path then rises diagonally to go through another wall at right angles to the first and then rises in zigzags keeping near the wall at first. The path then slopes up easily to arrive at the easiest way up on to the wooded col above, by means of some sticks set into a high wall next to a private hunting sign. Once on the top, turn right to reach the main path along the cliff edge and almost immediately fork left to reach the location known as Sa Bassa, where there is a large water tank, a *sitja*, and a ruined house. This is a significant reference point for the descent. Follow the path from here, rising slightly to reach in 10 minutes or so a thrush-hunting structure obstructing the path. About 100m further on there is a large *sitja* and a ruined shelter. Follow the path up left from here to reach the escarpment forming the summit ridge. At this point there is another thrush-hunting station with an impressive view down to Pastoritx. Continue along the ridge to the right to reach the rather indefinite tree-screened top, noting the route carefully so as to be able to retrace your steps.

Return to Sa Bassa. Follow the track NE passing a *sitja* and ignoring a branch left to reach a prominent bread-oven and another *sitja* where the track bends sharp right and starts to descend a steep gully in a series of tight bends, then makes some wide swings left and right. Ignore two turnings left and eventually go through a large opening in a wall which separates the wood from the cultivated terraces of Pastoritx. About 4 minutes later leave the main track where it makes a sharp bend left to take a path on the right and in a further 6 minutes turn right again. This track veers towards the gully previously descended and then swings left to enter the wood again. A large limekiln and a bread-oven are seen on the right and a *sitja* on the left.

Less than 10 minutes later go over a stile consisting of branches across a wire-netting fence with stone steps in the wall below. Descend the pleasant woodland path on the other side in a south-westerly direction. This turns right towards a wall. Go through a gap in the wall near a small stone trough. Turn right to reach the Font de Sa Predio. The path descends through a gateway then through open ground to join a road by the gates of Predio Son Veri. Turn right and follow the road back to Sa Coma and Valldemossa.

Valldemossa - Sa Bassa	1hr 20min
Sa Bassa - Moleta	25min
Moleta - Sa Bassa	20min
Sa Bassa - Son Veri spring	1hr 10min
Son Veri spring - Valldemossa	45min

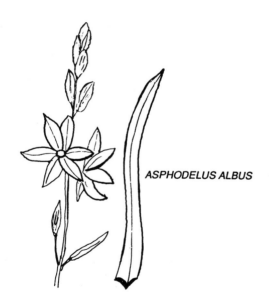

ASPHODELUS ALBUS

Andratx and The South

59. PORT D'ES CANONGE

The Port d'es Canonge is a small resort on the coast north of Banyalbufar, which can be reached by driving down a steep and narrow winding road. There is not much there apart from a few boats, an abandoned urbanisation and a restaurant which has a good reputation, Toni Moreno's. This circular walk from Banyalbufar is extremely attractive with views of typical countryside as well as the sea. Some large country houses are passed: Son Valenti, then Son Balagueret which has an old defensive tower approached through an inner courtyard, and finally the impressive manorial property of Son Bunyola, currently owned by Richard Branson. The best time for this walk is February, when sugar-pink and white almond blossom enhances the views. Some changes may be expected in this route as new fences are being built, but the management of Virgin Hotels Limited has assured the author that they 'have no wish to disturb the traditions of the area'.

Type of walk: Mostly very easy on narrow roads and wide tracks and paths. Some objective danger where the route passes below an unstable cliff.

Starting point:	Centre of Banyalbufar
Time:	4hr 25min
Distance:	13km
Highest point reached:	385m
Total height climbed:	460m
Grade:	C+
Map:	Esporles 1:25,000

From the bus stop in Banyalbufar, next to the shop Es Forn, go up the steps on the right to the Placa d'Espanya. Follow the narrow lane on the left, the Carrer Jeroni Alberti, which winds uphill steeply at first. The street name changes to Carrer de la Font de la Vila and this continues upwards. There is a short descent before the water channel from the spring crosses under the road, after which the ascent continues until the surfaced road ends at the gates of Ses Senutges, a former cement

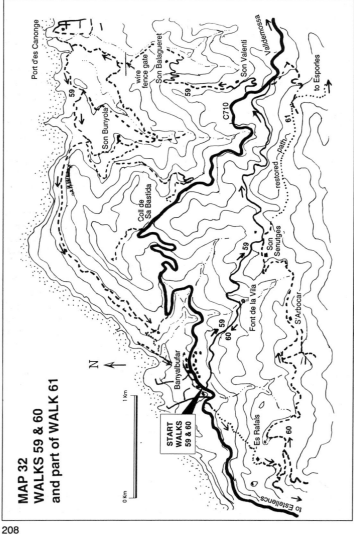

MAP 32
WALKS 59 & 60
and part of WALK 61

Port des Canonge

Son Bunyola

wire fence gate
Son Balagueret

Son Valenti

Valldemossa

to Esporles

C710

59

59

restored path 61

Coll de Sa Bastida

59

Son Senutges

59

Font de la Vila

S'Arbocar

60

Banyalbufar

59

60

N

1 Km

START WALKS 59 & 60

0 Km

Es Rafals

60

to Estellencs

works.

Follow the unsurfaced track to the left, contouring at a height of about 350m until it joins the C710 at K80.7. Turn left until the track to Son Valenti is reached shortly after the K81 stone. Go through the open gate and pass the large house , where the dogs are chained. The track goes behind the house and then descends, in about 25 minutes, to the old abandoned house Son Balagueret. Continue past the house for about 4 minutes, then take a left fork towards the stream-bed. The track goes gently downhill through a valley filled with almond trees and flowering shrubs. Red and yellow paint marks show the way and a right fork is taken to reach a new wall. A wire netting gate closing a gap in this wall can be opened at the left-hand side. One minute later join a major track at a T-junction and turn right. Follow this for about 9 minutes to meet another wide track at a T by a new fence. Turn right again and follow this across the dry stream-bed to a flat area adjoining the Port d'es Canonge.

To return to Banyalbufar recross the stream-bed and keeping near to the sea follow the little headland round to join the track which comes from Son Bunyola. At a branch track turn right and one minute after turn right again at a cross-track. This leads up to the foot of the high cliff and continues past the base of it for some 5 minutes. Not a place to linger as a glance at the large fallen rocks below will confirm. Once safely past, a wide and pleasant track now contours and then rises gently through the woods on the sloping hillside for about 2km to reach a gate which can be opened, although it appears locked. Keep on the main track until it bends sharp left at a house (Sa Cabarola). Immediately before the house turn right on a narrow descending path waymarked with red and white paint. About 6 minutes down this path watch out for a white arrow on a right bend where the route deviates from the old path. After reaching a wide track at the side of a house above the small harbour turn left and follow the lane back up into the village.

Banyalbufar - Ses Senutges		50min
Ses Senutges - Son Valenti		55min
Son Valenti - Canonge	1hr	
Canonge - Banyalbufar	1hr	40min

60. BANYALBUFAR CORNICHE WALK
Between Banyalbufar and the Mola de Planicie there is a terraced hillside with pines dotted among the old olive trees. The wide corniche track

which undulates round about the 350m contour gives good views over the trees and down to the sea. This was once the priniciple road used by the *carboneros* to take down the charcoal and bring in their provisions.

During the descent the Font de la Vila can be seen by going up a short stepped path on the left. Water gushes out of an opening into a narrow channel with branches off, the flow being controlled by boards at the entrance to these branches. This is the main source of water for the village and flows generously except in times of severe drought. At one time tomatoes were grown commercially on the splendid terraces, as well as vines, citrus fruit and almonds. Large water tanks or *estancas* are a conspicuous feature of the landscape here.

Type of walk: Easy, but the lane going up out of the village is very steep.

Starting point:	Bunyola centre
Time:	2hr 45min
Distance:	8km
Highest point reached:	368m
Total height climbed:	253m
Grade:	C
Map:	Esporles 1:25,000

Walk towards Estellencs from the centre of the village and take the first turn left up a narrow lane with an arrow on the right-hand wall. Keep to the main track which levels out and passes several *estancas* before rising steeply to end by a house with an unusual pink ceramic totem pole in the graden. At this point a grassy track continues upwards and leads to some old stone steps going up into a wood at the side of a high stone wall. Go through the wooden gate (which should be closed after you) and continue along the wide track to the large house Es Rafals. The track passes to the right of the house and above a threshing floor, then makes a rising traverse round a terraced valley before swinging sharp left. At this point ignore a track right with a chain across. About 500m further on another track is met. There is a notice reading 'Perros sueltos', which means loose dogs.

Go through the gate ahead and follow the 'corniche' track along past the S'Arbocar farm, where there is a chained dog. On the way out of this property there is a high gate, not locked. At Son Senutges there are a few empty houses and a derelict cement works. Go through the stone gateposts and turn left, following the winding lane back down into the oldest part of the village to arrive at the square in front of the town hall.

61. BANYALBUFAR TO VALLDEMOSSA
(for start see map 32 p209)

The countryside between Banyalbufar and Valldemossa contains no really high mountains but is a pleasant area with many quiet roads and paths. A short diversion can be made to the Mola de Son Pacs, a 731m top on a high rocky ridge, partly hidden in woodland. This linear walk can be done using the afternoon bus back from Valldemossa at 16.30 (or 17.30 in summer [check]), although in this case a start from Esporles is recommended because of the time factor. It can also be included as a stage in a long walk from the Andratx area to the north, and the walk from Banyalbufar to Esporles and back makes a pleasant short day.

Type of walk: Mainly on good paths, one of which is currently being restored, but other parts are disused and not easy to follow. In woodland the paths are confusing and a sense of direction and ability to read the land is more use than a map.

Starting point:	Centre of Banyalbufar
Time:	6hr 20min
Distance:	19km
Highest point reached:	731m
Total height climbed:	870m
Grade:	B
Map:	Esporles 1:25,000

From the centre of Banyalbufar walk up to Ses Senutges as in Walk 59 Port d'es Canonge. The partly restored footpath begins here, going uphill on an indefinite ridge. It bends left, then left again to reach a gap in a wall. Go over the gap and keep along the left-hand side of the wall, then recross the wall by a high ladder stile made of branches. The path continues in the same direction and rises gently. Fork left by a cairn, on to the edge of a wall with laid stones on a kind of causeway. Keep on the path which is cut by a forest track as it turns a corner and find the continuing path on the other side. The way continues through the wood, swinging round a valley and crossing a stream-bed, passing several *sitjas*. Go round the end of a wall by a broken stile and soon after this follow the zigzags downhill. About 10 minutes after passing a branch track left to a house go through a narrow gate in a wall, with rough

211

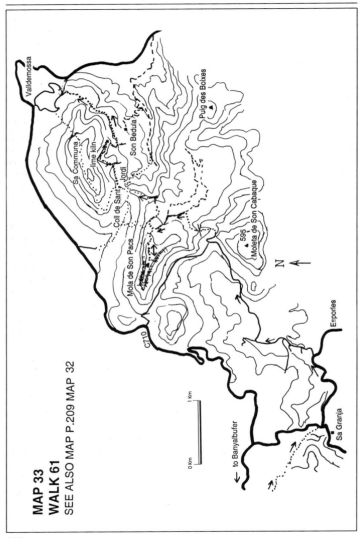

MAP 33
WALK 61
SEE ALSO MAP P.209 MAP 32

Valldemossa

Sa Communa

lime kiln

Son Bedula

Puig des Boixes

Coll de Sant Jordi

Moleta de Son Cabaque

595

Mola de Son Pacs

C710

N

Esporles

to Banyalbufer

Sa Granja

0 Km   1 Km

steps down the other side. Another track joins in on the left. At a fork, turn left and join the road by two gateposts exactly by the right turn sign approaching the Puigpuñent junction. Follow the road almost into Esporles, until it makes a sharp bend right on the northern edge of the town. If you are starting the walk from the bus stop in Esporles, then walk north towards Valldemossa to reach this point, then turn right over a bridge.

Go up the steps on the left almost immediately after the bridge. Keep straight on at the top then turn left at a T-junction. Ignore two branches left, the second of which is signed Es Noguerra. After going through two metal gates turn right through a third. (No locks or private signs.) Pass a large house called Son Danelo which seems mainly closed up but has cars and a chained dog. At the end of the drive turn left at a T and 2 minutes later go through a large open gateway with stone pillars, the entrance to Son Cabaspre. A sign says there is no entry for unauthorised vehicles. After about 50m turn right.

Continue up this narrow road which climbs uphill and then curves to the left after passing a house at the head of the valley called Finca Ca'n Buades. A couple of minutes later turn right on a track with a low gate and pedestrian access. This doubles back above the house and leads to a col at 457m. Just as the track starts to go downhill turn left up a good track leading to an old shelter and a *caseta*. When the concrete ends here look for a narrow path beginning on the right, marked with faded red paint signs. This goes up through the woods, turning left at a double *sitja* and then bending right to cross a wall by a crude stile. Turn left, then follow the path to the right and right again in the valley bottom at another *sitja*. About 8 minutes later the path arrives at a partial clearing on a large flat area where there are forestry operations. There is a high wall on the other side.

Turn left on a wide track parallel to this wall. About 5 minutes later take a left turn at a T-junction, in a roughly north-west direction. After passing a new shelter next to a covered *cisterna* a path-junction is reached by a bright green mossy *sitja*. At this point those wishing to take the diversion to the top of the Mola de Son Pacs should turn left, then return to this point. To continue the walk, turn right at the *sitja*. The path approaches a wall with a stile. Do not go over this stile but follow the path to the right, reaching in 4 minutes a significant cairn and a red arrow showing the way down a gully, which is one of the few breaks in the cliffs. At the foot of the gully traverse right below the cliff and then double back left, gradually descending to the Coll de Sant Jordi. Do not go through the gate, but continue alongside the wall for a minute or so to pick up a good track. Follow this on through the woods to reach a large limekiln, with a good wide track leading down to the right. Do not follow this down but turn left immediately opposite and follow an ill-defined path. This crosses a wall by a stick-stile and then reaches another good track by a large limekiln.

Follow this track down. It bends right and goes through a wall with a fence-type gate. Continue descending, ignoring a branch right. After a short traverse high above the large house Son Bedula, fork left up to a blue metal gate leading into open woodland. Keep along the old path which is adjacent to the wall. It contours and then rises slightly and after two short double bends descends between walls to join the old Palma road at a sharp bend. Turn left up the steep narrow lane at this junction. When it bends left go up the field path on the right to reach a lane with an aqueduct crossing it. Turn right, passing Ca'n Mossanya, then go left to reach Valldemossa.

Banyalbufar - Esporles	2hr	20min
Esporles - 457m col	1hr	20min
457m col - Sant Jordi	1hr	20min
Sant Jordi - Valldemossa	1hr	20min

62. ES PUNTALS

Es Puntals is a high top of 898m on a long narrow ridge between Galatzó and Planicie. The views from the escarpment edge and from the top are very fine. There are steep cliffs on both sides, although the ridge is not narrow enough to cause any problems and is easily reached from Banyalbufar as in route 62(a). This is because the area was once a highly productive centre for the production of charcoal and good tracks were needed to take the product down the mountain. Although charcoal has long been replaced by butane gas there are still good tracks as high as 800m which give good easy walking, although they have deteriorated in places. There are numerous examples of the charcoal workers' activities such as *sitjes, barrancas* and bread-ovens. There are a cluster of these at Ses Aljubets. An *aljub* is a covered water cistern where rainwater is stored for all purposes: cooking, drinking, washing, washing clothes and for animals to drink. There is a double one at Ses Aljubets with one rounded and one rectangular openings, making a distinctive landmark. When charcoal burning was taking place the fires required constant attention so the *carboneros* and their families lived up here for months at a time.

62(a). ES PUNTALS FROM BANYALBUFAR

Few of the paths used are marked on the published maps which means route-finding is not all that easy, the author and friends making several attempts at this route before succeeding.

Type of walk: Mainly easy walking on tracks and paths, but a hands-on scramble up a kind of chimney makes it hard.

Starting point:	Centre of Banyalbufar
Time:	5hr 30min
Distance:	15km
Highest point reached:	898m
Total height climbed:	800m
Grade:	A+
Map:	Esporles 1:25,000 and Sa Vileta 1:25,000

Walk along the road towards Estellencs and turn left by the village signpost, between a house and a high wall. This narrow lane rises, then bends right and levels before going up very steeply towards the woods. When the surfaced road ends a track continues and leads into the wood by some stone steps below a high stone wall. A pleasant path leads to a wire and wood gate giving on to a wider track which arrives at the large house of Es Rafals. Go to the right of the house and the left of a threshing circle and stay on the track which makes a big sweep round a terraced slope. After swinging right and then left, a branch track with a chain across it is passed on the right. In a further 500m, just before reaching a gate, turn right along a wide track and follow this all the way to the *finca* of Planicie.

The way goes in front of the house, where it is essential to ask permission to continue, so far always readily given. Pass round the far side of the building, through a little gate, then left up some steps by a waterpipe to reach the track behind the house. After roughly 10 minutes, keep straight on along the main track by the wall, ignoring the cairned path left which leads to Planicie and to Son Vic. Continue along the main track which swings right at a clearing with several *sitjes* and an old shelter. On reaching an abandoned car, turn left uphill and keep to the main track which rises with many bends through the woods. A wall is approached but before reaching it the track doubles back left. After a short level section, look out for a stone arrow pointing uphill, a key point where the path begins to rise more steeply. There are many branches, but the main route is well cairned. Higher up, near a steep

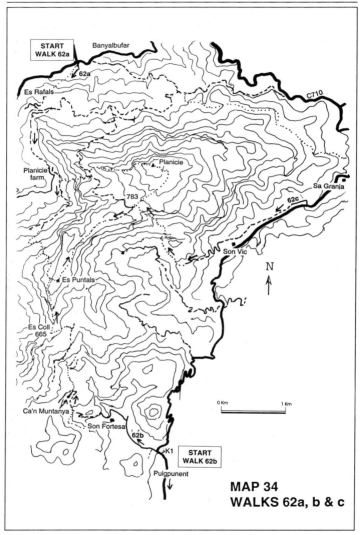

START
WALK 62a

Banyalbufar

62a

Es Rafals

C710

Planicie
farm

Planicie

783

Sa Granja

62c

Son Vic

N

Es Puntals

Es Coll
665

Ca'n Muntanya

0 Km   1 Km

Son Fortesa

62b

K1

START
WALK 62b

Puigpunent

MAP 34
WALKS 62a, b & c

rock, the path goes to the right and passes through a gap in a wall. After a further 200m look out for a second key landmark: a group of 3 roofless shelters clustered around a mossy *sitja* with a faint painted arrow on a boulder pointing upwards. This is the point where the route from Es Coll is joined.

The way now zigzags upwards, passing a large rocky outcrop on the left. Continue up steep ground with a deep layer of fallen leaves to the foot of the only feasible way to the top. This is a scramble which although easy is steep enough to deter those walkers unused to this activity. A dead tree chokes the direct line which is rather loose, so avoid this by going to the right and then back left over firm rock. Faint paint marks above confirm you are on the right route. At the top you find yourself on the lower 882m top of Es Puntals. The highest top is easily reached by crossing a shallow depression.

Continue the circular route by following the long ridge of the Serra des Puntals which curves away in a general NE direction. It is important to keep within sight of the cliff edge on the right in order to avoid descending a steep valley on the left. Soon a wide track is picked up, leading to a large flat col at 783m, between Es Puntals and Planicie, where there is a major path junction. This is where the path from Sa Granja arrives. Trees prevent a clear view and vegetation hampers route-finding, but a wide stony track leading down to the west is picked up here.

This track zigzags down to reach several *sitjas* just above Ses Aljubets. Continuing down past the water cisterns the track makes a sharp bend right then doubles back to the valley floor, bending left again by some more ruins. After passing a limekiln look out for two cairns on the left of the track, which show the way up from Planicie farm and which could be used as an alternative descent. Keep on the main track which is easy to follow, with occasional breaks in the trees giving rewarding views. After a level section the track descends towards S'Arbocar. When a wide track is met at a T, turn right and one minute later turn left on another wide track. This goes through an opening in a stone wall marked with an arrow and 5 minutes later the main Es Rafals - S'Arbocar track is reached between two houses. (Note that recent building work may result in some alterations here.)

Follow the main track back to Es Rafals, noting that an apparent short cut from a sharp bend left leads to a small *mirador*.

62(b). ES PUNTALS FROM PUIGPUNENT

This route could be used as part of a long walk from Andratx to Valldemossa, although it does involve a steep scramble which not everyone would like. So far an easier alternative has not been found, but route 62(a) could be used in reverse for a descent to Banyalbufar.

Type of walk: Without the final 10 minutes' scramble the walk makes a pleasant moderate day walk to a rocky viewpoint, returning the same way.

Starting point:	Puigpunent
Time:	4hr 45min
Distance:	11km
Highest point reached:	898m
Total height climbed:	630m
Grade:	A+ (or B omitting scramble)
Map:	Sa Vileta 1:25,000

At the north end of the village turn left where the main road bends right. (There is room for a couple of small cars to park in this lane.) Go through the gates which should be kept closed and walk up the surfaced road, turning left outside the high wall of Son Fortesa, a large manorial house. Follow the track as it doubles back behind the house and through the farm where a herd of goats is kept for milk. Follow the track on up to Ca'n Muntanya in the upper valley and there turn right, immediately opposite a branch track to the house. The track goes through a gap in the wall with a yellow paint mark. Two minutes later take a left fork which leads to a gate in a wall and on to join a cross-track. Turn right and follow this up to Es Coll, a flat wooded area on the main ridge between Galatzó and Es Puntals. On the way up, ignore a branch right and turn left uphill at a junction where there is a red arrow on a boulder pointing to the way down. When the track levels out on Es Coll look out for a branch path on the right, which is not particularly conspicuous but marked by a painted sign and a cairn.

This path is easy to follow and rises to an old gate in a boundary wall. On the other side of the wall the path contours or rises slightly along the west side of Es Puntals for about 20 minutes. After a brief descent, look out for a key landmark, the same one reached in 62(a), where a group of 3 shelters is clustered round a *sitja* and a painted red arrow on a boulder shows the way up. See the description above for the next section to the top. Those who do not fancy the scramble can more easily bear right to gain a rocky viewpoint without too much difficulty.

Return the same way to Puigpunent.

62(c). SA GRANJA TO BANYALBUFAR

This walk makes use of the bus that leaves Paguerra at 09.00 and Banyalbufar at 09.55, getting off at the junction with the Esporles road and transferring to the Esporles bus as far as La Granja. Either Es Puntals or Planicie can be climbed as a diversion from the col between the two, and this is the easiest way to the top of the former.

Type of walk: Mainly on good tracks but some rough paths.

Starting point:	Sa Granja
Time:	5hr
Distance:	15km
Highest point reached:	898m
Total height climbed:	650m
Grade:	B+
Map:	Esporles 1:25,000 and Sa Vileta 1:25,000

From Sa Granja walk along the road towards Puigpunent as far as K8. Turn right and go through the high iron gates of Son Vic, easily opened by a bolt on the inside. At Son Vic turn right in front of some outbuildings, then follow the track round to the right and back left. Keep on the main track as it climbs in bends up the hillside. At Ca'n Poma pass between the house and the farm buildings and go right between some gateposts, keeping to the left of a new concrete wall. Turn diagonally right across a field and in 20/25m pick up a path heading across a field to reach a little col with a threshing circle.

Go through the narrow wooden gate, from which there is a view into a high upper valley and the large house of Son Balaguer. The path is now rough and rocky and continues steeply upwards on the right-hand side of this valley, crossing a wide track twice. After going through a narrow gap in a stone wall, closed by a stick and stone stile, turn left and follow a narrow and overgrown path up through the wood to reach a col at 593m. This is the Coll del Pujol de Sa Coma and across it is a wide track going through a gap in a wall. Turn right and descend very slightly and then turn left on a path leading up into a narrow valley. At first it is overgrown, but soon improves and is easy to follow. Fork right after 3-4 minutes.

219

At the top of the steep zigzag path the ground levels out on the wide and confusing area of the 783m col between Planicie and Es Puntals. Follow the cairns and paintmarks which head straight on at first, then go left, cross a *sitja* and turn right. Turn left on a cross-track, and almost immediately look for a branch left at a small cairn. The painted arrow here is very faint but it is the way to Es Puntals. The way becomes a wide track with built-up edges and more or less contours to the north of the 844m top on the ridge at about 800m or so, to reach a small depression where there are several old shelters. Just beyond these the ridge narrows and there are views down a narrow valley bordered by steep cliffs. The path soon disappears after this but it is easy to find the way by keeping fairly close to the edge of the cliffs on the left. The 898m top is tree covered so continue a little beyond it to some bare rock which is a fine viewpoint.

Retrace your way back to the cairn on the main path, turn left and follow the descent as described in Walk 62(a).

63. GALATZÓ

Galatzó is the highest peak in the south-western mountains and the only one over 1,000m in this area. Because of its position it commands some outstanding views. It is seen as a prominent pyramid from many parts of the island. The most usual way up used to be from Son Fortuny near Estellencs by a good path but currently a signpost here directs you to K97, which is the way descibed in Walk 63(a), and it can also be climbed from Puigpuñent or Galilea.

63(a). GALATZÓ BY THE PAS DE COSSIS

The way described here was restored and signposted in 1991 and is an interesting route when combined with a descent to Son Fortuny to make a circular walk. The only disadvantage is having to walk 3km along the main road at the end of the day. This can be avoided if it is possible to use two cars and leave one in Estellencs, or by using the bus which leaves Paguerra at 09.00, returning from Estellencs at approx. 17.15 (changes seasonally, so check locally).

Type of walk: Strenuous and rough.

Starting point:	K97, Estellencs-Andratx road
Time:	5hr
Distance:	11km
Highest point reached:	1,027m

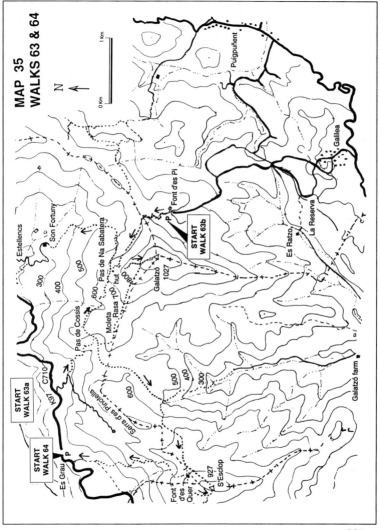

MAP 35
WALKS 63 & 64

N

0 km — 1 km

START WALK 63a
C710
K91

START WALK 64
Es Grau
P

Estellencs
Son Fortuny
300
400
500
Pas de Cossis
600
Pas de Na Sabatera
Moleta Rasa 700 hut
800
Galatzó 1027
900
Serra d'es Pinotells
600
500
400
300
Font d'es Quer
927 S'Esclop

Font d'es Pi
P
START WALK 63b
Es Ratzo
La Reserva
Galatzó farm

Puigpunent
Galilea

Total height climbed:	916m
Grade:	B+
Map:	Sa Vileta 1:25,000 and Andratx 1:50,000

Park near the K97 stone and walk up the restored track, passing a well and an informative signpost. At a track junction turn left and continue up the wide track to a picnic site with a reconstruction of a shelter for *carboneros.* From this point the footpath, cleared of vegetation and easy to follow, begins to rise more steeply with impressive views of steep cliffs. It reaches the top of the 'step' in about 15 minutes, on the high ground behind the Serra d'es Pinotells. At this point there is another signpost indicating right for S'Esclop and left for Galatzó.

Turn left and follow the path which rises at an easy gradient, swinging round towards the valley head and over a spur separating this valley from the Son Fortuny valley. The path then dips into a stream-bed before rising again. About 8 minutes later take the left fork to reach an important path junction at the foot of the Pas de Na Sabatera. The way straight ahead is the way down to Estellencs. Turn right uphill to reach the site of a ruined shelter, previously a prominent landmark. Ignore the path left which comes from Puigpuñent and head south to the top of Galatzó by the well-trodden and cairned route. At first easy ground leads to the foot of a rocky staircase where there is a red arrow painted on a white rock. The angle eases at the top of this but the path continues to rise up to a natural rock shelter with many paint signs which used to house a summit book. The top is reached in a few minutes by a litle rock scramble which is quite steep but not difficult. (The summit book was reported as buried near trig point in 1997.)

To descend, return down to the ruined shelter and continue down the Pas de Na Sabatera by the route of ascent. At the bottom turn right and follow this down into a shallow valley. A few minutes after reaching the woodland there is a large *sitja*, where it is important to bear left and not go straight on. Some unobtrusive paint marks on a tree branch show the correct path which leads in about 2 minutes to another bright green *sitja*. From this point it is a question of keeping to the main track, which is wide and gives pleasant walking. Some 20 minutes later a large water storage tank is passed. Another 20 minutes or so later turn right down a narrow path and go through a wooden gate. Further down there is some confusion where the path crosses some ploughed terraces and at this point there are two alternatives. The old way continued down in the same direction and went through a gap in a wall and on down to

Son Fortuny. This way still seems viable for a descent, although you cannot come up by this route. The new way which avoids the farm goes left at this point, then curves round to rejoin the road below Son Fortuny. Follow this down to Estellencs. Alternatively a short cut can be taken from about half-way down near a large water tank, where a field path leads down the side of the stream and then crosses it to reach the old houses of Estellencs. At the houses go right, left, then right again and continue down steps and paths to the centre of the village. The bus stop for Paguerra is a couple of minutes along the road to the left. To return to K97 it is about 3km along the road.

63(b). GALATZÓ FROM PUIGPUNENT

Puigpuñent is a delightful mountain village to the east of Galatzó. It is reached by very narrow winding roads either from Sa Granja, near Esporles, to the north or from Capdella and Galilea to the south. Although only short, this is a highly recommended route with splendid distant views and impressive rock scenery nearer at hand. The most difficult part of the route is finding the way to the starting point from the village.

To reach the starting point, take the road west from the village by a signpost for 'La Reserva'. This is easily seen if the village is entered from the south. From the north this junction is a little under 200m south of the junction with the Palma-Establiments road. Keep following the signs for the Reserva until after many twists and turns, some 3km from Puigpuñent, you come to a wide road junction on a col at 403m. At this point, instead of going left here turn right and follow the road uphill. Turn right again 200m after passing an old quarry. Keep climbing steadily until the surfaced road ends at a rough turning place with two minor roads going off to the right. Park here.

Type of walk: Easy path through woodland at first and then open ground. A traverse path crosses below crags to the north-east, then a well-marked route goes up steep and rocky ground to the top.

Starting point:	See sketch-map
Time:	2hr 45min
Distance:	6km
Highest point reached:	1,027m
Total height climbed:	530m
Grade:	B+
Map:	Sa Vileta 1:50,000

Purple paint signs, a little faded, and a newly painted red arrow at the road end show the start of the route. A stone arrow and a cairn show a right turn after a few minutes, followed shortly by a left turn. A very good path continues to zigzag upwards with numerous and somewhat superfluous paint signs. There is a marker stone at the point where the east ridge of Galatzó is reached and the traverse path crossing below the impressive north-east face begins here. This rises at the end to reach a ruined shelter, the same one passed on the ascent or descent from Estellencs.

The way up to the top continues to be well marked, at first up easy ground leading to the foot of a rocky staircase where there is a red arrow painted on a white rock. The angle eases at the top of this but continues to rise up fairly steeply to a natural rock shelter with many paint signs where there used to be a hidden summit book. The top is reached in 5 minutes by a little rock scramble, quite steep but no problems. Return the same way.

Road end - ruined hut	1hr
Ruined hut - summit	30min
Descent	1hr 15min

Note: the 'Reserva' is a kind of country park with laid paths and many amenities, worth visiting on an off-day.

64. S'ESCLOP

S'Esclop (the name means 'the clog') is at the southernmost end of the Sierra de Tramuntana. Although under 1,000m it is wild and rough and the ascent should not be undertaken lightly. Near the summit are the ruins of a stone hut where the French scientist Francois Arago lived while making a triangulation to measure the meridian in 1808. This route by the Pas de Cossis replaces the one decribed in the previous edition via the Galatzo farm, partly because permission was sometimes not given and partly because this is a more enjoyable and scenic route. The views on the way up include magificent rock scenery with impressive cliffs. On the way up there is a picnic site by a *sitja* and near to is a reconstruction of a charcoal workers shelter, roofed with *carritx* grass in the traditional manner.

There is a car park at the Restaurante Es Grau on the Andratx-Estellencs road, which can also be reached by the 09.00 bus from Paguerra (Mondays-Fridays). Return is approximately 17.30 in winter, 18.15 in summer.

Type of walk: A mountaineering route over rough ground.

Starting point:	Es Grau
Time:	4hr 20min
Distance:	9km
Highest point reached:	916m
Total height climbed:	727m
Grade:	A
Map:	Andratx 1:50,000

Begin by walking along the road towards Estellencs for 1km. At K97 turn right up a wide stony track, passing a notice-board bearing the name 'Son Fortuny', an estate belonging to the government. Nearby is a water supply. After 10-15 minutes uphill turn left where the main track leading to a farm bends sharp right. The signposted track leads to the picnic site. Beyond this follow the signposted and recently restored path signposted 'Pas de Cossis'. Cleared of vegetation it is easy to follow. At the top of the 'Pas', meaning a step, is a new wooden signpost indicating left to Galatzó and right to S'Esclop. Turn right and follow the path over bouldery ground, keeping a look-out for the occasional cairns and paint marks.

After rising up the broad ridge of the Serra d'es Pinotells, the marked way descends some distance down the south-east side of the mountain until it meets with the path coming up from the Galatzó farm. This path junction is at the head of a long valley with a steep headwall. From this point it rises in zigzags to arrive at a high col at the corner of a wall with a fence on top. The path continues uphill, crossing a threshing floor on a col behind the Peña Blanca. Five minutes later the Coll de Sa Font d'es Quer at 743m is reached.

From this point it is possible to make straight for the summit rocks, aiming for the furthest left of several sloping grassy ledges. The normal way is longer, but much more interesting and a little easier. Start off by crossing the col and descending slightly to pick up the contouring path towards the covered spring, the Font d'es Quer. Go straight to this spring, which is both a good resting place and a useful point of reference. Then back-track for about 50m to identify the path and faint paint sign to the Puig.

The path up is marked by cairns and rises steeply at first and then round a corner to the west or south-west side, finally reaching a high shoulder below the summit rocks. The path is indistinct in places, but passes by a large solitary pine which is a conspicuous feature. There is another old threshing floor on this shoulder with a ruined building alongside it. Looking at the summit rocks from here, at least two lines of weakness can be seen and scrambled up after following animal tracks leftwards, but recently another way has been waymarked, further to the right, so that when you reach the top you have to turn left to the trig point.

Retrace your steps to the spring. (After recent rain it is advisable to reverse the ascent route because the alternative descent described below can be unpleasantly slippery.) In front of the spring a steep and narrow path leads down to the left and then back right, at first through open ground and then through a dense thicket of thorny broom and large clumps of *carritx*. This is where it may be slippery underfoot. After about 20 minutes the path goes through an opening in a stone wall, then crosses the stream-bed to the right-hand side. The route now zigzags down an open hillside opposite steep cliffs and then enters a pinewood. After a steady descent terraced fields of almonds, olives and carobs are reached. Keep right, between the wood and the edge of the fields, then join the track from the Es Grau farm to the road. (The gate may be locked but the fence is old and easy to negotiate, at present.)

Es Grau - picnic site	40min
Picnic site - Galatzó-S'Esclop signpost	20min
Signpost - Font d'es Quer	45min
Font - summit	45min
Summit - font	40min
Font - Es Grau	1hr 10min

65. SA TRAPA

The area lying to the north-west of Andratx is wild and unspoilt, being devoid of the encroaching urbanizations which flourish elsewhere in the south of the island. There are two high points of interest on this walk. One is a really magnificent viewpoint on the Cap Fabioler overlooking the sea and the isle of Dragonera. The other is Sa Trapa, an abandoned Trappist monastery, now preserved and protected by GOB. There are impressively built terrace walls, and an old mill still with some of its machinery inside, and parts of an old irrigation system. A disastrous fire in 1994 set back the restoration programme but this is now continuing. The system of water channels, which made possible the growing of crops in this arid region, is also being repaired with the

Sa Trapa. Abandoned Trappist monastery

help of European funds. On the edge of the cliffs is a large circular area, a popular picnic place now, which was probably an old threshing floor.

65(a). SA TRAPA FROM S'ARRACO

Type of walk: Moderately strenuous, but on well-defined paths.

Starting point:	Centre of S'Arraco
Time:	5hr
Distance:	15km
Highest point reached:	450m
Total height climbed:	560m
Grade:	B
Map:	Andratx 1:50,000

The small village of S'Arraco between Andratx and San Telmo is a good starting point for many walks. It can be reached by bus (from Andratx at 10.15). From the bus stop by the church in S'Arraco walk towards San Telmo and turn right into the Cami des Castellas, signposted to the sports field. If arriving by car there is parking along this road. Follow the narrow unsurfaced road uphill and heading NW. After about 800m turn left, after which the track bends right (north) and

227

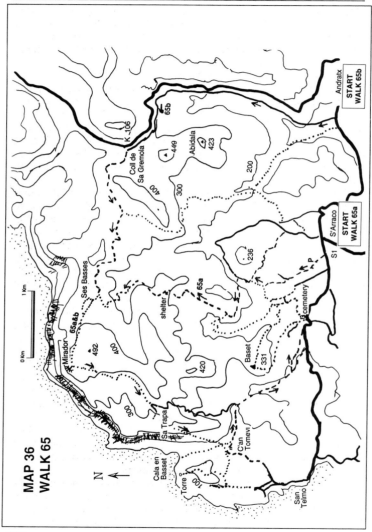

MAP 36
WALK 65

then swings west. Look out for a gate giving on to a narrow path, crossing fields on a col and then keeping to the edge of a pinewood. When a wide track is met at a corner, turn left and follow it uphill, rounding several bends to meet another track at a T-junction just above a restored *caseta* with a garden.

Turn left along the track, west at first and then swinging north-east and rising on to the right- hand side of a broad valley. A boundary wall is crossed by a private hunting sign. A few minutes later there is a *caseta* on the left of the track near some pine trees. The path levels off and contours into and out of a stream-bed. At a cairn with coloured paint marks the path begins to descend into the valley of the Torrent Gore d'en Betts which runs south to S'Arraco. On reaching the valley floor it turns left and climbs up again to reach the Ses Basses track about 150m from the houses.

Turn left and follow the good path which contours round the north side of Ses Basses. There are outstanding views NE along the coast, with S'Esclop dominating the scene inland. As the path rounds the headland there is a short diversion to a *mirador* overlooking Dragonera. Continuing towards Sa Trapa, the path contours and then descends, at first through open ground and then among pines. Fire damage has resulted in diversions round fallen trees in this area, but after about 30 minutes from the *mirador* a wide track is met at a bend. Turn right downhill to reach Sa Trapa in about 10 minutes.

After exploring the area follow the wide track back up from the main building to the first sharp bend left, where there is a signpost pointing the way to San Telmo and Ca'n Tomevi. The path slopes up to a high shoulder and then descends some rocky ground by a choice of routes. Keeping too far left can lead to some difficult scrambling although this way seems to have the most recent paint marks. There are no difficuties if you keep to the obvious route on the right. Once this bit is negotiated an easy path now swings round the head of a side valley, crosses a spur and swings round another corner before descending into the wooded area around Ca'n Tomevi. To avoid disorientation in this somewhat confusing area, avoid short cuts and keep on the main track until you come to a cross-track with two concrete gateposts on the right. Turning right here leads to Cala en Basset.

Turn left, opposite these posts and in a few minutes reach a wide track at a T-junction. There is a choice of routes now and if you wish to go down to San Telmo to catch a bus you can turn right here to Ca'n Tomevi and on down the main track into the village. To return to S'Arraco, turn left and follow the track east over a low col, where it swings SE. At a junction, fork left uphill to reach the main road near the cemetery. To avoid walking down the main road, a circuitous and interesting route can be used. At the cemetery turn left and then go immediately right at the far side of the cemetery. Ignore a branch left, cross a stream-bed and keep uphill to a ridge near a small stone building. The path contours and then descends to the valley floor. Turn left through some old almond trees until you see a way to cross he stream-bed and reach the track on the other side. Turn right and follow this down to the main road on the edge of S'Arraco.

65(b). SA TRAPA BY THE COLL DE SA GREMOLA

The walk does not make a complete circle and use is made of the bus which runs between San Telmo and Andratx. In winter there is only one bus each day so check timetables locally. More buses in summer from Monday to Saturday.

Type of walk: Very easy up to Gremola on an old metalled road. Then an easy and wide cart track to Ses Basses, followed by a narrow but well-defined path all the way to Sa Trapa and San Telmo. Between Sa Trapa and the Coll de Cala en Basset there is a bit of a scramble down some rock, but it is not difficult.

Starting point:	Andratx, bus station
Time:	5hr 40min
Distance:	14km
Highest point reached:	c.420m
Total height climbed:	c.480m (in reverse, 580m)
Grade:	B
Map:	Andratx 1:50,000

Walk out of Andratx on the road to San Telmo and take the first turn to the right, the Calle de Barcelona. Follow this old road up, ignoring turnings, until it makes a sharp turn right. At this point, where there are painted signs on the wall, turn left on a cart track which goes through several gates before arriving at the Coll de Sa Gremola at K106. From the clearing at the side of the road take the right-hand track, where there is a 'No entry' sign saying 'prohibido el paso, excepto proprietarios'. (This refers to cars, not walkers, so do not be concerned. The route is a well-known and popular walk. Unauthorised cars are in any case prevented from using the track by a padlocked chain a little further on.)

This track is very pleasant walking, on earth rather than stones, and contours with only a few ups and downs at about 400m. Be careful to follow the main track which is drivable to Ses Basses and which runs mainly west. From Ses Basses follow the description in Walk 65(a).

Andratx - Coll de Sa Gremola	1hr 40min
Gremola - Cap Fabioler *mirador*	1hr 40min
Cap Fabioler - Sa Trapa	50min
Sa Trapa - San Telmo	1hr 30min

66. SAN TELMO AND PORT ANDRATX

There is a hinterland of rough country between San Telmo and the Port of Andratx which provides some satisfying walks. The top named on the map as the Penyal d'Enric has a long curving ridge and the trig point is on the 323m top at the west end. There are steep cliffs on the north side, breached by a good ledge path, the Pas de Vermell, which is the key to the way linking the two resorts on foot. There are excellent views of S'Esclop and Dragonera from the top. Two walks are described and other variations can be worked out.

66(a). SAN TELMO TO PORT ANDRATX BY THE PAS DE VERMELL AND ENRIC

Type of walk: mainly easy on good paths, but one steepish section near the top.

Starting point:	San Telmo
Time:	3hr 15min
Distance:	9km
Highest point reached:	323m
Total height climbed:	350m
Grade:	B
Map:	Andratx 1:50,000

From the sharp bend to the right where the road from Andratx meets the coast, walk back inland to the first turning to the right. Follow this new road south along the coast until it ends. Continue along a rough track which swings left and uphill to arrive at a flattish col. Do not turn right along the obvious broad track, but take the narrow path at right angles to it and marked by a stone arrow. Turn right at a cross-track into a narrow lane outside an enclosed field of carobs, almonds and figs. There are some colourful paint marks here. When the track begins to swing left ignore a narrow path on the right (which only leads to a

231

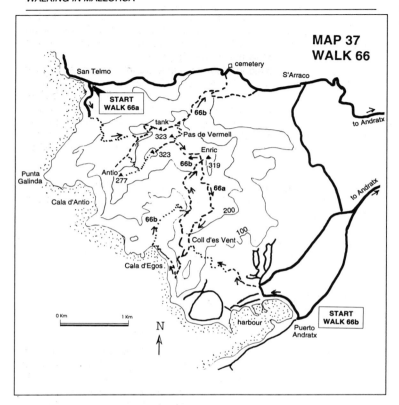

MAP 37
WALK 66

San Telmo

cemetery

S'Arraco

START WALK 66a

to Andratx

tank

66b

323

Pas de Vermell

323

Enric

66b

319

Antio

277

66a

Punta Galinda

200

Cala d'Antio

66b

100

Coll d'es Vent

Cala d'Egos

0 Km   1 Km

N

to Andratx

to Andratx

harbour

START WALK 66b

Puerto Andratx

terrace by a ruined house). Instead, stay on the main track which leads uphill and goes through a gate made of wooden branches and over a chain across the track.

About 15 minutes later there is a cross-track with stone arrows pointing left uphill. A big field house is passed on the left. After this the way is quite clear, joining another track and turning left to join yet another track, all now leading uphill and in the right direction. Keep along the main track which runs below the steep crags of the Enric ridge, ignoring branch paths. The track rises to a col on which is a water storage tank. As the track begins to descend, look out for a branch path right, near

232

two fire-blackened gateposts. Red and yellow paint marks show the way steeply uphill and lead to the attractive ledge path at the foot of the cliffs. Go through the breach to join the red earth path on the south side, turn right and follow this to the trig point.

To continue, return along this wide path and continue past the branch path from the Pas de Vermell. The way to Port Andratx is easy to follow. Stay on the good wide track which keeps to a high level before descending to the Coll d'es Vent. Follow the main track down the valley to reach a surfaced road with lampposts and a sign 'Prohibido buscar setas' (It is forbidden to pick mushrooms). When this road stops and joins a cart-track turn left to join the main road by the Carrer de Cala d'Egos. A right turn and then left lead into the port.

66(b). PORT ANDRATX TO S'ARRACO BY CALA D'EGOS

Cala d'Egos is a small attractive bay with no access by road so it is unspoilt and quiet.

Type of walk: Easy but fairly strenuous.

Starting point:	The marina in Port Andratx
Time	4hr
Distance:	10km
Highest point reached:	323m
Total height climbed:	490m
Grade:	B
Map:	Andratx 1:50,000

From the bus stop by the marina walk away from the port to the west and follow the main road as it bends sharp right. When it makes a second bend right in 200m turn left along the Carrer de Cala d'Egos. In about 3 minutes turn right on to a surfaced road at the end of which is a rough track. Five minutes later there is a chain across to stop cars. Follow the winding track up to the Coll des Vent, taking occasional short cuts on an older track on the left.

At the col descend towards the sea, turning left at the first junction. (The track to the right could be followed to give a longer but easier route.) Follow the track down left and then back right until it ends. A narrow path continues in the same direction to reach Cala d'Egos, getting steeper at the end. To continue the walk go up the wide track on the right (true left) of the stream-bed. This is crossed twice and then a series of big bends leads up to join the lower track coming from the

Coll d'es Vent. Turn left and about 15 minutes later turn left again on to an old track with various private notices. This goes up fairly steeply to reach the upper track from the Coll d'es Vent, just below the east top of Enric. Turn left and continue along to the end of this wide track to reach the trig point on the west top. Return along the wide track for about 5 minutes and turn left along the narrow footpath leading over the ridge to the ledge path, the Pas de Vermell. This slopes down easily below the cliffs and then zigzags down to a wide cross-track. At this point you could turn left to go down to San Telmo, which is Walk 66(a) in reverse, but for S'Arraco turn right and after about 20 minutes fork right on to a narrow surfaced road. (The left fork leads to the main road near the cemetery.) Turn left at a T-junction to join the main road, then right to reach the bus stop in S'Arraco.

This walk can also be used as a circular walk from Port Andratx to Enric, returning as in Walk 66(a).

67. DRAGONERA

The island of Sa Dragonera lies off the SW coast of Mallorca opposite the small resort of San Telmo (also known as Sant Elmo). The highest point at Na Popi is 360m and it is crowned with an abandoned lighthouse. There are two other lighthouses at the north and south of the island. On the west side vertical cliffs plunge straight down to the sea and are one of the sites where Eleanora's falcons can be observed giving superb flying displays as they prepare to head off to Madagascar for the winter. Dragonera was bought by the Consell Insular in 1988 in order to protect it from development; plans for a 'de luxe' urbanisation had been put forward in 1974. Approval for Natural Park status was given in 1995 and it is in the care of GOB, Spain's largest bird and conservation organisation.

The island is very arid and only a small area was ever cultivated, with a few olives, almonds, figs and other fruits. The vegetation is typically Mediterranean with lentisc, rosemary, *Erica multiflora*, pink and white cistus and wild olive. There are more than 20 endemic Balearic plants incuding *Limonium dragonericum*. Goats have been eliminated so all the plants are flourishing. Besides birds there is little wildlife except for the millions of tiny indigenous lizards known as *sarganta* in Mallorquin.

The island is reached by a regular ferry service from San Telmo, or from the Port of Andratx where the *Margarita* sets off at about 09.30

every day except Sunday, then plies back and forth from San Telmo to the island. A full day is recommended. (Note that the boat will not go out in bad weather conditions.)

Dragonera is a small island and can be fully explored in a day. There and back to the northern lighthouse takes about an hour and to the southern lighthouse 2hrs, in each case along a narrow lane with no traffic and encroached on both sides by flowering shrubs.

67(a). NA POPI

The walk up to the top, Na Popi, takes a little longer and 3hrs should be allowed. This route is up a good wide path built during the last century by prisoners during the construction of the lighthouse. This ceased to function in 1910, so the path is now beginning to deteriorate. Some care is required where the retaining walls have collapsed.

Starting point:	Cala Llado (boat landing)
Time:	3hr
Distance:	6km
Highest point:	360m
Total height:	360m
Grade:	C+
Map:	Andratx 1:50,000

For this route set off from the cross-track above the boat landing place by turning left towards the Far de Llebeig. After about 250m turn right where the main track bends left. The path heads almost north up a shallow valley, the Comellar des Coll Roig. After passing a stone building the route goes up terraces towards the col before turning south, then winds up to the top in two series of tight bends linked by a traverse.

67(b). DRAGONERA ISLAND SKYLINE

This is a classic mini-expedition which provides a most satisfying experience. The route traverses the ridge from one lighthouse to the other, following the crest of the sea-cliffs throughout. There is no path but a way can be found along the edge or near to it all the way. A good head for heights is a prerequisite as these cliffs are vertical. Wearing shorts should be avoided as it is often necessary to push through prickly vegetation. For maximum time ashore, choose the first and last ferry crossings.

Starting point:	Cala Llado (boat landing)
Time:	c.6hr

**MAP 38
WALK 67**

Cap de Tramuntana

Puig d'es Far
343

Cala Llado
(boat landing)

311
Puig des
Aucells

200

100

N

Cala Cuco

Far de Llebeig

Torre de Llebeig

0 Km   1 Km

Distance:	10km
Highest point reached:	360m
Total height climbed:	c.650m
Grade:	A+
Map:	Andratx 1:50,000

From the boat landing, take the signed gravel road to the lighthouse on the Cap de Tramuntana. Access to the cliff edge is easy through patches of thorny scrub. The route along the edge is obvious, but occasional detours inland must be made to get round gullies or avoid dense bushes. It is best to stop moving when you want to take in the stunning views.

On reaching the col at Es Coll Roig, follow the substantial wall. At the corner, where you will be able to join the normal path to Es Popi if you want to escape, the direct route picks a line up the hillside ahead, keeping to rock outcrops where possible. On reaching the final vertical rock headwall, traverse left for 70m across slabs, then ascend mixed ribs and grooves on easy rock to arrive at the path just below the summit. Beyond the summit buildings continue SW following the cliff edge over another top, the Puig des Aucells, and on to the lighthouse at the Cap de Llebeig. Allow a good hour for the walk back to the jetty along the gravel road.

It is possible to escape from the ridge down the south-east slopes almost anywhere, but be prepared to fight your way through gorse and thorny broom in places.

68. PUIG D'EN GARRAFA

Garrafa is a low hill to the east of Andratx. It consists of a long ridge running almost north-south and has several rocky tops known as *geps*. There are impressive cliffs on both sides but a path provides an easy walk along the ridge which is partly wooded. The top is clear of trees and is an excellent viewpoint, especially of S'Esclop and Galatzó.

Type of walk: The ascent is quite steep and the path very stony. Easy walking along a well-trodden path along the ridge is followed by an easy descent on a wide track.

Starting point:	Andratx
Time:	3hr 25min
Distance:	7km
Highest point reached:	462m
Total height climbed:	420m
Grade:	B
Map:	Andratx 1:50,000

If arriving in Andratx by car, park near the school and the bus station at the north-eastern side of the town. If by bus, ask for the *gasolinera*.

From the petrol station, walk back up the road towards Palma and in about 15 minutes turn left along the old road, reached just before the Coll Andritxol. In about 2 minutes turn left along a path to a locked gate which is easily bypassed on the right. Ignore the wide track running south and take the disused track left which leads into a narrow wooded valley, the Coma de Sa Teva. The track soon narrows and becomes steeper, but is marked with cairns and paint spots. In any case it is easy to follow as it more or less keeps to the centre of the valley floor. (After heavy rain it must also function as a stream-bed.)

The path arrives on a flat top to the south-west of the main summit. This top has a large cairn and a stone with a painted red arrow showing the way back down. Follow the narrow path left to reach the main top in about 15 minutes. There is a small shelter on the top near the trig point.

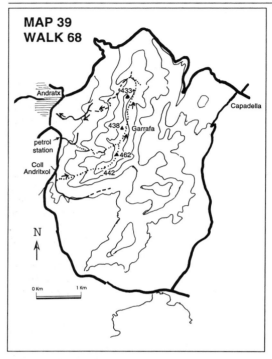

MAP 39
WALK 68

Andratx

Capadella

433

438 Garrafa

petrol
station

Coll
Andritxol

462

442

N

0 Km   1 Km

Continue along the path which first descends to an obvious col with a cairn indicating an alternative way up or down. (See note at end.) The main path then runs almost north along the ridge passing *geps* of 438m and 433m, largely unseen because of the trees. After about half an hour the path begins to descend the east side of the ridge, then swings back left (west) to go through a gap in a wall and arrive at a small grassy col between pine trees. From this point a cart track begins to descend a cultivated valley, the Coma de S'Ermita. The track used to go through two gates near a small field house, but has now been diverted along a narrow fenced path outside the enclosure. It is well marked by yellow paint signs. Shortly after the diversion the main track swings left.

At the bottom of the hill turn left at a cross-track. (In reverse, look out for a right turn by an olive tree with a white house on the right.) A little further another track comes in from the left. Follow the surfaced road into Andratx near a school by the Calle Juan Riera. Turn right into Carrer de Son More to reach the bus terminus.

Andratx - Coll Andritxol		15min
Coll Andritxol - south top	1hr	
South top - main top		15min
Main top - end of ridge		45min
End of ridge - Andratx	1hr	10min

Note: An alternative way up begins almost opposite the petrol station, through a wide gateway on to a track which goes right, skirting a field edge. When it makes a sharp bend to the left, a waymarked path leads up a gully and is easy to follow. A pleasant route, but sometimes the gate is locked.

69. PORTALS VELLS AND MORRO D'EN FELIU

Portals Vells is a quiet, attractive little bay with a small sandy beach protected by encircling rocks. The most remarkable feature is the series of caverns on the south where the stone used for building Palma Cathedral was quarried out of the rock. These are best appreciated from within; there is no difficulty. On a tiny peninsula below the quarry is a small square room cut out of the rock. It was used as a fort to protect the stone workers from attack by pirates.

Punto Catius is the southern tip of the Calvia peninsula and has an old watchtower on the edge of the cliffs, looking across a small bay to a lighthouse. Nearby is a military installation with four cannon making an interesting object of exploration, on the occasions when it is unoccupied. Machinery for raising shells up to the gun emplacements is still intact. But the best part of this walk is still to come, along the edge of the cliffs in the only truly unspoilt and undeveloped part of the Calvia coast, with views of the steep cliffs of Rafeubetx normally only seen from the sea.

The starting point is reached by bus from either the Palma direction or from Santa Ponsa direction. (If you have a car then parking by the stone sign at the Portals Vells junction is recommended, saving 5km. An advantage is that the track at the edge of the golf course, made obnoxious by rushing dumping, is thereby avoided.)

Type of walk: Easy, along dirt tracks, metalled roads and a marked path. The path requires care and a bit of clambering in one place at Cala Figuera.

Starting point:	Son Ferrer
Time:	5hr (or 3hr 45min)

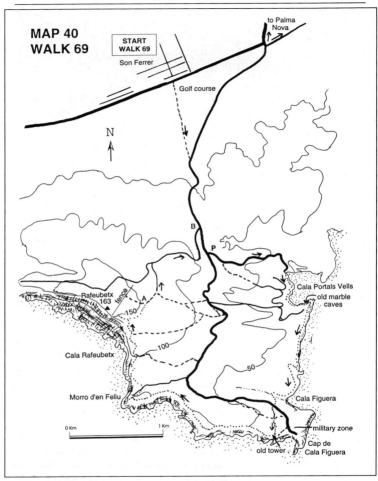

MAP 40
WALK 69

START
WALK 69

Son Ferrer

to Palma Nova

Golf course

N

B

P

Rafeubetx
163

fence

A

150

100

50

Cala Portals Vells

old marble caves

Cala Rafeubetx

Cala Figuera

Morro d'en Feliu

military zone

0 Km   1 Km

old tower

Cap de
Cala Figuera

Distance:	19km
Total height climbed:	About 200m
Grade:	C+
Map:	Illa del Toro y Cap de Cala
240	Figuera 1:25,000

Carved rock in marble quarry, Portals Vells

From Son Ferrer take the rough track running towards the wooded hill by the edge of the golf course. When the metalled road is reached follow it to the right, looking out for a short cut aross the bends. Turn left at the large stone sign for Portals Vells, and walk down the wide road on to a promontory where some ruins on the left are the remains of a film set used for filming *The Magus* in the 1960s. Turn right and walk down to the small beach where there is a bar. Go past this and continue round the coast past some wind-sculpted rocks to another small bay, and continue round this on the narrow path to the quarries. After visiting the caverns return along the path towards the beach, and look for a way to scramble easily up to the cliff top. Here will be found a path running south to along the cliff top, marked by yellow paint signs. This leads first to a small headland with a deep inlet on the right, Cala en Beltran. The small path bypassing this may not be noticed at first, but will be found on returning from the headland if you overshoot. This delightful path now leads south again to arrive at Cala Figuera. Here, although the descent appears a little difficult, yellow spots show an easy way along rock ledges down to the head of the cove where there are a few small boats.

241

The caves noticed in the cliff opposite are said to have been inhabited 2,000 years ago. Cross the narrow shingle beach and yellow marks will be found showing a path up the cliffs, with steps cut out of the rock in places. Turn left along the lighthouse road at the cliff top, which leads past the military establishment, and follow the track on to the old tower on the cliff top. When the military are in occupation, there is a guard on the gate and another way must be used. This is a rough path beginning some 20m from the old fence and leading through shrubs and old walls in a confusing way to arrive at the old watch-tower outside the fenced area.

To continue the walk set off in a westerly direction along the edge of the cliffs. Easy walking places can be found, occasionally turning inland a little to avoid dense clusters of pines growing right up to the edge. At the Punta des Captius the direction becomes north-west and then curves around the next bay to reach a headland, the Morro d'en Feliu, a superb viewpoint. On the way here, a wide track is picked up and followed for a while. To continue, head along a track north-east at first, then pick up a branch path at first north-west and then north, gradually rising towards Rafeubetx. It is not possible to reach the top itself, which is in a military zone and is fenced off. If you come to the fence it can be followed to the right to meet a good track which is followed to the right, or you can branch off right before this to come to the same point, shown as point A on the sketch map. Keep on this in a northerly direction to a T-junction and turn right to join the lighthouse road at B, if you are walking back to Son Ferrer. If you are returning to a car you can take a short cut across to the parking area as this road swings north.

70. PUIG D'EN SARAGOSSA

This low hill in the south-west of the island is a natural garden of flowering shrubs. In February there are brilliant yellow splashes of thorny broom and the air is fragrant with dense spikes of lavender. An outstanding viewpoint, with the peaks of S'Esclop and Galatzó to the north and the sea nearly all round. It is best to shut one's eyes to the unsightly resorts along the coast and it provides a pleasant half day out for anyone finding themselves in this area. On the top is a bunker dating from the Civil War and also remains of earlier fortifications. The second top overlooks the Coll de Batalla where a historic battle took place in 1229, when the Moors were defeated by Jaime I of Aragon.

Type of walk: easy up to the first top, then a rough intermittent path to the second summit.

Starting point:	Sa Porassa, Bar Ca'n Miguel
Time:	2hr 45min
Distance:	6km
Highest point reached:	187m
Total height climbed:	216m
Grade:	B
Map:	Calvià 1:25,000

From the bus stop in Sa Porassa walk north along the road for 1km until opposite the wide road from Magalluf. (Cars can be parked here, or this point can easily be reached on foot from Palma Nova or Magalluf across the open ground by the cricket club.)

Go through the metal gate exactly opposite the Magalluf road. Leave this gate as found; when closed a notice reads 'no passing' but normally applies to cars. (If the landowner happens to come by it is advisable to request permission and point to your destination at the top!). In any case avoid turning left on the track which leads to the farm and keep

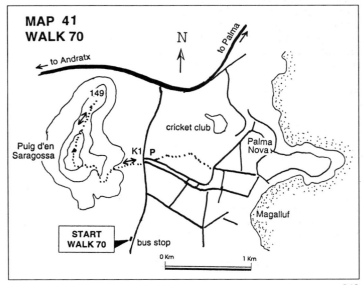

MAP 41
WALK 70

to Andratx

to Palma

N

149

cricket club

Puig d'en Saragossa

K1 P

Palma Nova

Magalluf

START WALK 70

bus stop

0 Km   1 Km

straight ahead. In a few minutes a curious building is seen on the right, probably an old limekiln converted to a weekend retreat. Continue up the track which becomes somewhat steeper then rises more gradually through a profusion of flowering shrubs. There is no mistaking the way to the main top. To reach the second top follow the faint yellow paint marks along the ridge, down to a saddle and then up again to the final top of 149m on which is a ruined *talaiot* (tower). There is no path and a good deal of thorny vegetation, so if this does not appeal you can spend longer on the top.

Return the same way. A slight variation can be made by taking a branch path left within a couple of minutes of leaving the main top. This goes down to a semi-ruinous building which probably dates from the same time as the gun emplacements on the top. A path continues below to rejoin the main track.

71. MIRADOR DE N'ALZAMORA FROM VALLDURGENT

This *mirador* lies on the end of a ridge curving round from the Coll d'es Pastors and the Puig d'en Bou; it is not as shown on the new 1:25,000 map but about 800m further south. From the terrace outside the stone shelter there are panoramic views across the cultivated Calvià valley to S'Esclop and Galatzó. Although so near Palma the area is very quiet and peaceful, but it is an area popular with hunters. Among the luxuriant vegetation there is an abundance of *Arbutus unedo*, the strawberry tree.

Type of walk: Easy, at first on roads and tracks, then a good path.

Starting point:	K7 on Calvià-Establiments road
Time:	3hr 20min
Distance:	10km
Highest point reached:	c.430m
Total height climbed:	c.200m
Grade:	C
Map:	Calvià 1:25,000

From the bend at K7 two roads lead off to the south. Take the left-hand one (the other road leads to the large *finca* of Valldurgent). After 2km of steady uphill walking leave the road by a wide track beginning at a U-bend and well indicated by painted arrows. This track sweeps round the head of the valley, rising very slightly to reach a large clearing after another track has joined it from the left. A few minutes later go straight on at another cross-track. The track now narrows and begins to descend towards a stream-bed. After climbing up again on the other side of the stream it continues to rise to meet a cross-path marked by a cairn on the ridge. Turn right and 10m further on notice another cairn marking another path on the left. (Take note of this point in anticipation of your return.) The *mirador* is reached in less than 10 minutes' walking from here.

For an easy walk, return by the same way.

Alternative return by the Puig d'en Bou

The Puig d'en Bou at 503m makes an alternative way back which is a bit more strenuous and somewhat rougher walking. In this case, start walking back along the ridge and take the second path on the right.

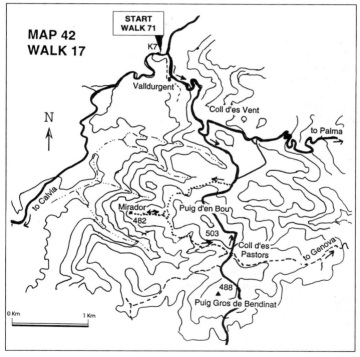

The top of the Puig d'en Bou is almost due east from here, so leave the path and make for it, picking the best line through the scrub and trees. From the top find a convenient way down to join the broad track a little over 100m to the east. Turn left and follow this track until you join the route of ascent.

A third way back is to keep on the above path and follow it to the Coll d'es Pastors which it reaches after descending into a gully and up again. (It becomes very indefinite until after the gully.) Turn left to reach the col and left again at a major cross-track. This contours along the side of the Puig d'en Bou and is followed to join the route of ascent. Another option is to include the ascent of Bendinat from the track leading to the Coll d'es Pastors.

K7 - Mirador	1hr	40min
Mirador - K7	1hr	40min
Mirador - K7 (by Puig d'en Bou)	2hr	
Mirador - K7 (by Coll d'es Pastors)	2hr	

72. BURGUESA RIDGE

Although close to Palma and many resorts along the south coast, the Serra de Na Burguesa is not well known. This low range of hills is a world away from the crowded coastal scene and some quiet and pleasant walks can be found. Although devastated by forest fires in recent years, the flowering shrubs have quickly recovered and new trees have been planted. Since these serious fires, access tracks have been cleared and a new fire tower built on the Pi de Ses Creus. Important archaeological discoveries have been made in hidden caves in these hills. Although crossed by some wide and easy tracks there are deep, steep-sided valleys filled with almost impenetrable scrub and a chaos of rocks. This walk makes use of a major track running along the ridge from the conspicuous statue of Na Burguesa on the Puig Caragol to the television and radio masts on the Pi de Ses Creus in the west. To reach the start, take the No.4 bus to Genova from the Plaza de la Raina or the Plaza del Port in Palma.

Variations of this walk can easily be found, for example there are two ways on to the ridge from Costa d'en Blanes or Portals Nous.

Type of walk: Very easy, except that the descent path is a little rough and stony in places.

Starting point:	Crossroads in Genova
Time:	4hr 15min

Distance:	12km
Highest point reached:	450m
Total height climbed:	470m
Grade:	C
Map:	Calvià 1:25,000

From the crossroads at the edge of the village take the uphill road signposted to Na Burguesa and then the first road to the right. This surfaced road leads quite steeply uphill to the conspicuous statue where there is a restaurant. Shortly before arriving at the road end take a track to the left and then a path on the right which leads up on to the ridge between fences, passing several masts. The track then follows the crest of the ridge at first and then keeps on the north side, rising gently and then contouring to the Coll d'es Pastors. Turn sharp left here and in a couple of minutes the track from the Mirador de N'Alzamora comes in on the right. About 200m further on turn right. (The track straight on continues over a low col and then descends to Bendinat. A diversion could be made to the top of the 488m top of the Puig Gros de Bendinat from the col.)

The track we are following descends to the Coll de Bendinat in about 1km. From this point it makes a wide sweep around to the south side of an unnamed hill, making a left bend opposite a disused path on the right. Turn right after about 100m and keep on the main track, which now runs west, for about 600m. After swinging south the track turns west again and passes an old shelter, often spolit by abandoned litter. Five minutes later the junction with the Costa d'en Blanes track is met: there is a yellow paint sign 'Pi', short for the Pi de Ses Creus, pointing to the right. Follow this track towards the radio masts, but look out for the path junction on the left, marked by a paint sign on a pine tree and some cairns. This is about 800m from the last junction and after passing the fire tower.

This narrow path goes steadily downhill, dropping into the valley on the right, then back left and down a broad ridge to an old shelter on a flat area. The path turns left here and zigzags down into a stream-bed. Another track joins it and the main track contours along below a steep crag to reach a ruined building with several water tanks. Just below this ruin there is a cross-track with a large cairn in the middle. Ahead is a conspicuous pylon. Turn left and continue downhill to join a narrow surfaced road by an old building. Turn right and go under the motorway, then turn right at the old main road to reach the bus stops at Son Caliu.

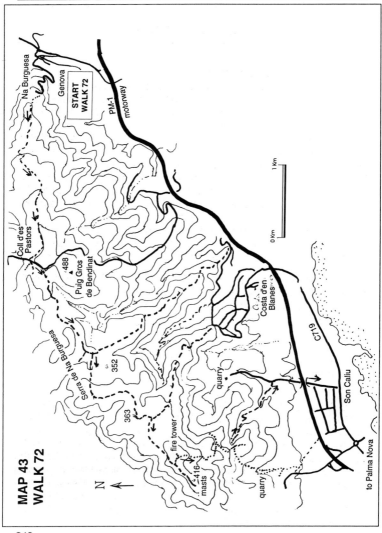

MAP 43
WALK 72

N ←

Na Burguesa

Genova

START
WALK 72

PM-1 motorway

Coll d'es Pastors

488
Puig Gros de Bendinat

Serra de Na Burguesa

352

363

fire tower

416
masts

quarry

Costa d'en Blanes

C719

quarry

Son Caliu

to Palma Nova

1 Km

0 Km

Outlying Areas

73. TALAIA DE SON JAUMELL

The old tower of Son Jaumell is on a superb viewpoint at 271m, on a headland between two bays of pure white sand, Cala Agulla (aka Cala Guia) and Sa Mesquida. The area is a protected SSSI with attractive pinewoods and dunes, in autumn carpeted with meadow saffron. Although the tower is ruinous the near views of the coast and the distant views which extend to Formentor make it a fine excursion. The jewel-like colours of the sea on a sparkling winter day, jade and turquoise, have to be seen to be believed. The beach at Cala Agulla is a perfect swimming place on a hot day, but likely to be crowded in summer. For a shorter easier walk, going over the Coll de Marina to Cala Mesquida and back, takes about one hour each way.

To reach the starting point drive through Artà and Cala Ratjada, then follow signs to Cala Agulla which is on the north side of the Capdepera peninsula. There is a pay parking area at the road end.

Type of walk: Mainly easy tracks and well-marked mountain paths, but the last pull up on to the ridge is quite steep.

Starting point:	Cala Agulla
Time:	2hr 50min
Distance:	8km
Highest point reached:	271m
Total height climbed:	356m
Grade:	B
Map:	Artà 1:25,000

From the car park walk through the woods to the north end of the beach where there is a white building on the neck of a narrow rocky peninsula, Es Guyo. Turn left here and in 2 minutes go through a gateway. Three minutes later take a left fork, where purple paint spots mark the route. After about 10 minutes ignore a right turn near a limekiln which is the return route. The wide track continues over the Coll de Marina, passing a ruin and another limekiln. On the descent towards Mesquida turn right at a T and almost immediately fork left. Ignore the next fork left and continue on the right-hand side of the wall to a gap, where the path turns left and descends to the beach.

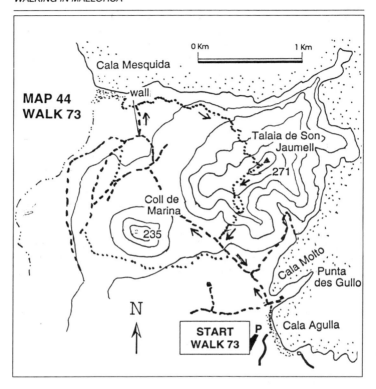

To continue, return to this point where several paths and animal tracks lead away from the wall. Look for the one liberally splashed with blue paint, at first roughly parallel to the coast. After passing some scattered trees the path turns inland, rising towards the ridge on the right hand side of a shallow gully. The tower is clearly visible all the way. Near the top the path veers left into the gully where it becomes rather steep but is not difficult. When the ridge is reached the tower is about 100m away to the left. (Note that if reversing this route this point is not clearly marked.)

From the tower follow the path back along the ridge and continue past the point of ascent. At the end of the ridge there are two main variants, both of which are quite easy to follow. They meet lower down and then rejoin the main track to the Coll de Marina by the prominent limekiln. For anyone going up this way this path is clearly marked with signs hanging in the trees. Follow the outward route back to the start.

Cala Agulla - Cala Mesquida   1hr
Cala Mesquida - tower   55min
Tower - Cala Agulla   55min

74. TORRE DE AUBARCA

This is one of the best coastal walks on the island with views of the colourful sea all the way. The old watch-tower on the cliffs is in a fine state of preservation and there is even a spiral staircase, a little precarious, leading to the large circular viewing platform on top, on which is an old cannon. The walk continues on to Sa Font Celada, a small sandy bay between rocky points where the sea is a pale turquoise; in winter this can be enjoyed in solitude.

The walk begins at Cala Estreta which is reached by turning left at the junction signposted to Cala Torta, just outside Artà on the road to Cala Ratjada. Pass the football ground and turn right. The road is badly potholed for most of the 10km to Cala Estreta. Park where the road bends right at the bottom of the hill.

Type of walk: Moderately easy on coastal paths, but a little rough in places.

Starting point: Cala Estreta
Time: 3hr
Distance: 9km
Highest point reached: 74m
Total height climbed: 250m
Grade: C+
Map: Cap Ferrutx 1:25,000

Cross the stream-bed and pick up the narrow fisherman's path heading round the coast. This goes through a gate on a headland and then crosses the inlet of Cala Dentol. Further on there is a fine overlook of Cala Matzoc from the headland Na Brotada. Follow the path down to the beach and across to the other side where a continuing path leads up the rocky ridge to the tower. To continue, follow the track SW from the tower and after about 350m look for a cairn among the trees which shows the start of a path which descends almost to the sea and then

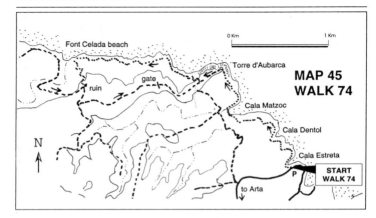

rises again to the next headland. On this headland the path goes through a gate in the fence and then continues along a rocky path to the Font Celada beach.

Although it is probably more rewarding in terms of scenery to return the same way, the first part to the tower can be varied by an inland route. From the western side of the beach follow the track inland, swinging sharp left and rising to reach a ruin at a sharp bend right. (Or you can take a short cut to this point from the east side of the beach.) Five minutes later turn sharp left at a cross-track and follow this to the east. Last time the author was here, this track had been ploughed up in places so its future status is uncertain. After about 1km a locked gate can be circumvented on the right. Either keep on the main track to the tower and retrace your steps from there, which is the most attractive alternative, or take a right turn down through the woods to Cala Matzoc and pick up the outward route at that point.

Cala Estreta - Torre	50min
Torre - Font Celada beach	45min
Font Celada beach - Cala Matzoc	50min
Cala Matzoc - Cala Estreta	35min

75. BEC DE FERRUTX AND THE ERMITA DE BETLEM

The mountains of Artà are the highest of the Serra de Levant, the discontinuous chain of mountains bounding the central plain of Mallorca on the east. Although only of the order of 500m they have many of the characteristics of the higher Serra de Tramuntana and are certainly wild and unfrequented. The Bec de Ferrutx is not the highest of these hills, Morey being 561m, but it is certainly the most spectacular. The mountain tops are all very stony and arid with a garigue type vegetation; many asphodels, flat-topped thistles, sparse clumps of carritx and some dwarf fan palms. There are wide and dramatic views across the bay of Alcudia to the Sierra de Tramuntana from this walk.

The walk can easily be split into two shorter walks if required. From Betlem to the Ermita and return is short and easy. Allow three hours including Sa Coassa. There is a narrow but adequate driveable road from Artà to the Ermita, (best avoided at weekends) enabling those who think the full walk too strenuous to walk to Ferrutx and back from there. The way through the narrow streets of Artà is now reasonably well signposted.

Type of walk: Not strenuous, and no route-finding difficulties. Mainly tracks and paths and all fairly easy walking. There is some pathless ground, but it is open and not too stony.

Starting point:	Betlem
Time:	5hr 20min
Distance:	12km
Highest point reached:	522m
Total height climbed:	c.580m
Grade:	B
Map:	Artà 1:50,000 or Colonia de Sant Pere 1:25,000 and Artà 1:25,000

To reach the start of the walk, drive towards Artà on the C712 and turn left at K7.8 towards Colonia de Sant Pere (San Pedro). The best way to identify the start is to continue past San Pedro to the roundabout at the beginning of Betlem and then return the same way for 300m. The path begins by a cross-track on the left and is marked by a cairn. There is a very deep oval well surrounded by a high stone wall quite near the beginning. The track veers right at some old farm buildings and some yellow paint marks show the way. About 15 minutes after passing the farm the path turns uphill by some carob trees on terraces, then goes through a wall and levels out as it enters a deep-cut valley. Follow the well-marked path up this wild valley, devastated higher up by forest fires. (In September 1990 we had to retreat from this walk when we could see a fierce fire raging up near the *ermita* and charred and burning

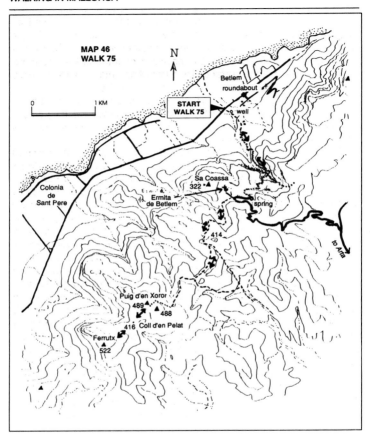

MAP 46
WALK 75

N

0   1 KM

Betlem
roundabout

**START
WALK 75**

well

Colonia
de
Sant Pere

Sa Coassa
322 ▲

Ermita
de Betlem

spring

414

to Artà

Puig d'en Xoror
489 ▲   ▲ 488

416 Coll d'en Pelat

Ferrutx
522

vegetation began to rain round us. A continuous stream of flying boats were dousing the fires with water, but seemed to be having little effect.)

The path rises at a moderate gradient, zigzagging up to the left of a steep headwall to reach a wide upper valley. After going through gaps in two walls, the path continues up towards a field shelter made out of a boulder. Before reaching this, it crosses the stream to join a wide cart track and rises towards the *ermita*. When a double stone gateway is seen, do not go through it but follow the track left to reach a spring. There is a shrine and a picnic table by the clear water of the *fuente* which is roofed over and provided with a chained iron ladle. Follow the track from here to the gates of the *ermita*, 5 minutes or less from the spring. It is here that the surfaced road from Artà ends and where there is some parking space for those starting the walk here.

Those making the short walk will have plenty of time to visit the chapel and to go up to the hill behind it, Sa Coassa (322m), where there are panoramic views of land and sea. There is an old semi-roofless building offering some shelter here.

To continue the main walk take the track beginning at the gates of the *ermita*. This leads west then south into a shallow valley, crossing a stream-bed then swinging back right to a shoulder. The old track descends into another valley and becomes a wide, bulldozed one which is now mellowed and easily followed. About 40 minutes from the *ermita* a wire meshed fence across the track can be lowered at the right-hand side and easily stepped over by those on foot. When a T-junction is met, turn right and follow the track through a gently-sloping upper valley with many heaps of stones. Continue until the track ends near the south-east extremity of Xoroi. Ahead is a fence. The easiest way to cross this barrier is to turn right at the track end and follow a level path along a sloping ledge between two rocky escarpments. The low fence can be stepped over, or bypassed at the point where it drops sharply downwards a little way to the right. Walk along the ledge to the far end and then go up towards a large overhanging rock. This is easily passed on either side. Continue over the Xoroi ridge and down (south-west) to the Coll d'en Pelat, on the far side of which is a conspicuous and solitary pine tree. Continue in the same direction to the trig point on the top of Ferrutx. There is no path but the walking is easy on stony ground between clumps of *carritx*. To fully appreciate this spectacular mountain continue along to the end of the north-west ridge which is the true mountain top.

Betlem - Ermita	1hr	
Ermita - Xoroi	1hr	10min
Xoroi - Ferrutx		40min
Ferrutx - Ermita	1hr	45min
Ermita - Betlem		45min

76. MOREY

At 561m Morey is the highest point on the Artà peninsula. On a good day the views are outstanding and it is almost like being on a island with sea to the west, north and east. Although not high it is the culminating point of a long escarpment of imposing cliffs on which are some good scrambling routes. The hinterland is rough and stony ground scattered with ruined buildings and tumbled terraced walls, evidence

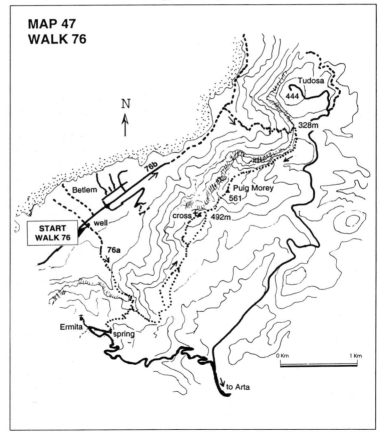

**MAP 47
WALK 76**

N

Tudosa
444

328m

76b

Betlem

Puig Morey
561

well

cross 492m

**START
WALK 76**

76a

Ermita

spring

0 Km   1 Km

to Arta

of cultivation in times gone by. To reach the start drive along the road towards Betlem on the Artà peninsula and park 300m south of the roundabout by the Pobla de Pescadors.

76(a). A LINEAR WALK TO THE TOP AND BACK

Type of walk: Mainly pathless and rough on stony ground or overgrown paths, but no real difficulties.

Starting point:	Pobla de Pescadors
Time:	4hr 30min
Distance:	9km
Highest point reached:	561m
Total height climbed:	566m
Grade:	B+
Map:	Artà 1:25,000 and Cap Ferrutx 1:25,000

Start up the track used in the approach to the Ermita de Betlem as in Walk 75. After going through the gaps in two walls continue up the main path until just before it turns right and crosses the stream-bed to go up to the *ermita*. At this point an old path rises up a kind of ridge on the right-hand side of a side valley, crossing the highest point, which is an old stone wall. Although much overgrown with long grasses, the path can be followed to reach a ruined stile at the right-hand side of this wall. A landmark on the way is an isolated plane tree, conspicuous among the scattered pines in this otherwise treeless valley.

From the stile the path rises across the valley head between walls and in 5 minutes goes through a broken gate. Turn right at the gate towards a prominent ruined building, then veer left towards another ruin. Continue in the same direction past this to arrive in a few minutes at the fenced escarpment edge. Follow this edge to the right to the lower top of Morey (492m) on which is a prominent cross with a summit book in a metal case.

Descend to the 447m col (about 10 minutes), traverse round the right-hand side of a large pinnacle and then ascend to reach the escarpment edge again. Continue up quite steep but easy ground to reach the trig point on the main top.

To return, go back the same way to the 447m col, then continue towards the escarpment edge, bypassing the top with the cross. A line of cairns can be picked up and these can be followed back directly to join the route of ascent just below the prominent ruin, or the same line followed back to the broken gate.

76(b). A CIRCULAR ROUTE

Type of walk: Tricky route-finding and some easy scrambling make this a route for the adventurous.

Starting point:	As for Walk 76(a)
Time:	5hr
Distance	10km
Highest point reached:	561m
Total height climbed:	605m
Grade:	A+
Map:	Artà 1:25,000 and Cap Ferrutx 1:25,000

Walk along the road straight through Betlem and when the surfaced road ends continue along the rough track which leads to Es Calo. After about 1km turn right along a wide track towards a ruined building and go past this to the end of the track. At this point there is not much of a path, but keep going upwards by the best way you can find to reach the base of the layered cliff at the head of the valley. There is no mistaking this point as on either side there are steep and broken cliffs seamed by gullies, some of which can be climbed but are loose and not recommended. In contrast, the layers of this headwall, which average about 1m thick or less, are easy to surmount by following various ledges between the layers, the way often marked by cairns. At the top is a 328m col between the Puig de sa Tudosa, crowned with masts on the north side, and our objective, Puig Morey, to the south-west. Turn right and follow the escarpment edge to the top. The descent is by the same way as in Walk 76(a). Those who have already made the ascent by this route will find it much easier than those who have not!

77. RANDA

This flat-topped hill in the centre of the Mallorcan plain is known as the Holy Mountain. It has three sanctuaries, the oldest of which, the monastery of Nuestra Señora de Cura, was founded in 1275. The great Mallorcan scholar Ramon Llull lived there for about ten years while writing the first of more than 250 books in Catalan. The library still holds collections of old music books, missals and medieval manuscripts. Cura is right at the top of the hill and the church is open at all times. The museum is opened to visitors who must attract attention by pulling on a bell at the hours of 10.00, 11.00, 12.00, 13.00, 16.00, 17.00 or 18.00. A bar-restaurant is open throughout the year but is closed on Mondays. From the large terraces there are panoramic views. It is said that 32

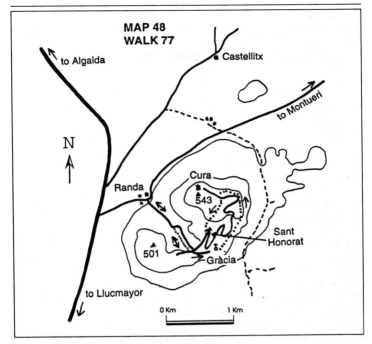

**MAP 48
WALK 77**

to Algaida

Castellitx

to Montueri

N

Randa

Cura
▲543

Sant
Honorat

▲501

Gràcia

to Llucmayor

0 Km   1 Km

towns and villages can be seen on a clear day. Sant Honorat is another monastery with an attached church, 1.5km below the top. The third monastery, the fifteenth century Gràcia, is built under an impressive overhanging rock on the west side.

Although there is a drivable road to the top, the easy walk from Randa village, following the road but taking advantage of a number of obvious short cuts, makes a pleasant half day. The walk described here is a variation, which is more of a challenge, using a rough path which follows the base of the crags for a considerable distance. There are a number of shallow caves, but a close inspection is not advised as the rock here is very loose.

Randa village is reached from either Algaida, Montueri or Llucmayor. Park in the reasonably wide street entering the village, after passing a bar.

Path below cliffs of Randa

Type of walk: Easy, except for the section from Gràcia to the top at the north end, which is by a rough path not always easy to follow. The start of this path is also quite steep and loose, although it improves and levels out further on.

Starting point:	Randa village
Time:	2hr 45min
Distance:	7km
Highest point reached:	543m
Total height climbed	250m
Grade:	B
Map:	Porreras 1:50,000

Take the signposted road towards Cura. Go through a metal gate at a hairpin bend and follow the path until it rejoins the road near the entrance gate of Gràcia. Follow the road in front of Gràcia to the end of the terrace. Go through the gap in the wall and up the steep scree path. This bit is soon over and a comparatively good path is found among some colourful shrubs including lavender, pink-flowered cistus and yellow euphorbias. The path has some ups and downs but is mainly contouring. At times it seems to disappear, but can always be found again with the aid of occasional painted arrows and cairns. Eventually the path turns east, still below the crags, but now rises onto the grassy summit plateau and joins another path which comes up from the Albenya-Randa road.

Follow this path southwards and then turn right along the surfaced road to reach the large group of buildings at the top. To return, follow the road and whatever short cuts appear worthwhile on the way back down to Randa.

Randa - Gràcia	30min
Gràcia - Cura	1hr 15min
Cura - Randa	1hr

Appendixes

APPENDIX 1: A High Level Walk from Valldemossa to Pollensa

Every year Mallorquin walkers organise a very tough three-day walk from Andratx to Pollensa. This is usually only attempted by the very young and the superfit, and still very few actually complete the rather gruelling course. The following walk from Valldemossa to Pollensa has been devised for those who indulge in walking for pleasure rather than regarding it as a challenge. Even so it is quite a strenuous undertaking requiring skills in route-finding and some easy scrambling.

This walk takes in several mountains over 1,000m. It can be done in three days with overnight stops at Soller and Lluc, but the section from Soller to Lluc is very long. If preferred, it could be done in two stages by providing for an overnight bivvy at the attractive spring, the Font d'es Prat.

The route only touches surfaced roads for very short distances at Soller, Cuber and Lluc. Otherwise it takes the walker through wild country, reaches the tops of Teix, Sa Galera, L'Ofre, Sa Rateta, Massanella and Tomir and enjoys some spectacular scenery. In part it follows an ancient track once used by pilgrims travelling on foot to the monastery of Lluc from Soller.

Day 1

The walk begins in Valldemossa, easily reached by bus from Palma. Leave the village by Son Gual and head up the Cairats valley to the Font des Poll. Opposite this a signpost labelled Serra des Cairats points the way up a wide path which soon doubles back, rising through woodland and eventually up to Teix (1,062m) by the SW ridge. There is a short, easy descent to the little plain known as the Pla de Sa Serp, where there is a freshwater spring. The route now rises slightly over the Puig d'es Vent at 1,004m and follows the crest of the ridge along bare rock with superb views over to the Puig Mayor and the peaks that will be followed on the next stage of the trek. This ridge runs north-east, and before it rises to a final top a right-angled left turn is made to Sa Galera.

The descent to Soller begins by going down to the col between Sa Galera and the Puig des Morro. From here route-finding is fairly complex. Go down the centre of the valley floor to reach a *sitja* (an old charcoal hearth) and a ruined building. An overgrown track leads out to the right and down the right-hand side of the valley. A cairn at the end of an uphill section shows where to leave this track and turn left. After passing a branch back up the valley and another one leading down, the path seems to end at a brushwood fence. This is easily stepped over and the way found down to another little path which leads in zigzags to a small enclosure. After going over a stile of branches the path descends to a marker post where we turn right. The path soon improves, going through a gate with a stile leading below the cliffs and down to some cave houses built under them.

Now a drivable road, the route winds through terraces. Go through a gate by a water tank at a T turn right, then after about 100m go left through a gate into a wood. When an old stepped path is joined turn left. Cross the railway twice, then join a tarmac road and turn right then left to reach Soller by the petrol station. The centre of the town is about 10 minutes away. The Hotel Guia next to the station is recommended if it is open.

Day 2a

Next day walk along to the village of Biniaraix. By the washplace at the end of the village there is a signpost showing the way to the beautiful walk up the *barranc,* the gorge which falls from the tiny upland hamlet of the Cases de L'Ofre. The cobbled and stepped path winds enchantingly up through terraces of olive trees into the ever-narrowing valley below the towering cliffs of Cornadors.

Before reaching the Cases de L'Ofre there is a path diversion on the left, clearly signposted. Follow this track up to the Coll de L'Ofre, and just before the col take the track right which contours round to the south side of L'Ofre. Shortly after going through a gap in a wall red waymarks show the route up to the top of L'Ofre.

From the top there is a delightful walk along the ridge and over the Puig Franquesa to Sa Rateta. To the left there are views over the Cuber Reservoir to Puig Major and to the right across the Comasema valley to the striking sugarloaf peaks of S'Alcadena and Alaró. From the top of Sa Rateta the way down to the Cuber dam is roughly north-east (steep crags prevent any wandering astray): a cairn shows the entrance to a hidden valley with a cairned path leading downwards. Lower down cairns show the place to strike left, crossing a gully and then going through a fence to easier ground.

From the dam walk to the main road and turn right. Continue for about 150m then leave the road to follow a large open *canaleta* for about 2km. At this point a path coming up from Almalutx is met. This crosses over the open channel by a bridge. The path now leads over the Coll des Coloms and on to the Font des Prat. The delicious freshwater here is under a stone roof and protected by an iron railing and door. (Possible bivouac site.) An alternative possibility is to follow the path round to the Tossals Verds hut, fully equipped and offering accommodation and meals for walkers, with places for 30.

Day 2b

From the spring a waymarked path leads up an attractive and uninhabited valley, the Comellar des Prat, right up to the Coll des Prat and down over the other side to Comafreda. This way is the way of the pilgrims and quite pleasant and easy to follow.

However, the ascent of Massanella is one of the highlights of this walk and should not be missed. Before the col is reached there is a big red M for Massanella painted on a boulder. This shows the way up to the col between Massanella and the Puig de Ses Bassetes. There isn't exactly a path, but several painted waymarks show the general direction. To reach the col itself it is necessary to scramble up a little rock wall several metres high. There is nothing difficult about it but it does involve trusting one's boots on sloping holds with nothing much for the hands until, after a couple of steps up, a good jug can be gripped with the right hand. Once this little rock scramble is negotiated there is nothing as difficult on the rest of the route.

Make a rising traverse across scree to the foot of a rocky spur and go up this until a way can be found leading back left to the ridge. There are some cairns but they are hard to see in the rocky wilderness so it is best to rely on your own judgement to pick out the best way. Once on the ridge it is easy walking along to the top of Massanella.

There are two ways of descent which will no doubt be familiar to those who have been to Mallorca previously. For newcomers it is probably easiest to follow the waymarked path down from the top to the sloping plateau below the summit. When the engraved stone is reached follow the path south, rather than go down to the spring, the Font de S'Avenc. Either way, the route is very well marked down to the Coll de S'Arbona. Turn left on the col and after about 15 minutes of descent look out for paint marks, recently renewed, showing a short cut down through the woods to Comafreda. The farm track leads down to a gate onto the road near the petrol station.

From the Coll de Batalla go down a minor road to the monastery of Lluc. There are rooms to be had very reasonably, and a restaurant serving evening meals from 20.00hrs. There are also self-catering facilities. If the weather is cold ask for a room *con calefaccion* (with heating).

Day 3

To begin the last stage of the walk go out of the main gate and turn left, then left again, then first right into the football ground. Go through the fence and follow the track until it joins the main road. After turning left for 150m along the main road turn right along the minor road leading to the Binifaldo bottling plant. (It is worth mentioning that an easier option for the last day is to follow the old road from Binifaldo as in Walk 24.)

The route up Tomir starts between the gate to the plant and the forest fence. The way is well marked and easy to follow. On reaching the summit ridge a left turn is made to reach the summit. Go down towards the col between Tomir and the Puig des Ca. This passes the remains of a large snow-pit. Follow the track south along the broad col and, after going through a boundary wall, turn left into a shallow gully. There is an easy way up the little crag at the top by means of a sloping ledge. From the west top double back, then go over the main top and on down the ridge towards the Coll de Miner. It is necessary to come down on the north side of the wall which crosses this col, as there is a high locked gate in it. In this area too, it is as well to keep a low profile as walkers are not too welcome.

Avoid following the new track to Fartaritx del Raco and, where it bends left, cut over the hill to pick up the track that contours along the high cultivated plateau of Fartaritx. When the enclosing wall of Fartaritx Gran is reached, look for the way down to the left shortly after crossing a stream. A delightful mule track winds down through a wild garden of flowering shrubs and arrives in the Vall den Marc by a house known as Ca'n Huguet.

Now follow the track alongside the stream. Shortly after it turns left and crosses the stream, turn right along a rather overgrown footpath leading to Pollensa. The stream must be crossed again and as the footbridge has collapsed long ago, it may have to be paddled. Most often the stream-bed is dry, but on rare occasions there is a raging torrent and in this case recourse must be had to going round by the main road. In the town, follow the Calle de la Huerta towards the centre, turn left by the Banco Central, then right and left again to arrive in the main square where very welcome refreshment may be had. Rooms are usually available at the Hostal Juma at a corner of the square. (Due to re-open after extensive refurbishment.)

Further details of the route may be found by reference to the following walks: 57, 55, 45, 43, 29(c), 24, 21, 20 and 19.

Addendum: Using some of the new walks described in this edition, it is possible to make a three-day walk from Andratx to Valldemossa, making a six-day walk in all.

Day 1. Use the bus to reach Es Grau on the coastal road and walk down the road for 1km to K97, then follow Walk 63 over Galatzó, descending to Puigpuñent. (There are one or two small places offering accommodation but I have no details.)

Day 2. Follow Walk 62 over Es Coll to Banyalbufar, including the scramble up to the top of Es Puntals or not. (Accommodation recommended at the Mar i Vent.)

Day 3. Walk up to Ses Senutges and on the newly restored path to Esporles and continue to Valldemossa as in Walk 61.

APPENDIX 2: Alphabetical Reference Section

Accommodation

For the benefit of those who prefer to travel independently, here are the names and telephone numbers of some selected hotels. (This information has been taken from Tourist Office publications and has not been personally verified.) (H = Hotel, HS = Hostal, R = Residencia, which is a hotel without a restaurant.)

Cala San Vicente	Open	Rooms	Tel.no.
Molins H****	1.05-1.11	90	53 02 00
Cala San Vicente H***	1.04-31.10	38	53 02 50
Don Pedro H***	1.04-31.10	136	53 00 50
Simar H***	1.05-31.10	120	53 03 00
Niu H*	1.04-31.10	24	53 01 00
Mayol HS**	1.04-31.10	40	53 04 40
Oriola HS**	10.02-31.11	23	53 19 98
Pinos, Los HS**	1.04-31.10	19	53 12 10
Vistamar HSR* (Annexe of Don Pedro)	1.04-31.10	11	53 00 50
Puerto de Pollensa			
Daina H***	1.4-31.10	60	53 16 00
Illa D'Or H***	1.4-31.10	119	53 11 00
Pollensa Park H***	1.4-31.10	316	86 13 50
Pollentia H***	1.4-31.10	70	53 12 00
Ses Pins HR***	1.1-31.10	55	53 10 50
Uyal H***	1.4-30.09	105	53 15 00
Pollensa			
Juma HSR*	1.1-31.12	8	53 00 07
Puerto de Soller			
Rocamar H*			63 13 83
Los Geraneos			63 14 40
Marina			63 14 61
Eden H***			63 16 00
Eden Park H***			63 12 00
Miramar H*			63 13 50
Monte Azul H*			63 15 13
Atalaya Club			63 14 03
Hostal Es Port HS***			63 16 50
Soller			
Pension 'La Guia' H*			63 02 27
Pension 'Nadal'			63 11 80
Monumento			63 01 18

Estate agent: Immobiliaria Alcover, Paseo Es Traves, 07108, Puerto de Soller. Tel 63 18 67. English spoken, and usually have flats to let in the port for long or short periods.

Tour operators: Major tour operators such as Thomson and Intasun normally offer winter holidays in the above resorts. But try Alternative Mallorca who offer apartments and hotels in lesser-known places as well as courses in bird-watching, painting and other activities. Enquiries to Michael Walsh at 60 Steinbeck Road, Leeds LS7 2PW. Classic Collection Holidays also have a brochure on Mallorca with hotels in small and attractive places such as Deià, Valldemossa, Banyalbufar and Estellencs. May to October. Enquiries to Classic Collection Holidays, Travel and Leisure Limited, 9 Liverpool Terrace, Worthing, West Sussex BN11 1TA.

Banks: Most of the main resorts have several banks, but there is only one in Cala San Vicente. Opening hours are 09.00 to 14.00, but they also may close for lunch from 11.30 to 12.30. There are fairly frequent holidays when the banks close all day and most hotel notice-boards give this information. Changing money is simple, using travellers' cheques or Eurocheques. Passports must be shown and they usually want to know where you are staying. The exchange rate is usually more favourable in banks than in hotels and travel agencies.

Boats: There are several regular boat services running in summer which can be very useful to walkers. The following timetables operate in summer only. (When summer begins and ends may depend on the weather.) Times may vary from year to year so it is advisable to check the notice-boards displayed in the ports.

Formentor - Daily service, except Sundays
Journey time 30 minutes

Dep. Pto. de Pollensa	Dep. Formentor
10.00 11.00 13.00 15.30	10.30 11.30 13.00 15.00 16.00 17.00

Sa Calobra and Torrente de Pareis - Daily service
Journey time 50 minutes

Dep. Pto. de Soller	Dep. Sa Calobra
10.00 12.30 15.00	12.00 14.00 16.45

Deià - Tuesdays only
Journey time 30 minutes

Dep. Pto.de Soller	Dep. Deià
10.00 15.00	12.30 17.15

Cala Tuent - Saturdays only
Journey time 50 minutes

Dep. Pto. Soller	Dep. Cala Tuent
10.00	16.45

Bus travel: Although walkers are strongly advised to hire a car for getting to the start of walks, there are some occasions when public transport can be used. The best place to get hold of timetables is at a bus station, although some tourist offices supply them and many hotels display local ones. Sometimes they are posted up on bus stops. Many services are locally organised and bus companies only supply timetables for their own services.

The following timetables give an indication of frequency and times. Although there seems to be little change from year to year, there are usually some minor alterations. More buses run in the summer, from the beginning of April to the end of September, but vary according to demand. Walkers are not well served by buses, especially in the mountains. Although there is a service from Soller along the C710 to Puerto Pollensa, returning in the evening, this only runs at weekends in winter. In summer there is a daily service from Ca'n Picafort to Puerto Soller, which would be a great benefit to walkers in the winter.

There are many buses from Palma radiating in all directions, details of which can easily be obtained if you are staying in Palma. Most walkers will be based in the north of the island so only timetables relevant to this area are included here.

Timetables: (N.B. Readers are reminded that they may be changed at any time and advised to collect an up-to-date version from any tourist office.)

Airport - Palma: For those who book flights only it is useful to know that an airport bus runs into the Plaza España in Palma right to the bus station where buses leave for the north, and the railway station where trains depart for Soller. Buses leave the airport every 30 minutes from 07.05 to 24.05 and leave the Plaza España for the airport from 06.30 to 23.30.

Palma - Pollensa - Puerto Pollensa: The bus stop in Palma is in the bus station next to the Inca railway station in the Plaza España.

	Monday - Saturday				Sundays/Holidays		
Palma	10.00	13.30	17.30	19.15	10.00	16.30	20.30
Pollensa	11.00	14.30	18.30	20.15	11.00	17.30	21.30
Puerto Pol.	11.15	14.45	18.45	20.30	11.15	17.45	21.45
Puerto Pol.	07.15	09.00	14.00	17.30	08.00	14.45	18.45
Pollensa	07.30	09.15	14.15	17.45	08.15	15.00	19.00
Palma	08.30	10.15	15.15	18.45	09.15	16.00	20.00

Pollensa - Puerto Pollensa: There is a bus station in Pollensa, 2 minutes' walk downhill from the main square. The bus stop in Puerto Pollensa is on the sea-front opposite the bar YUM YUM. The journey takes 15 minutes and only the starting times are given.

Pollensa - Puerto Pollensa
Weekdays
06.45 07.30 08.15 09.30 10.15 11.00 12.30 13.30 14.30 15.45
16.30 17.00 17.45 18.30 19.15 20.15
Sundays/Holidays
07.30 08.30 09.30 10.15 11.00 12.00 13.00 14.15 16.00 16.30 17.00 17.30
18.15 19.15 20.15 21.30

Puerto Pollensa - Pollensa
Weekdays
07.15 08.30 09.00 10.00 11.00 11.45 12.45 14.00 15.00 16.00 16.45 17.30
18.00 19.00 19.30 20.45
Sundays/Holidays
08.00 08.45 10.00 11.00 11.45 12.45 13.15 14.45 16.15 16.45 17.45 18.45
19.45 20.45 21.45

Pollensa - Cala San Vicente: In Cala San Vicente the bus stop is outside the Bar Miguel in the Calle Temporal, not far from the bank. Sometimes it picks passengers up outside the Don Pedro but in busy times it is best to walk to the bus stop.

Pollensa - Cala San Vicente
Weekdays	08.15 11.15 14.30 18.30
Holidays	09.30 12.15 17.30

Cala San Vicente - Pollensa
Weekdays	08.45 12.30 14.45 18.45
Holidays	10.00 12.30 17.45

Cala-San Vicente - Puerto Pollensa - Llenaire: This is a daily service, except Sundays, and in summer only.

Llenaire - Cala San Vicente
09.50 11.50 15.50

Puerto Pollensa to Cala San Vicente
09.15 10.00 12.00 16.00 18.15

Cala San Vicente - Puerto Pollensa - Llenaire
09.30 10.15 12.15 16.15 18.30

Puerto Pollensa - Alcudia - Ca'n Picafort: This service is especially useful to birdwatchers as it can be used to get to the Albufera. This is a winter timetable, from 1 November to 31 March.

Pto. Pollensa		10.30	12.00		16.45
Alcudia	09.25	10.45	12.15	15.30	17.00
Pto. Alcudia	09.30	10.50	12.20	15.35	17.05
Tucan	09.35	10.55	12.25	15.40	17.10
Ciudad Lagos	09.40	11.00	12.30	15.45	17.15
Ca'n Picafort	09.55	11.15	12.45	16.00	17.30
Ca'n Picafort	09.45	11.15	12.45	16.00	17.30
Ciudad Lagos	10.00	11.30	13.00	16.15	17.45
Tucan	10.05	11.35	13.05	16.20	17.50
Pto. Alcudia	10.10	11.40	13.10	16.25	17.55
Alcudia	10.15	11.45	13.15	16.30	18.00
Pto. Pollensa	10.30	12.00		16.45	

Palma - Valldemossa - Deià - Puerto Soller: This service is very useful to walkers based in Soller, especially when the 09.30 bus from Puerto Soller is running. (Not on Sundays in winter, but check locally.) In Palma tickets can be obtained from the Bar Ca'n Meca, at the corner of Avda Juan March, and the Calle Archiduque Luis Salvador. The bus leaves from the opposite side of the road. In Soller this bus stops in the Plaza America and not near the railway station where other buses depart.

Winter service 1 November - 30 April

Palma	07.30*	10.00	12.00*	15.00	19.00
Valldemossa	08.00*	10.30	12.30*	15.30	19.30
Deià	08.15*	10.45	12.45*	15.45	19.45
Puerto Soller	08.45*	11.15	13.15*	16.15	20.15
Puerto Soller	07.30	09.30*	14.30	16.00*	17.30
Deià	08.00	10.00*	15.00	16.30*	18.00
Valldemossa	08.20	10.30*	15.30	17.00*	18.30
Palma	08.50	11.00*	16.00	17.30*	19.00

* Not on Sundays and Holidays

Summer service from 1 May to 31 October

Palma	07.45	10.00	12.00	16.15	19.30
Valldemossa	08.15	10.30	12.30	16.45	20.00
Deià	08.30	10.45	12.45	17.00	20.15
Puerto Soller	09.00	11.15	13.15	17.30	20.45

Puerto Soller	07.30	09.30	14.30	16.00	18.00
Deià	08.00	10.00	15.00	16.30	18.30
Valldemossa	08.20	10.30	15.30	17.00	19.00
Palma	08.50	11.00	16.00	17.30	19.30

Soller - Puerto Pollensa: This very important service for walkers in the Soller area unfortunately only runs at weekends in winter, from approximately 1 November to 31 March, but is a daily service in summer. The bus stop is outside the railway station in Soller, but check locally as it has been known to change. (In good weather on Sundays the bus can be full when it arrives in Puerto Soller.)

Soller	09.00	18.25	
Puerto Soller	09.30	18.10	
Ses Barques	09.45	17.50	
Army base	10.05	17.35	
Escorca	10.20	17.20	
Lluc	10.35	17.00	
Pollensa	11.20	16.20	
Cala San Vicente	11.30	16.10	
Puerto Pollensa	11.45	16.00*	* 1 hour later in summer

Ca'n Picafort - Alcudia - Puerto Soller: A daily service in summer, from 2 May to 31 October.

Ca'n Picafort		09.15	15.15
C. Lagos		09.30	15.30
Pto. Alcudia		09.40	15.40
Alcudia	07.00	09.50	15.50
Pto. Pollensa	07.10	10.00	16.00
Cala San Vicente		10.10	16.10
Pollensa		10.25	16.25
Lluc		11.00	17.00
Soller		11.50	17.50
Puerto Soller	(approx.)	12.00	18.00
Return from Pto. Soller	09.30	16.30	

Paguera - Estellencs - Banyalbufar - Valldemossa: A daily service all year round.

Departures		*Returns :* 1 Oct - 31 Mar.	1 April - 30 Sept.
Paguera	09.00		
Andratx	09.10	17.45	18.30
Estellencs	09.40	17.15	18.00
Banyalbufar	09.55	17.00	17.45
Valldemossa	10.30	16.30	17.15

Car Hire: Some package holidays offer 'free' or reduced car hire as part of the deal, especially during the winter months. (It's not really free as you find you have to pay the insurance.) If this does not apply, then it is cheaper to hire locally than to book a car in advance with one of the international companies. The smallest and cheapest cars are the Seat (i.e. Fiat) Pandas, which are good for driving along narrow mountain roads, but sometimes have starting problems. Note that the spare wheel, jack and wheel brace are under the front bonnet. International driving permits are no longer required, but a current driving licence and your passport must be produced when hiring a car.

Chemists: The sign for a chemists shop is a green cross. Many medicines for which a prescription would be required in Britain can be bought over the counter. However, these are not handed over just for the asking and a detailed description of symptoms will be required. Staff are usually very helpful and many speak English. After normal hours, one chemist in each town is usually open until late at night. Details are posted in the windows of all chemists.

Complaints: All hotels, shops, bars, garages and any place offering services to the public are compelled by law to have a supply of a complaints form or *hoja de reclamaciones* (pronounced 'O-ha day rek-lam-ath-ee-oh-neys'). These are only for very serious complaints and should only be resorted to after every attempt has been made to get things put right in a friendly way. If a polite approach to a manager or owner has not worked, then simply asking for the form may bring about a dramatic change of attitude as it is a very serious matter to have a complaint registered. The forms are in triplicate: one copy for the offending organisation, one to be sent to the Oficina de Turismo, Avenida Jaime III, Palma, and one copy to be retained by the complainant.

Currency: The monetary unit is the peseta (pta). There are coins of 5, 10, 25, 50, 100, 200 and 500 pesetas and banknotes of 1,000, 2,000, 5000 and 10,000 pesetas. During the last six years, the rate of exchange has varied between 170 and 240 pesetas to the pound. An easy rule-of-thumb for those who dislike mental arithmetic is to pretend that 200 ptas = £1.00.

Drinks: There are no licensing laws as in Britain and there are very many bars where drinks are served all day. All bars also serve coffee and soft drinks and often food as well. All supermarkets and most village shops sell wine, beer and spirits. Some good Mallorquin wines are made at Felanitx and at Binisalem by Franje Roja. Beer, *cerveza* (pronounced 'thair-baytha') is generally good. Draught is *de barril* or *a presion*.

Driving: Getting to the start of the walks often means driving along narrow winding roads. The roads themselves are mainly good, but there can be problems when coaches going in the opposite direction are met with. The drivers are always very good and expert at edging past with only an inch or two to spare. The worst place for this is the narrow winding corniche road between Deià and Soller, but at the time of writing this is being improved. Another problem when driving about the island is the lack of signposting and lack of advance warning of turns. Go very slowly when you know you going to make a turn and expect it to be a sudden one.

Driving offences: The traffic police are very strict and on-the-spot fines are very high. It is as well to be aware of the following Spanish laws:

1.   Always use the seat belts.
2.   Always indicate you are pulling out when overtaking anything, including parked cars and cyclists, and allow 1m clearance at least.
3.   Always dip headlights when coming up behind another vehicle as well as when approaching.
4.   Pay particular attention to all *ceda el paso* (give way) signs and to 'Stop' signs. Some road junctions can be confusing, but 'Stop means Stop' as the author was told by the policeman charging an on-the-spot fine at the Tucan crossroads near Alcudia. (This junction has since been changed.)
5.   Give way to all vehicles coming from the right.
6.   Keep to the speed limit of 110km on C roads and 90km on other roads, or other speeds as shown locally.
7.   Never cross unbroken white lines in the centre of the road. 'No overtaking' signs back up these white lines.

8.   Do not park facing oncoming traffic or within 3m of a corner.

9.   Obey the priority signs on narrow roads and bridges. You have priority at a sign with a white arrow pointing up and must give way at a sign with a red arrow pointing up.

10.   Each car in Spain should carry a set of spare bulbs, but car hire companies do not provide these. Any fine incurred will be refunded by the car hire company.

If you are stopped by the police for any offence whatsoever it is no use pleading ignorance of the law and highly inadvisable to argue. The best course of action is to apologise: *lo siento*, or *lo mucho siento*. If it is not a very serious offence then you may be let off with a warning, but it is far more likely that you will be charged and required to pay a fine *(una multa)*. If this is the case you will be given a slip of paper, explaining what is to happen. The policeman booking you will then fill in a form describing the offence and ask you to sign it. He will sign it too and give you a copy to keep.

Food: *(See also markets and restaurants)* Mallorquin cuisine is similar to that of Catalonia on the mainland. Fish dishes are a speciality and so are *tapas*, which are wonderful titbits served with drinks in many bars. They are usually laid out behind glass on the counter and you can point to the ones you want. Small or large helpings are offered and a large one can make quite a substantial meal. Food in hotels catering for English people sometimes tends to be rather bland, although the tendency now is for most meals to be self-service and there is often an excellent buffet with a good salad selection.

You may like to sample the following dishes when you have the opportunity:

Angulas: small eels fried whole in batter

Arroz brut: rice soup with meat

Bacalao: dried codfish with tomatoes in a casserole

Butifarra: Catalan spiced sausage

Calamares: squid, usually served *a la romana* or deep fried, in rings

Caldera de peix: fish soup with rice and slices of bread

Capo a lo Rei en Jaume: capon, cock or turkey stuffed with marzipan and sweet potatoes and slightly fried

Caracoles: snails cooked in a garlic mayonnaise sauce

Chorizo: a strong spicy sausage

Coca mallorquin: a kind of pizza, often including fish

Empanada: meat and vegetable pie

Ensaimada: a very light flaky bun sprinkled with icing sugar, often eaten for breakfast or taken on picnics

Escaldums: a casserole of chicken and potatoes in an almond sauce

Espinagada: a savoury pie of eels and highly seasoned vegetables

Frito mallorquin: a fry-up of liver, kidneys, green peppers, leeks and garlic

Gambas: prawns

Gazpacho: a cold soup made from tomatoes, onions, peppers, cucumbers, garlic, oil and vinegar

Graixonere: fish with vegetables and eggs

Greixera: mixed pressed cold meats with egg, artichokes, peas, beans and herbs

Guisantes a la catalana: peas fried with ham and onions

Langosta a la catalana: lobster sautéed in wine and rum with herbs and spices

Lechona asada: roast suckling pig (the most famous speciality)

Lenguado: sole, usually grilled with fresh herbs

Mejillones a la marinera: mussels cooked in a spicy sauce

Pa amb oli: bread spread with oil and topped with ham and tomatoes

Paella: a classic Spanish dish. The best are cooked to order and take at least half an hour. It is a combination of rice with poultry, various seafoods, and pork, plus onions, tomatoes, peppers and garlic. Normally served in an iron dish straight from the oven.

Paella catalana: spicy sausage, pork, squid, tomato, chilli pepper and peas

Paella marinera: fish and seafood only

Paella valenciana: the traditional dish with chicken, mussels, shrimps, prawns, peas, tomatoes and garlic

Salmonetes: red mullet

Sobrasada: pork-liver sausage, bright red with pimento

Sopa mallorquina: a very filling soup, almost a stew, made from garlic, onions, vegetables in season and bread

Tortilla española: omelette with potatoes

Trempo: a summer salad with mixed vegetables

Trucha a la navarra: trout stuffed with bacon or smoked ham

Tumbet: a type of ratatouille with aubergines, peppers, tomatoes and potatoes cooked in olive oil

Zarzuela: a mixture of various fish in a hot spicy sauce

Markets: Anyone self-catering will enjoy buying fresh fruit and vegetables at the open markets. There is a superb selection, even in the depths of winter, and the prices are very reasonable. They are good places to buy food for packed lunches too, especially the local oranges. A visit to one of these markets is a colourful and entertaining event and highly recommended. Most of them open early in the morning and finish by lunch time.

Alcudia	Tuesday, Sunday	Pollensa	Sunday
Andratx	Wednesday	Puerto Pollensa	Wednesday
Calvià	Monday	Sa Pobla	Sunday
Inca	Thursday	Sineu	Wednesday
Palma	Saturday		

Medical matters: When booking a holiday make sure that you have adequate insurance cover. Note that if you intend rock climbing it is often excluded from insurance cover so that special arrangements should be made, for example with the BMC. There are doctors in all towns and a hospital in Palma, which can be reached in under two hours from the most distant parts of the island. First class specialist and emergency treatment is available. (*See also Chemists.*)

Photography: Bring all the film that you are likely to need as it is a lot more expensive to buy in Mallorca. Colour prints can be developed in 24 hours. Kodak transparencies can be sent to Madrid and should be returned within a week. Remember that the light is very bright and it is easy to overexpose, especially near the sea or white buildings.

Police: There are three different police forces in Spain and all are armed. The *Policia Municipal* wear blue uniforms and are attached to local town halls and the *Policia Nacional* wear brown uniforms and berets or hats with a red stripe. The national police force is the *Guardia Civil*, whose uniforms include patent leather hats. (The *Guardia Civil* have the most power.) All three services may be called upon if you need help.

Post Offices: The post offices, *correos*, are open from 09.00-14.00 and from 16.00-19.00, Monday to Saturday. It is best to buy stamps (*sellos*) at a tobacconist (*estanco*) or from any shop selling postcards or from a hotel reception desk. Mail boxes are yellow with a red stripe. A box labelled *extranjero* is for foreign-bound mail. Mail can be sent to a post office to be collected if you do not know what your address will be. The form of address is:

Mr and Mrs A.B. Smith
Lista de Correos
Puerto Pollensa
Mallorca
Baleares Spain

Telephones are quite independent of post offices. (q.v.)

Railways: *(See trains)*

Restaurants: There is a wide choice of places to eat in every resort. Many bars also serve meals and most hotels offer meals to non-residents. Your own hotel will probably offer specialities at extra cost which can be ordered instead of the standard fare. Menus and prices are usually posted outside the entrance so that you can see what is available before deciding where to eat, but it is a good plan to ask someone with local knowledge to recommend somewhere. There is a wide range of prices but paying more does not always mean a better meal, but may mean a more elaborate service. In tourist places the menu is often in several languages including English. In smaller places with more authentic local cooking it pays to know some of the words which may be on the menu. (See *Food* and *Language notes*.) The *menu del dia* is always very good value. This is a two or three course meal including bread and wine.

Shops and shopping: *(See also Markets)* Shopping for food is easy everywhere on the island. Even the smallest villages have a general store and they are nearly all self-service. Hours are 09.00-13.00 and 16.00 or 16.30-20.00. Some shops close on Saturday afternoons. If you go to Palma for a day's shopping and sightseeing, remember the long *siesta*. Even the cathedral closes in the afternoon .

Taxis: These are cheaper than in Britain and can be good value for four people sharing. They are usually found in main squares or in front of hotels, or the reception desk at the hotel will call one. The green sign *Libre* means free and any taxi displaying this can be flagged down. There is usually a board near the taxi rank displaying the standard fares to nearby places. If you want to go on a long journey you will probably have to pay the fare both ways even if you are not returning. It is best to agree on the price before setting off. Tips of 10% of the fare are customary.

Telephones: The telephone system has been modernised and most telephones have automatic dialling systems and can be used for international calls. They take 25-, 50-, and 100-peseta coins, which are lined up on top of the dialling box which is a push-button type. Coins not used are refunded when you hang up. Most bars have telephones which can be used for local calls. The dialling tone is a single intermittent note and the engaged sign a very rapid intermittent note. To make a call to England, first dial 07 for the international line, pause until a continuous high-pitched tone is heard, dial 44 for Great Britain, then the area code omitting the first 0 (e.g. 161 for Manchester, not 0161). A good supply of 50-peseta coins are needed, but it is cheaper after 20.00hrs and before 08.00, after 14.00 on Saturday and all day on Sunday. If the coins won't go in the slot it means the box is full and you will have to find another telephone. Hotels will usually make calls for you, but there is often a surcharge. To make a personal call ask the operator for *persona a persona* and to reverse the charges ask for *cobro revertido*.

Theft: In Palma and the busy resorts of the south coast it is necessary to be on guard against handbag-snatchers and pickpockets, as in many places today. Never accept a free carnation for your buttonhole; this is a ploy to gain free access to your wallet. Car thieves operate in many areas all over the island and it is never safe to leave valuables or anything at all in a car when you go off walking for the day. Leave the car empty, with the seats tipped foward to show there is nothing hidden underneath. Many friends have had cars broken into and all sorts of items taken, from cameras and good clothes to old trainers and a few groceries.

Toilets: There are very few public toilets in Mallorca and most people use those in bars and restaurants. There are usually pictorial signs for men and women, some of them a bit ambiguous. A useful phrase to know is *dónde estan los servicios, por favor* (where are the toilets, please?).

Tourist offices: The Spanish National Tourist Office at 57, St. James' St., London SW1A 1LD (tel: 0171-499-0901) will supply lists of accommodation and a brochure but do not undertake bookings. The main tourist office in Palma is in Avenida Jaime III, 10, tel. 71-22-16. There is also a kiosk in the Plaza España offering some information and maps of Palma. There are local tourist offices in some of the resorts, although some of these only open in summer.

Trains: There are two railway lines on the island, Palma-Inca and Palma-Soller. The line to Artá was closed some years ago. It is the Soller line which is of special interest to walkers and may be used by the independent traveller going to stay in Soller, or by walkers staying in Palma to get there for the day. The two lines have adjacent stations in the Plaza España. From the bus station, go past the Inca line to reach the station for Soller. The Soller line was built in 1912 and although now electrified it still uses very old and attractive carriages with brass fittings. The train ride itself is highly recommended for its own sake. The 10.40 train from Palma is a special tourist train which stops at a viewpoint high above the Soller valley for 10 minutes while everyone leaps out with their cameras. This train can be very crowded, especially at peak holiday times, and unless you are early at the station you may find that it is standing room only on the platforms between the carriages. There is also an old tram which runs between Soller and the port, which gives an exciting and scenic ride.

Train times

Palma	08.00	10.40	13.00	15.15	19.45	22.00*
Bunyola	08.26	11.08	13.26	15.40	20.10	22.25*
Soller	09.00	11.45	14.00	16.15	20.45	23.00*

* Sundays and holidays only

Soller	06.45	09.15	11.50	14.10	18.20	21.00*
Bunyola	07.15	09.45	12.15	14.35	18.45	21.25*
Palma	07.45	10.15	12.50	15.10	19.20	22.00*

* Sundays and holidays only

Tramway

Departures from Soller

05.55	07.00	08.00	09.00	10.00	11.00	11.30	12.00	12.30
13.00	14.00	15.00	16.00	16.30	17.00	17.30	17.55	19.00
20.00	20.45							

Departures from Puerto

06.20	07.30	08.25	09.30	10.30	11.30	12.00	13.00	13.25
14.30	15.30	16.30	17.00	17.30	17.55	18.30	19.30	20.20
21.10								

Water: Although it is perfectly safe to drink the tap-water, in some of the coastal resorts it is often quite strongly saline and has an exceedingly unpleasant taste. Best to buy the excellent spring water available everywhere in 5-litre bottles.

APPENDIX 3: Language Notes and Glossary

Introduction

Many people in Mallorca speak some English, especially in the major tourist centres and in large hotels. Many others, particularly in the smaller villages and in the country, do not know a single word of English or any other languages except Castilian Spanish and Mallorquin. (Some older country people only speak Mallorquin.) These are the people most likely to be met while walking and it is well worthwhile taking the trouble to learn a few words and phrases so as to be able to pass the time of day with them.

The official language of Mallorca is about to change from Castilian Spanish to Mallorquin. Mallorquin is a dialect of Catalan and includes words of French and Arabic origin. The written language can be mastered, for reading purposes, by those with a little knowledge of French and Spanish, but the spoken language is another matter entirely. Between themselves, most of the islanders speak Mallorquin, so that overheard conversations on buses and in bars and shops are frequently totally incomprehensible to visitors. However, if you try and speak a little Spanish in shops and so on, you will find that people are delighted that you are making the effort and will help you all they can.

One of the best ways of learning is to listen to cassettes or radio programmes such as the BBC sometimes produce. Castilian is pronounced exactly as it is spelt, so that if the rules are known a reasonable attempt at pronunciation can be made. Stress is on the last syllable unless indicated otherwise by a stress accent.

Key to pronunciation

The following guide is given for reference and to introduce a few words of vocabulary. It is no substitute for listening to people talking on cassettes, radio or in real life.

a	between a in lass and in father	*adiós*	goodbye
b	as English	*banco*	bank
c	before i and e like **th** in thin	*cinco*	five
	before anything else as in cat	*cliente*	customer
ch	as in church	*chico*	boy
d	at beginning of word, like **d** in dog	*dos*	two
	in other places, like **th** in though	*verdad*	true
e	as in men, but at end of word as in day	*leche*	milk
f	as English	*fácil*	easy
g	before a,o,u, or consonant, as in gas	*gasolina*	petrol
	before e & i as **ch** in loch	*gente*	people
gu	before a, like gw	*agua*	water
h	always silent	*hombre*	man
i	between i in bit and in machine	*litro*	litre
j	like **ch** in loch	*ajo*	garlic
k	as in English	*kilo*	kilo
l	as in English	*libro*	book
ll	like **lli** in million	*me llamo*	I'm called
m	as English	*mantequilla*	butter
n	as English	*naranja*	orange
ñ	as ni in onion	*los niños*	the children
o	between top and for	*oficina*	office
p	as English	*pan*	bread
q	like English k	*quizás*	perhaps

r	slightly rolled	*el norte*	the north
rr	strongly rolled	*carretera*	main road
s	voiceless, as in sin	*seis*	six
t	as English	*tienda*	shop
u	as in boot	*usted*	you
v	like a soft English b	*vaso*	glass
x	at end of word, like tch	*Felanitx* (placename)	
	between vowels, like gs	*taxi*	taxi
y	like y in yes	*mayor*	main
y	the word y, as the i in machine	*y*	and
z	as th in thick	*manzana*	apple

N.B. The three double letters ch, ll and rr are considered as separate letters by the Spanish Academy so they have separate sequences in Spanish dictionaries.

Brief glossary

Some very basic words and phrases are included here because it can be useful to have reference to them without carrying a separate phrase book in your rucksack. Note: Question marks and exclamation marks are always used upside down at the beginning of a question or exclamation.

Everyday words and expressions

hello	*hola*
good morning	*buenos días*
good afternoon	*buenas tardes*
goodnight	*buenas noches*
goodbye	*adiós*
see you tomorrow	*hasta mañana*
see you later	*hasta luego*
yes/no	*si/no*
please	*por favor*
thank you	*gracias*
that's all right	*de nada*
thank you very much	*muchas gracias*
excuse me, sorry	*perdoneme*
I'm sorry	*lo siento*
I'm English	*soy Inglés (man) soy Inglesa (woman)*
I don't understand	*no comprendo*
would you repeat please?	*¿puede repetir, por favor?*
more slowly, please	*más despacio, por favor*
what did you say?	*¿qué dijo?*
what is that	*¿qué es eso?*
do you speak English?	*¿habla Inglés?*
I don't speak Spanish	*no hablo Español*
there is, there are	*hay*
is there a bank near here?	*¿hay un banco por aquí?*
where is the post office?	*¿dónde esta correos?*
where are the toilets?	*¿dónde estan los servicios?*
men	*señores/hombres/caballeros*
women	*señoras/mujeres*
open/closed	*abierto/cerrado*

today/tomorrow/next week	*hoy/mañana/la próxima semana*
where can I buy...?	*¿dónde se puede comprar...?*
a newspaper, stamps	*un periódico, sellos*
I'd like that	*quiero eso*
I'll have this	*tomo esto, llevo esto*
how much is it?	*¿cuánto es?*

Accommodation

do you have a room?	*¿tiene una habitación?*
double, single	*doble, individual*
tonight	*esta noche*
for two/three nights	*para dos/tres noches*
how much is the room?	*¿cuanto es la habitación?*
with bath/without bath	*con baño/sin baño*

Bar and restaurant

drinks	*bebidas*
breakfast	*desayuno*
lunch/dinner	*comida/cena*
I'd like/we'd like	*quiero/queremos*
I'll have/we'll have	*tomo/tomamos*
a black coffee	*café solo*
two black coffees	*dos cafés solos*
white coffee	*café con leche*
three white coffees	*tres cafés con leches*
tea with milk	*té con leche*
tea with lemon for me	*té con limón para mi*
beer	*cerveza*
the house wine	*el vino de la casa*
a glass of red wine	*un vaso de vino tinto*
white wine	*vino blanco*
a dry sherry	*un jeréz seco*
a bottle of mineral water	*una botella de agua mineral*
fizzy/still	*con gas/sin gas*
orange juice	*zumo de naranja*
soup	*sopa*
hors d'oeuvres	*entremeses*
eggs, egg dishes	*huevos*
fish, fish dishes	*pescados*
sea food, shell fish	*maríscos*
meat, meat dishes	*carne*
game	*caza*
vegetables	*verduras/legumbres*
cheese	*queso*
fruit	*fruta*
ice-cream	*helados*
desserts	*postres*
sandwich	*bocadillo*
anything else?	*¿algo más?*
nothing, thank you	*nada más, gracias*

the bill, please	*la cuenta, por favor*
packed lunches	*picnics*
two packed lunches	*dos picnics*
for tomorow	*para mañana*

Getting about

by car, on foot	*en coche, a pie*
how can I/we get to Soller	*¿cómo se llega a Soller?*
where is. ..	*¿donde esta...*
the bus station?	*la estación de autobús?*
the bus stop?	*la parada de autobús?*
for Pollensa	*para Pollensa*
how much is the fare?	*¿cuánto vale el billete?*
return	*ida y vuelta*
single	*sencillo/solamente ida*
where is the road to Inca?	*¿donde esta la carretera de Inca?*
how do I/we get to Alcudia?	*¿para ir a Alcudia?*

Especially for walkers

where is the footpath to...?	*¿donde esta la senda a...?*
may we go this way?	*¿se puede pasar por aqui?*
is it far?	*¿esta lejos?*
how far?	*¿a que distancia?*
how long?	*¿cuanto tiempo?*
very near?	*¿muy cerca?*
left/right	*izquierda/derecho*
straight on	*todo recto*
first left	*la primera a la izquierda*
second right	*la segunda a la derecha*
in front of the church	*en frente de la iglesia*
behind the hotel	*detrás del hotel*
at the end of the street	*al final de la calle*
after the bridge	*después del puente*
where are you going?	*¿adonde va/van?*
I'm going/we're going to	*voy a/vamos*
a right of way	*derecho de paso*
private hunting	*coto privado de caza*
please close	*cierren, por favor*
dogs on guard	*cuidado con el perro*

Car travel

where can I/we rent a car?	*¿donde se puede alquilar un coche?*
how much is it per day?	*¿cuánto es por día?*
how much is it for a week?	*¿cuánto es por una semana?*
petrol	*gasolina*
petrol station	*gasolinera/estación de servicio*
car repair shop/garage	*taller/garaje*
standard/premium petrol	*normal/super*
fill it up please	*lleno, por favor*
10, 20, 30 litres	*diez, veinte, treinta litros*
may I/we park here?	*¿se puede aparcar aquí?*

Road signs

Most are international, but you may see these:

¡Alto!	*Halt!*	Despacio	*Slow*
Aparcamiento	*Parking*	Desviación	*Diversion*
Calzada deteriorada	*Bad road*	Desprendimientos	*Falling stones*
Calzada estrecha	*Narrow road*	¡Pare!	*Stop!*
Ceda el paso	*Give way*	Peligro	*Danger*
Cruce peligroso	*Dangerous crossroads*	Prohibido adelantar	*No overtaking*
Curva peligrosa	*Dangerous bend*	Prohibido aparcar	*No parking*
Cuidado	*Caution*	Puesto de socorro	*First aid post*

Emergencies

Help! Fire!	*¡Socorro! ¡Fuego!*
Police	*Policia, Guardia Civil*
I've had a breakdown	*mi coche se ha estropeado*
there's been an accident	*ha habido un accidente*
call a doctor quickly	*llamen a un medico, rapidamente*
it's urgent	*es urgente*

Placenames

Most places in Mallorca have two names, Castilian and Mallorquin, both of which are in common use. At the time of writing Mallorquin is about to become the official language. Whether this means that placenames become standardised remains to be seen. It seems probable that both names will continue to be used, as after all both names have appeared in many books, maps and other printed material which still exist. The names are fairly similar as a rule, such as La Calobra, Sa Calobra, and La Puebla, Sa Pobla.

Some placename pronunciations

Cala San Vicente	*Kah-lah San Bee-then-tay*
Lluc	*L'yook*
Mallorca	*My-orka*
Pollensa	*Pol-yen-sa*
Soller	*Sol-yair*
Ternelles	*Tern-ell-yes*
Valldemossa	*Vall-day-moh-sah*

Days of the week

	Castilian	Catalan
Monday	*Lunes*	*Dilluns*
Tuesday	*Martes*	*Dimarts*
Wednesday	*Miercoles*	*Dimecres*
Thursday	*Jueves*	*Dijous*
Friday	*Viernes*	*Divendres*
Saturday	*Sabado*	*Dissabte*
Sunday	*Domingo*	*Sabat*

The Catalan has been given for the days of the week because notices about opening times of shops, museums etc. are often only given in this language.

APPENDIX 4: Further Reading

Walking guidebooks

Beese, Gerhard. *Richtig wandern: Mallorca*. 2nd ed. Koln. Dumont, 1990.

Crespi-Green, Valerie. *Landscapes of Mallorca: a countryside guide*. 4th ed. London. Sunflower Books, 1997.

Heinrich, Herbert. *12 classic hikes through Majorca*. Palma, Editorial Moll, 1987.

ICONA. *Son Moragues: guia de paseo*. Palma, 1982.

Llofriu, Pere. *Caminant per Mallorca*. (Manuals d'introduccio a la naturelesa, 8.) 2nd ed. Palma. Editorial Moll, 1989.

Palos, Benigne. *Itineraris de Muntanya: excursions a peu per la Serra de Mallorca*. 2nd ed. (Manuals d'introduccio a la naturelesa, 5). Palma. Editorial Moll, 1984.

Palos, Benigne. *Valldemossa com a centre d'excursions*. Mallorca. Editorial Moll, 1989.

Ponce, Paco. *Mallorca: ein Mallorquiner zeigt seine Heimat*. Gerlen, 6601 Saarbrucken-Ensheim, West Germany, Repa-Druck. 2nd ed. n.d.

Natural history books

General

Parrack, James D. *The naturalist in Majorca*. Newton Abbot. David & Charles, 1973. (o.p.)

Birds

Bannerman, David & Bannerman, W. Mary. *The birds of the Balearics,* illus. by Donald Watson. Croom Helm, 1983.

Busby, John. *Birds in Mallorca*. Christopher Helm, 1988.

Hearl, G. and King, J. *A birdwatching guide to Mallorca*. Arlequin Pubns, 1995.

Heinzel, Herman & others. *The birds of Britain and Europe with North Africa and the Middle East*. London. Collins, 1972.

Peterson, Roger, & others. *A field guide to the birds of Britain and Europe*. 4th ed. London. Collins, 1983.

Serra, Joan Mayol. *The birds of the Balearic islands*. Tr. from the Catalan by Hannah Bonner. Mallorca. Editorial Moll, 1990.

Stoba, Ken. *Bird watching in Mallorca*. Milnthorpe, Cumbria. Cicerone Press, 1990.

Watkinson, Eddie. *A guide to bird-watching in Mallorca*. 2nd ed. Alderney, J.G. Sanders, 1982.

Flowers

Beckett, Elspeth. *Wild flowers of Majorca, Minorca and Ibiza;* with keys to the flora of the Balearic island. Rotterdam. Balkema, 1988.

Bonner, Anthony. *Plants of the Balearic island*. (Manuals d'introduccio a la naturelesa, 1). Palma. Editorial Moll, 1982.

Polunin, Oleg and Huxley, Anthony. *Flowers of the Mediterranean*. Chatto and Windus, 1972.

Polunin, Oleg. *Flowers of Europe; a field guide*. Oxford U.P., 1969.

Straka, Herbert, & others. *Führer zur Flora von Mallorca/Guide to the flora of Majorca*. Stuttgart/New York. Gustav Fischer Verlag, 1987. (In German, English, Spanish and French.)

Geology

Adams, A.E. *Mallorcan geology: a geological excursion guide*. Cardiff. Dept. of Extra Mural Studies, University College, 1988.

Jenkyns, H.C. & others. *A field excursion guide to the geology of Mallorca*. (Geologists Association Guide), ed. by C.J. Lister, 1990.

General interest

Berlitz travel guide: *Majorca and Minorca*. English ed. dist. by Cassell, 1982.

Facaros, Dana & Pauls, Michael. *Mediterranean island hopping: the Spanish islands; a handbook for the independent traveller*. London. Sphere Books, 1981.

Fenn, Patricia. *Entree to Mallorca*. Quiller Press, 1993.

Foss, Arthur. *Majorca*. Faber and Faber, 1972.

Graves, Robert and Hogarth, Paul. *Majorca observed*. London, Cassell, 1965.

Lee, Phil, *Mallorca and Menorca*. Rough Guide, 1996.

Sand, George. *Winter in Majorca*. Trans. and annotated by Robert Graves. Valldemossa, 1956.

Thurston, Hazel. *The travellers' guide to the Balearics: Majorca, Minorca, Ibiza and Formentera*. London. Jonathan Cape, 1979.

Language

BBC. *Get by in Spanish: a quick beginners' course for holidaymakers and business people*. 1977.

Ellis, D.L. & Ellis, R. *Travellers' Spanish*. Pan Books, 1981.

Oliva, Salvador, & Buxton, Angela. *Diccionari Català-Angles*. Barcelona, 1985.

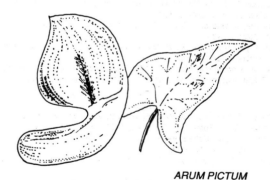

ARUM PICTUM

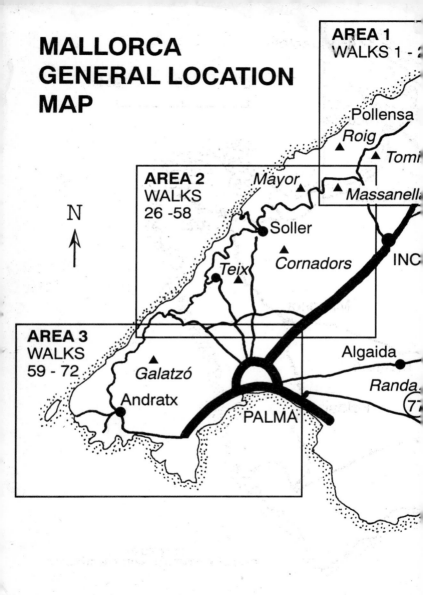